Myne awne good cardinall I recomande
me vnto yow as hartely as hart can thynke /
so it is that by cause writtyng to me is somwhat
tedius and paynefull therfor... the most
off thes besynes I have commyttyd to bur
trusty coseler thys berrar to be declaryd to yow
by mowthe whyche we wolde yow shulde
gyff credens / neverthelesse to thys that
folowith I thowght nott best to make hym
pryve nor non other but yow and I whych
ys that I wolde yow shulde make good
wache on the duke off suffolke on the duke
off bukyngam on my lord off northcombertlan
on my lord of darby on my lord off wylshyre
and oth ys whyche yow thynke suspecte
to se what they do with thys mes/ no more
to yow at thys tyme but sapienti pauca
wryttyn wt the hand off yowr lovyng
mastter. Henry R

RIVALS IN POWER

Copyright © 1990 by Toucan Books Limited

Published by Grove Weidenfeld
A division of Grove Press, Inc.
841 Broadway, New York,
New York 10003-4793

Published in Canada by General Publishing Company, Ltd.

Library of Congress Cataloging-in-Publication Data

Rivals in Power / [compiled by] David Starkey. — 1st ed.
    p. cm.
    ISBN 0-8021-1282-X (alk. paper)
    1. Great Britain—History—Tudors, 1485-1603—Sources.
    2. Great Britain—Court and courtiers—History—16th century—Sources.
    3. Great Britain—Nobility—History—16th century—Sources.
    4. Great Britain—Court and courtiers—Correspondence.
    5. Great Britain—Nobility—Correspondence.
I. Starkey. David
DA310.S77 1990   90-38019
942.05—dc20   CIP

Manufactured in Spain by Cayfosa, Barcelona.

First American Edition

10 9 8 7 6 5 4 3 2 1

Conceived, designed and produced by Toucan Books Limited, London

LIVES AND LETTERS OF THE GREAT TUDOR DYNASTIES

Rivals in Power

EDITED BY DAVID STARKEY

Grove Weidenfeld
New York

Acknowledgments

The reality of many co-operative books belies their name.
This one has not. Academically, it would be invidious to single out any of
the contributors, for I have learned much from all of them.
But it would be equally unfair not to mention Alasdair Hawkyard's
further contribution to the editing of the book. His hidden hand
appears as often as my own, and more discreetly.
But books are not only written but produced.
This book was conceived by Robert Sackville-West. He has kept a gentle,
but never slack, rein as I have taken it over and turned it
into what the French (who have a word for most of the
things that we lack) call 'high vulgarization'.
I could not have done this without the help of Catherine Bradley and
Jane MacAndrew, the successive text editors of this book;
John Meek, its designer, and Christine Vincent, the picture researcher.
Finally, outside this cosy circle of co-writers and the production team,
I must acknowledge a deeper and more personal debt
to Jenny and Bill Sessions of Atlanta, Georgia.
Jenny provided me with hospitality of the warmest and the most relaxing
(the two do not always go together) at a crucial stage of my work on this book.
At the same time, my discussions with Bill reshaped my
views of the Earl of Surrey and so, in effect, of the whole Tudor nobility.
In particular, it his view of the rivalry in image between
Surrey and Henry VIII which is reproduced here.
I am very grateful for his tolerance in allowing me to borrow an idea
without which this book would have been much poorer.

David Starkey

Highbury, London. July 1990

The numbering of Peers, for example, Thomas Howard, 4th Duke of Norfolk, is by creation and follows the numerical
order in G.E. Cokayne, *The Complete Peerage*.

Endpapers: Left, A formal letter from Queen Elizabeth I to her envoy in Scotland in 1566 (hence the signature at the top).
The letter deals with the delicate question of precedence which had arisen when the Scots appointed Lord Home,
a mere baron, as commissioner when his English equivalent was the Earl of Bedford.
Right, An informal, autograph letter from Henry VIII to Cardinal Wolsey, 1518-21 (hence the signature at the bottom).
The King, as he says, found 'writing ... somewhat tedious and painful'. So letters in his own hand were saved up for
special occasions, like this warning to Wolsey to 'make good watch' on five leading nobles.

Contents

Chronology

22 Aug 1485	Battle of Bosworth
c. 1503	Betrothal of Brandon to Anne Browne
1507	Marriage of Brandon with Dame Margaret Mortimer
1508-10	Marriage of Brandon with Anne Browne
22 April 1509	Death of Henry VII; accession of Henry VIII
11 June 1509	Marriage of Henry VIII with Catherine of Aragon
18 Aug 1510	Execution of Edmund Dudley
15 May 1513	Brandon created Viscount Lisle
9 Sept 1513	Battle of Flodden
2 Feb 1514	Lisle created Duke of Suffolk; Earl of Surrey created second Duke of Norfolk
15 Sept 1514	Wolsey appointed Archbishop of York
9 Oct 1514	Marriage of Princess Mary with Louis XII of France
1 Jan 1515	Death of Louis XII
Feb 1515	Marriage of Duke of Suffolk with Princess Mary
10 Sept 1515	Appointment of Wolsey as Cardinal
24 Dec 1515	Appointment of Wolsey as Lord Chancellor
18 Feb 1516	Birth of Princess Mary, later Queen Mary
17 May 1518	Appointment of Wolsey as Papal Legate
7-24 June 1520	Field of Cloth of Gold
1522-24	Scottish War
Nov 1523	Edward Seymour and John Dudley knighted
Mar-May 1524	Amicable Grant
21 May 1524	Death of second Duke of Norfolk
1529	Downfall of Cardinal Wolsey
c. Jan 1531	Appointment of Thomas Cromwell as Councillor
Jan 1533	Marriage of Henry VIII with Anne Boleyn
April 1533	Appointment of Duke of Norfolk as Earl Marshal
24 June 1533	Death of Mary, Duchess of Suffolk
Sept 1533	Marriage of Duke of Suffolk with Catherine Willoughby
7 Sept 1533	Birth of Princess Elizabeth
Nov 1533	Marriage of Lady Mary Howard with Duke of Richmond
April 1534	Appointment of Thomas Cromwell as King's Principal Secretary
1536	Betrothal of Lord Thomas Howard to Lady Margaret Douglas
7 Jan 1536	Death of Catherine of Aragon
19 May 1536	Execution of Anne Boleyn
30 May 1536	Marriage of Henry VIII with Jane Seymour
5 June 1536	Sir Edward Seymour created Viscount Beauchamp
22 July 1536	Death of Duke of Richmond
Oct-Dec 1536	Pilgrimage of Grace
1537	Death of Lord Thomas Howard
12 Oct 1537	Birth of Prince Edward, later Edward VI
18 Oct 1537	Beauchamp created Earl of Hertford
24 Oct 1537	Death of Queen Jane Seymour
1540	Downfall and execution of Thomas Cromwell
28 July 1540	Marriage of Henry VIII with Catherine Howard
8 Aug 1541	Marriage of William Cecil with Mary Cheke
13 Feb 1542	Execution of Queen Catherine Howard
12 March 1542	Sir John Dudley created Viscount Lisle
14 Dec 1542	Death of James V of Scotland; accession of Mary, Queen of Scots
12 July 1543	Marriage of Henry VIII with Catherine Parr
1544-51	Scottish and French Wars
22 Aug 1545	Death of Duke of Suffolk
21 Dec 1545	Marriage of William Cecil to Mildred Cooke
21 Jan 1547	Execution of Earl of Surrey; imprisonment of Duke of Norfolk
28 Jan 1547	Death of Henry VIII; accession of Edward VI
31 Jan 1547	Hertford created Duke of Somerset, Lisle Earl of Warwick and Sir Thomas Seymour Baron Seymour
early May 1547	Marriage of Lord Seymour to Catherine Parr
7 Sept 1548	Death of Queen Catherine Parr
20 March 1549	Execution of Lord Seymour
Oct 1549	Ending of the Protectorate
4 June 1550	Marriage of Robert Dudley to Amy Robsart
11 Oct 1551	Warwick created Duke of Northumberland; the Marquess of Dorset created Duke of Suffolk; William Cecil knighted
29 March 1551	Marriage of Henry Sidney with Lady Mary Dudley
1 Oct 1551	Henry Sidney knighted
22 Jan 1552	Execution of Somerset
May 1553	'Device for the succession'
21 May 1553	Marriage of Guilford Dudley with Lady Jane Grey
6 July 1553	Death of Edward VI followed by the succession crisis
22 Aug 1553	Execution of Duke of Northumberland
Jan-Feb 1554	Wyatt's Rebellion
12 Feb 1554	Execution of Guilford and Jane Dudley
23 Feb 1554	Execution of Suffolk
25 July 1554	Marriage of Queen Mary and Philip of Spain
25 Aug 1554	Death of third Duke of Norfolk
April 1556	Appointment of Sir Henry Sidney as Vice-Treasurer of Ireland

1558	Loss of Calais
17 Nov 1558	Death of Queen Mary and accession of Elizabeth I
11 Jan 1559	Appointment of Lord Robert Dudley as Master of the Horse
Jan-May 1559	'Settlement of Religion'
Aug 1559	Royal Injunctions to the Clergy
1560	Appointment of Sir Henry Sidney as President of the Council in the marches
8 Sept 1560	Death of Amy Dudley
28 Sept 1560	George Talbot succeeds as sixth Earl of Shrewsbury
Nov/Dec 1560	Marriage of Lady Catherine Grey with Earl of Hertford
26 Dec 1561	Lord Ambrose Dudley created Earl of Warwick
29 Sept 1564	Lord Robert Dudley created Earl of Leicester
13 Oct 1565	Appointment of Sir Henry Sidney as Lord Deputy of Ireland until 14 Oct 1567
9 Feb 1568	Shrewsbury marries Elizabeth Hardwick
17 April 1568	Appointment of Sir Henry Sidney as Lord Deputy of Ireland until 1 April 1571
16 May 1568	Flight of Mary, Queen of Scots to England, and subsequent imprisonment
Dec 1568	Shrewsbury appointed keeper of Mary, Queen of Scots
1569	Rebellion of the Northern Earls
Oct 1569	Arrest of fourth Duke of Norfolk
25 Feb 1571	Cecil created Baron of Burghley
5 June 1572	Execution of fourth Duke of Norfolk
24 Aug 1572	Massacre of St Bartholomew's
late 1574	Marriage of Earl of Lennox with Elizabeth Cavendish
late 1575	Birth of Arabella Stuart
5 Aug 1576	Appointment of Sir Henry Sidney as Lord Deputy of Ireland until 14 Sept 1578
22 Sept 1576	Succession of Robert Devereux as second Earl of Essex
21 April 1577	Marriage of Mary Sidney with second Earl of Pembroke
Nov 1577-Sept 1580	Circumnavigation of the Globe by Sir Francis Drake
21 Sept 1578	Marriage of Earl of Leicester with Countess of Essex
24 Feb 1580	Succession of Philip Howard as thirteenth Earl of Arundel
19 Sept 1580	Death of Catherine, Duchess of Suffolk
13 Jan 1583	Philip Sidney knighted
20 Sept 1583	Marriage of Sir Philip Sidney with Frances Walsingham
Aug 1584	Shrewsbury replaced as keeper of Mary, Queen of Scots
Sept 1584	Conversion of Earl of Arundel to Roman Catholicism
1 Nov 1584	Appointment of Earl of Leicester as Lord Steward
1585	Appointment of Sir Philip Sidney as Governor of Flushing
April 1585	Arrest of Earl of Arundel
Autumn 1585	English military intervention in the Netherlands under the command of Earl of Leicester
19 Oct 1585	Death of Earl of Arundel
25 Jan 1586	Appointment of Earl of Leicester by the Dutch as Governor General
5 May 1586	Death of Sir Henry Sidney
22 Sept 1586	Battle of Zutphen
17 Oct 1586	Death of Sir Philip Sidney
24 Nov 1586	Return of Earl of Leicester to England
8 Feb 1587	Execution of Mary, Queen of Scots
16 Feb 1587	Funeral of Sir Philip Sidney
May 1587	Appointment of Earl of Essex as Master of the Horse
July-Nov 1587	Return of Earl of Leicester to Netherlands
July-Aug 1588	The Spanish Armada
4 Sept 1588	Death of Earl of Leicester
5 April 1589	Death of Lady Burghley
1590	Marriage of Earl of Essex with Frances, Lady Sidney
21 Feb 1590	Death of Earl of Warwick
6 April 1590	Death of Sir Francis Walsingham
18 Nov 1590	Death of Shrewsbury
1591	English military intervention in North France
20 May 1591	Robert Cecil knighted
25 Feb 1593	Appointment of Earl of Essex as a Privy Councillor
May-Aug 1596	The Cadiz Expedition
5 July 1596	Appointment of Sir Robert Cecil as Principal Secretary of State
Aug-Oct 1597	The 'Islands Voyage' to the Azores
Dec 1597	Appointment of Earl of Essex as Earl Marshal and Master General of Ordnance
4 Aug 1598	Death of Lord Burghley
12 March 1599	Appointment of Earl of Essex as Lieutenant and Governor-General of Ireland until 25 Sept 1599
Feb 1601	Essex's Rebellion
25 Feb 1601	Execution of Earl of Essex
24 March 1603	Death of Elizabeth I and accession of James I

Rivals in Power

THE TUDORS AND THE NOBILITY

'Dynasty' originally meant power. Then, because power was normally held by ruling families, the word assumed its principal modern meaning of royal house. But the root sense of power is never far from the surface. Dynasties, whether they rule kingdoms, noble estates or industrial corporations, are *power families*. And from Texas to Tudor England their behaviour varies little.

This book tells the story of eight great Tudor families: the Brandons and the Greys, the Howards, the Seymours, the Dudleys, the Cecils, the Talbots, the Sidneys, and the Devereux. Their histories - interwoven with each other and with that of the royal family itself - are the history of Tudor England. It is a story of high politics and low cunning; of the love and loathing of close relations; of wealth and poverty; of ambition and failure; of crownings and beheadings. In it, everything becomes political. Praying is politics; marrying is politics, and dying may be the most politic act of all. The arts themselves were handmaidens to statecraft as poetry, painting, and architecture, even needlework, spelled out messages to the initiated. Finally everything is sacrificed for power: brothers and daughters are offered up on the altar and human beings are shifted like chessmen in the deadly game to control the family firm that was Tudor England.

It is, of course, a story that has often been told before. We tell it differently in two ways. The first is that wherever possible we use their words. They were one of the most rhetorically gifted of ages. So it seems only common sense to let them speak for themselves: they will do it better than any historian. And second, having borrowed their words we try to understand their values. All these master-players of the political game were, or became, noblemen. For most of them this fact was of enormous significance: it embodied their descent; it registered their achievements; it guaranteed the status of their posterity. We try to take their nobility as seriously as they did. And with good reason. For noble titles, honorific offices, pedigrees and tables of precedence were the score-cards of the power game; while magnificence and honour, chivalry and courtly love supplied its rules - and those of the games proper - jousting, hunting and love-making - which, then as now, the élite played almost more seriously than the game of politics itself.

We begin, not with the battle of Bosworth on 22 August 1485, when the crown really was snatched from a hawthorn bush and placed on the head of the victorious Henry VII, the first King of the House of Tudor, but with the untroubled accession of his son, Henry VIII, on 22 April 1509. Actually it is the latter which is the extraordinary event. In the fifteenth century usurpation had become the usual means of ascending the throne, and the last smooth transfer of power was almost ninety years earlier, in 1422, when the infant Henry VI succeeded his great father Henry V.

There are two reasons for starting the story at its second chapter. The first is a question of evidence. This book is based on letters. Letters are almost as old as royal government itself, and many of the documents contained in the majestic series of parchment rolls, which, from the late twelfth century, record the increasingly elaborate operations of the King's government, law courts, and Parliament, are letters in form and name: the letters patent, by which the King granted patronage; the letters close by which he issued instructions, and the writs which set in motion the complex procedures of the Common Law courts. But all these 'letters' were more or less formal and formulaic: they contain facts in plenty but few frills.

Then, in the later fifteenth and sixteenth centuries, a great change came about: letters in our modern sense appear and, still more importantly for the historian, are preserved in quantity. Every aspect of business is recorded in new and vivid detail. The new sort of letter was first used for private business; then, as part of the 'privatization' of government which was as much a feature of the late fifteenth century as it is of the late twentieth, the King and his Councillors went over to letters as well. The result is a hiccough in our knowledge, as the old-style records peter out before the new-style ones fully get going. The prime casualty is the reign of the first Tudor, Henry VII (1485-1509). Its politics are a blank which can be filled in only by the utmost technical virtuosity, and even then inadequately. With the accession of Henry VIII, however, the great stream of correspondence begins and swells relentlessly thereafter: the printed *Letters and Papers* for the reigns of Richard III and Henry VII comprise two modest volumes; those for Henry VIII's reign take up thirty-seven volumes and parts of volumes.

The second reason is that 1509 marks, and was felt to mark, a new start - particularly for the nobility. Henry VIII's accession on the eve of St George's Day; his marriage to Catherine of Aragon on 11 June, and the joint coronation of the young couple (he was eighteen; she was twenty-four) thirteen days later on Midsummer Day was the replacement of the Winter King by the Spring Prince. The contrast is caught by our first two documents: on the one hand, Bishop John Fisher's funeral sermon for his old and now despised master, 'Ah, King Henry, King Henry! If thou wert alive again, many one that is here present would now pretend a full great pity and tenderness upon thee' (p. 28); on the other, Thomas More's celebratory Latin poem for the new King's coronation day: 'If ever there was a day, England, ... for you to give thanks to those above, this is that happy day ... Now the nobility ... lifts its head and rejoices in such a King ...; long scorned ... [it] recovered the ancient rights of nobles on our Prince's first day' (p. 29).
Fisher proved the truer prophet, but what is striking about More's paean is the prominence accorded to the noblility. In his mature works, like *Utopia*, More was to see their pride, ostentation and appetite for war as the principal obstacles to reform; now in contrast he seems to think that the nobility's recovery of 'their ancient rights' was the symbol of the restoration of good government.

Henry VIII thought so too. He was determined to be a real King. At home, that meant taking part in the knightly pastimes of jousting and courtly love - and beating the best;

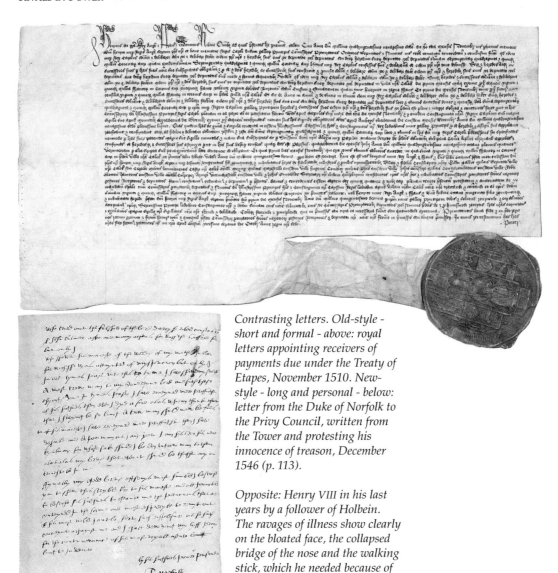

Contrasting letters. Old-style - short and formal - above: royal letters appointing receivers of payments due under the Treaty of Etapes, November 1510. New-style - long and personal - below: letter from the Duke of Norfolk to the Privy Council, written from the Tower and protesting his innocence of treason, December 1546 (p. 113).

Opposite: Henry VIII in his last years by a follower of Holbein. The ravages of illness show clearly on the bloated face, the collapsed bridge of the nose and the walking stick, which he needed because of his ulcerated leg.

abroad, it meant triumph in war. Both needed the nobility. They would provide him with his worthiest opponents in the tournament; and, in default of a standing army, they alone could provide the troops for war - as well as being themselves the natural choice as admirals and generals. Two of our families, the Brandons and the Howards, benefited enormously from Henry VIII's early honeymoon with the nobility.

They stood at opposite ends of the social spectrum that in Continental, though not in strict English, usage was regarded as 'noble'. In Continental Europe the whole of the chivalric class was considered to be noble; in England, they were divided into two very uneven groups. The lesser in rank but much the greater in size was the gentry. Gentility

was very ill-defined: effectively anyone who could behave, and could afford to behave, as a gentleman was accepted as such - or at least his sons were. On the other hand, the nobility proper was both small and tightly defined. In early sixteenth-century England there were some 1,500 or 2,000 gentry families, but only forty or fifty noble ones. And of those only the head of the house, who sat in the Upper House of Parliament, was a noble in the full sense. But despite, or rather because of, the strictness of the line of demarcation between gentleman and nobleman, the line was frequently crossed in both directions. The younger sons of noblemen, and their descendants, became gentry; conversely, the fact that peerage titles could ordinarily descend only in the male line, coupled with contemporary demographic patterns, meant that noble families lasted on average only three generations. The nobility therefore needed constant replenishing, which came, of course, from the gentry.

The career of Charles Brandon exemplifies much of this. The Brandons were an East Anglian gentry family which had distinguished itself in the previous generation by service to Henry VII. That got Charles off to a good start. But his essential qualities were of body and character. He was the only man big enough and skilled enough to offer Henry equal competition in the joust; he was equally sure-footed, and a good deal more delicate, socially. He charmed women off their feet (p. 44), and men out of their jealousy. The result was that his rise from gentleman to duke in five years aroused none of the fear and loathing directed, for example, at James I's favourite, the Duke of Buckingham, who took a year longer to travel the same road.

The Howards (also from East Anglia) had made the transition from gentry to nobility in the middle of the fifteenth century. Marriage to a sister of the Mowbray Duke of Norfolk, the extinction of the direct Mowbray line, and devoted service to the Yorkist Kings Edward IV and Richard III had brought the Howards the dukedom of Norfolk in 1483. Two years later the duke lost everything, including his life, at Bosworth. His son Thomas regained the earldom of Surrey from Henry VII; now Henry VIII's appetite for war offered him the chance of a full restoration. In 1513 war broke out on two fronts: the King and Charles Brandon, now Viscount Lisle, went off to fight the French; Catherine of Aragon and Surrey were left at home to deal with the Scots. The home team was much stronger: Henry and Brandon won a skirmish in France; Surrey, as Catherine wrote exultantly to her husband (p. 34), crushed the Scots and killed their King, James IV.

The rewards were equal, however. On 2 February 1514 Charles Brandon was created Duke of Suffolk and Thomas Howard Duke of Norfolk. The account of their creation is incomplete (p. 37), but the ceremony clearly followed the form laid down when dukedoms were first introduced into England in the later fourteenth century for the sons of Edward III. Each new duke would have been invested with a robe, a sword, a cap of estate, a coronet and a gold rod; henceforth, he would be addressed as 'Your Grace'; while his formal style would be 'Right High and Mighty Prince'. A dukedom remained, as the origins of the rank suggested, quasi-royal.

That presented problems with a King who grasped royalty as wholly and jealously as Henry VIII came to do. There was the added difficulty that Henry was giving his trust to a very different sort of figure: the humbly-born cleric, Thomas Wolsey. After a brilliant start at Oxford, Wolsey's career had stagnated until he had been talent-spotted by Richard Fox, Bishop of Winchester, the ablest of the Councillors whom Henry VIII had inherited from his father. Fox was fighting a vigorous rearguard action against the war-party led by Surrey. And it is as Fox's lieutenant that Wolsey wrote his first surviving official letter in September 1511 (p. 52). The tone is stridently partisan: Wolsey denounces the influence of Surrey's son, Sir Edward Howard, the Lord Admiral, who 'marvellously incenseth the King against the Scots'; rejoices that Surrey had quit the Court after a bad reception from the King, and proposes that the exclusion be made permanent by depriving the earl of his right to lodgings in the palace. Within a year much had changed. Wolsey had realized that it was also Henry VIII who wanted war and that nothing would stop him. He shifted ground accordingly and made his name by the efficiency with which he organized the French campaign. Four days after Brandon and Surrey were created dukes, Wolsey was made Bishop of Lincoln. In quick succession thereafter he became Archbishop of York, Chancellor of England and Cardinal.

There remained an undercurrent of unease in Wolsey's relations with the nobility. This was a natural response to the rule of a Cardinal-Minister. Such tensions did not of course exclude co-operation at moments of mutual convenience: Wolsey and Suffolk, both 'new men', were immediate natural allies against the Howards (p. 53); while the manner of Suffolk's marriage to Henry VIII's sister Mary - abroad, surreptiously, and without royal permission - reduced the duke to the minister's client (p. 48). Within a few years, however, the position had reversed: there was a close working relationship between Wolsey and Norfolk, while Suffolk was one of 'the great personages' under suspicion. In the letter from the King's Secretary, Richard Pace, to Wolsey of 1518 (p. 55), we see King and minister working themselves into a security scare about the arrival of the nobility at Court for the celebrations for Easter. Such incidents culminated in the trial (presided over very reluctantly by Norfolk) and execution of the Duke of Buckingham in 1521. But despite all this, the nobility were indispensable: whether for fighting wars abroad (pp. 60-64), or for putting down the disorder at home provoked by war taxation (p. 65).

The most serious internal disorder was caused by the exquisitely misnamed Amicable Grant of 1525. The centre of the disturbances was East Anglia, where both Norfolk (this is the third duke, who had succeeded in 1524) and Suffolk had their territorial base. Writing jointly from Lavenham after they had got the worst of the trouble under control, the two dukes advised Wolsey that the King should 'call his Council unto him, to debate and determine what is best to be done' (p. 65). This highlights the other aspect of the nobility's role: they did not only see themselves as the King's natural companions at Court and on the battle field, they were also his 'born councillors' (*consiliarii nati*).

In the most formal sense, this was unchallenged: the nobility formed the temporal (or lay) side of the upper house of the King's 'great council' of Parliament; while the bishops and mitred abbots made up the larger 'spiritual' (or clerical) side. In addition, Great Councils proper - that is, the House of Lords without the House of Commons - were still summoned fairly regularly. But the position of the nobility within the King's working Council of advisers was far more fluid, as indeed was the Council itself. Wolsey was the Chief Councillor and dealt directly with the King. This left the Council in attendance on the King's minister, rather than the King, and meeting at Westminster rather than at Court (usually Greenwich Palace, Henry VIII's favourite residence).

Norfolk and Suffolk were calling instead for the Council to meet at Court with the King. Six months later, in January 1526, their proposals were embodied in the Eltham Ordinances, which envisaged a high-powered Council resident at Court. But Wolsey had built enough exceptions into the scheme for him to frustrate its operations. On his fall, however, in 1529, it was immediately put into effect. It was further elaborated by an Act of Parliament passed in 1530, which created the office of Lord President of the Council Attendant on the King's Person. The first incumbent of the new post, which ranked third in the official hierarchy immediately behind the lord treasurership held by Norfolk, was Suffolk (p. 68).

It was not, of course, the aristocratic conciliarism of Norfolk and Suffolk that had brought Wolsey down. Instead, it was the King's determination to divorce his first wife, Catherine of Aragon, and marry Anne Boleyn. Wolsey failed to procure the divorce and was discarded. The divorce also divided the conciliar regime which had replaced him. The new Lord Chancellor, Sir Thomas More, opposed both the divorce and the general threat to the power and independence of the Church which it implied. Suffolk was happy enough to bash the Church, but he, and more particularly his wife Mary, loathed Anne Boleyn. Norfolk, on the other hand, was Anne's uncle and saw in her advancement a stepping-stone to power. At first all went to plan and Norfolk used Anne's coronation in 1533 to recover the only piece of his family inheritance to have eluded him.

From the days of Thomas 'of Brotherton', son of Edward I, from whom the Howards claimed descent in the female line, the earl marshalship of England had been the hereditary possession of first the Earls and then the Dukes of Norfolk. The Marshal had originally been deputy of the Constable, but Buckingham's execution in 1521 had extinguished the hereditary claim to the constableship and the office was never revived. This left the Earl Marshal unchallenged as commander-in-chief, master of ceremonies, and head of the College of Heralds, who had the crucial task of allowing or disallowing claims to bear coats of arms as testimonies of gentility. Henry VIII had made the second duke Earl Marshal, but only for life, and on his death in 1524 the position was given to Suffolk. Now, with the leverage of a niece as Queen, Norfolk got it back (p. 72).

But that was the high-water mark of Norfolk's gains from the Boleyn marriage. He soon got on the wrong side of Anne's tongue; more seriously, he was on the wrong side of the religious divide which had opened up after the divorce. Nothing had been further from Henry VIII's mind than to patronize heresy, which he detested. But events pushed him in that direction. To effect the divorce Henry had finally been driven to break with Rome and proclaim himself Supreme Head of the Church in England. Naturally, supporters of the 'new' in religion were the most enthusiastic advocates of the Royal Supremacy. The two most important were Thomas Cranmer, the new Archbishop of Canterbury, who, against Catherine's passionate resistance, formally freed Henry from his first marriage; and Thomas Cromwell, Wolsey's former factotum, who replaced him as chief minister. In addition, Anne added her powerful influence in support of the 'new'.

With this advocacy in high places, the 'new' made rapid advances. The first monasteries were dissolved and popular religious observances, like pilgrimages and miracle-working images, were attacked. The result was the massive rebellion in the north known as the Pilgrimage of Grace. It was the supreme challenge to the Tudors, and, whatever their private doubts about the policy, Norfolk and Suffolk (and most of the rest of the nobility) rallied to the dynasty in its hour of need. Suffolk dealt with the rebellion in Lincolnshire (pp. 80-82); Norfolk first negotiated with the main strength of the rebels in Yorkshire; then, when it was safe to do so, broke his word and crushed them.

Henry VIII never forgot Suffolk's services and 1536 marks a second watershed in his career. Out of favour, impoverished by the financial settlement he and Mary had been driven to make with the King, and squeezed out locally by the superior territorial power of Norfolk, for years Brandon had been on the margin of things. Now, however, he shifted his landed base from East Anglia to Lincolnshire, where he already held a great estate in the right of his fourth wife, Catherine Willoughby. With the move sanctioned by the King, Suffolk emerged as a great local power unchallenged by any rival (pp. 84-85). His rehabilitation at the centre took longer, however, until the fall of Cromwell.

Cromwell's background was much the same as Wolsey's. Yet his ministry was much more contentious. The ideological struggles of the Reformation made politics more bitter; while the concentration of politics about the King's person made them more intense. But there was also the fact that Cromwell was a layman. Wolsey's status as an upstart was overlaid and to some extent made acceptable by the fact that as Cardinal he was a Prince of the Church (even Norfolk told him he honoured him for that). The nakedness of Cromwell's origins had no such fig-leaf and they were made more, not less, blatant by the titles of honour bestowed on him: Baron in 1536, Knight of the Garter in 1537 and finally Earl of Essex in 1540. The outrage of the nobility exploded at the moment of his arrest in the Council Chamber in June 1540: led by Norfolk, they tore the emblems of the Garter from his person; subsequently they charged him with *scandalum magnatum*, or seditious abuse of noblemen, and, if they could, would have had him subject to the full horrors of castration and dismemberment, rather than the gentler death of beheading which was normally conceded to noble traitors (p. 97).

But a noble reaction, in some ways comparable to the heady days of Henry VIII's accession, was already under way before Cromwell's fall. It was signalled by the Act of Precedence of 1539. Precedence, that is ranking, was central to an aristocratic society and the Act effected the first radical changes in the nobility since it had first crystallized into a parliamentary peerage in the late fourteenth century. This peerage was differentiated into ranks which governed precedence in Parliament: dukes sat above marquesses; marquesses above earls; earls above viscounts, and viscounts above barons. Within each rank precedence was determined by 'ancienty', that is by the antiquity of the creation of the title by which a nobleman sat: the older the higher. The Act of 1539 overlaid the principles of title with those of office. The offices of state were put into a single order of precedence. The holders of the first four - the Lord Chancellor, the Lord Treasurer, the Lord President of the Council and the Lord Privy Seal - were to sit above all peers whomsoever, apart from royal dukes; while the incumbents of the next seven, headed by the Great Chamberlain and Earl Marshal, were to rank above all nobles of their grade, whatever the 'ancienty' of their title. This order of precedence was also to apply outside Parliament to all meetings of the Council, which, according to another Act of this Parliament, would be made up predominantly of the great office-holders.

The rules of the game had changed. Henceforward, at the head of the English peerage would be a group of noble great office-holders. Politics (alongside marriage) had always been the way to promotion in and to the peerage. Now politics meant specifically service in the Council. At the same time, the organization of the Council was tightened up to reflect its place as the principal centre of politics and power. The Household Ordinances of Christmas 1539 did what the Eltham Ordinances had promised and made the Council a Court Council: its members were to have lodgings in the palace, to meet there, and to dine communally in their own Council Chamber. Finally, immediately after Cromwell's fall, the Council's powers of summons, secretariat, and record keeping were put in order. Taken together, the changes gave the Council both a new corporate identity and (effectively) a new name: it was now the Privy Council, and, as such, would form the corporate governing board of England until the Civil War.

Viewed in another perspective, of course, the fall of Cromwell was only another incident in Henry VIII's long saga of matrimonial and religious reverses. Anne the Reformer had fallen in May 1536 in a particularly dramatic and bloody court coup (p. 77); she was replaced by the religious conservative Jane Seymour. Jane did not live long enough for her religious opinions to matter, as she died in 1537 after giving birth to Henry VIII's longed-for heir, Prince Edward (p. 90). Two years later Cromwell took advantage of the international situation to steer the King into a marriage with Anne, the sister of the heterodox Duke of Cleves. It was loathing at first sight and (after sorting out another divorce) Cromwell went to the block. Henry quickly consoled himself with Catherine Howard; she meantime consoled herself with one of the young Gentlemen of his Privy Chamber. In late 1541 all was revealed and early in the new year she became the second of Henry VIII's wives (and Norfolk's nieces) to go to the block (pp. 103-7). In 1543 Henry married his last wife, the already-widowed and religiously-reforming Catherine Parr. She outlived him. Henry engaged in another piece of recidivism in these last years and returned to the wars against France with which he had begun the reign.

Aristocratic revival under the Stuarts: The coats of arms as Knights of the Garter of left, Robert Sidney, now created Viscount Lisle (claimed through his Dudley mother); and right, Thomas Cecil, as Earl of Exeter (a promotion which he at first resisted and to which he had no claim).

From this kaleidoscope of events emerged a relatively simple pattern as Norfolk and his son (and Henry VIII's godson) Henry Howard, Earl of Surrey, confronted Edward Seymour in a struggle for power under the old Henry that would lead to power over the young Edward. The Seymours had been a substantial Wiltshire gentry family, whose head in the late fourteenth century had married the sister and eventual heiress of Lord Beauchamp of Somerset. This was recalled when, after his sister's marriage to Henry, Edward Seymour was made Viscount Beauchamp; six days after Jane had given birth to Prince Edward he was promoted to Earl of Hertford. At first, despite a possible contretemps with the prickly Surrey, relations between Hertford and Norfolk were good. But in the 1540s they deteriorated rapidly. On the one hand, Hertford put himself at the head of the 'new' in religion; on the other, the wars in France and Scotland turned into a duel for military supremacy between Hertford and Surrey. Hertford won hands down (p. 109).

In the last months of the reign Surrey took on a bigger opponent and seems to have entered into a direct political rivalry with Henry VIII himself. Surrey's aristocratic pride and poetic imagination fused to create a vision of a reforming aristocracy. It would be an aristocracy indeed, that is the rule of the best, rather than the rule of the worst, as under a King like Henry VIII. The earl's final full-length portrait by William Scrots deliberately sets out to challenge Holbein's overwhelming representation of the King as Supreme Head in a superb body. There could only be one outcome. In December-January 1546-47 Surrey and Norfolk were arrested: Surrey was executed and Norfolk was spared only because the King's death on 28 January 1547 made his execution redundant as well as unseemly (p. 113).

The future belonged to the Seymours. The machinery of Henry VIII's will, which Hertford had helped to frame, worked smoothly (p. 116). With the unanimous 'assent' of the Council, he was made Lord Protector and Governor of the King's Person on 31 January; on 16 February he was created Duke of Somerset. But Seymour's power was not to be unchallenged. Another family rose and rose phoenix-like from the wars and faction strife of Henry VIII's last years: the Dudleys. John Dudley always struck contemporaries as two-faced; the doubleness extended to his ancestry. His father was the gentleman-lawyer Edmund Dudley. He had become Henry VII's chief minister in the last years of his reign, but had been disgraced and executed in the reaction of Henry VIII's accession. So his father brought John Dudley tainted gentility; from his mother, however, he inherited unimpeachable nobility. She was Lady Lisle in her own right; she also had a good claim to the mighty earldom of Warwick. Dudley's own quality was a fine tactical sense, which stood him in good stead in both the battlefield and the no less savage faction fights at Court. In 1542-3 he succeeded as Viscount Lisle; was appointed Lord Admiral and became a member of both the Privy Council and the Privy Chamber. The Privy Chamber, which supplied the King's most private attendants, was the other power centre of Tudor England: Lisle was the first nobleman to hold a salaried post in it.

With Edward VI's accession, Dudley quickly established himself as the second power in the land. In the division of spoils which marked the begining of the reign, his share was one of the largest; he also got both the earldom of Warwick and the symbolically important Warwick Castle. He was able to move from second place to first thanks partly to Somerset's overweening pride and arrogance (exceeded only by the pride of his Duchess Anne (p. 129)), and partly by the division within the Seymour family between Somerset and his brother Thomas, Lord Seymour of Sudeley. Successively Seymour tried to use the Queen Dowager Catherine, the Princess Elizabeth, and King Edward himself to get even with his brother (pp. 121-7). At length Somerset was driven to execute him. Fratricide damaged much of the Protector's credit; the remainder was destroyed by his mishandling of the rebellions of 1549. He fell in slow motion: first he was deprived of the Protectorate; then he was restored to the Council by Warwick for his own reasons; finally he was executed in 1552 for plotting against Warwick. The end was inglorious but Somerset's career did have long-term importance. His great London palace, Somerset House, was the first (and for long the last) rigorously classical building in England; he also espoused a self-consciously 'popular' programme of social reform which earned him the title of the 'good duke'. Stylistically and politically he was pursuing a policy of 'aristocratic reform': Surrey's enemy had stolen Surrey's clothes.

Warwick was far too clever a politician to don this shirt of Nessus, or to assume the equally tainted Protectorate. Instead, he played politics by the rules of 1539 and became supreme ring-master of the game. Richard Scudamore, secretary and court agent of Sir

Rivals in image (1): left Holbein's 'cartoon' or working drawing for the 1537 fresco in the Privy Chamber in Whitehall of Henry VIII as the embodiment of divine and patriarchal kingship; right, William Scrots's 1546 portrait of the Earl of Surrey as the aristocratic restorer of Roman virtue (the broken classical column) to an England out of joint (the ruinous battlements behind).

Philip Hoby, was an informed spectator who kept careful tally of the score. 'These be all that lately hath altered their offices and received higher dignities', he noted in his account of the reshuffle of February 1550, in which Somerset's spoils were divided up. In the reshuffle, which followed the strict letter of the Act of Precedence, Warwick's share was the lord presidency of the Council and the great mastership of the King's Household. Warwick had spotted the potential of these posts in the early 1540s, when they had been held by the Duke of Suffolk, and had angled for them (unsuccessfully) after Suffolk's death. Now he had them it was natural that a dukedom should follow and in 1551 he was made Duke of Northumberland.

Northumberland was not the reckless adventurer of legend; instead he was a politician who played by the rules. And when circumstances forced him to break the rules he lost his touch - and his head. There were two interlinked problems: the succession and religion. Henry VIII's will laid down a clear order of succession: first came his own children, Edward, Mary and Elizabeth, and then the children of his younger sister Mary by her marriage to Charles Brandon, Duke of Suffolk. The children of his elder sister Margaret, who had married James IV of Scotland, were excluded because they were foreign born. All this became a matter of urgent moment when Edward, who had been a healthy boy, suddenly fell ill with tuberculosis. The other, complicating factor was religion. Somerset cautiously and Northumberland more aggressively had pursued a Protestant policy. And Edward had been more enthusiastic than either of them. But Mary, his half-sister and appointed successor, was equally vehemently Catholic. Someone - was it Northumberland or Edward himself? - resolved to cut the Gordian knot by excluding both Henry VIII's daughters (who were still technically bastards) from the succession and turning instead to the descendants of Mary Tudor. Her union with Brandon had produced two daughters, the elder of whom, Frances, had married Henry Grey, third Marquess of Dorset. Dorset, who was himself quasi-royal as a descendant of Edward IV's stepson, had first flirted with Thomas, Lord Seymour, but in the struggle between Somerset and Warwick, he threw his weight on Warwick's side. His reward was his elevation to his father-in-law's dukedom of Suffolk. The couple's eldest daughter, Jane, was highly educated, fanatically Protestant and unmarried. She was quickly married to Northumberland's son, Lord Guilford Dudley, and after Edward's death on 6 July 1553 she was proclaimed Queen. Mary had been advised to flee. Instead she proved a Tudor, raising East Anglia and sweeping to power at the head of the only successful sixteenth-century rebellion (pp. 140-1).

Northumberland, who had been oddly indecisive, surrendered at Cambridge. In his scaffold speech he went further and renounced Protestantism (p. 142). Jane had only scorn for his weakness and met her own fate steadfastly when she and her husband were executed after Wyatt's unsuccessful rebellion(p. 145). Mary's vengeance stopped there and even Northumberland's younger sons returned to favour in the French campaigns waged by Mary's husband and consort, King Philip of Spain and England (p. 148). What the future of the Dudleys in a Catholic England would have been we can only guess.

For Catholic England died with Mary. Her appointed successor was Elizabeth, and she, just as Mary herself had been, was determined to undo what her predecessor had done.

Nor did the problem of the succession solve itself with Elizabeth's accession in November 1558. For Elizabeth would not marry. Still worse Mary, Queen of Scots, fled to England in 1568. She was granddaughter of Henry VIII's elder sister Margaret, and, though her line had been excluded by Henry's will, she was much the most plausible successor to Elizabeth. She also became flamboyantly Catholic. The resulting uncertainty proved too much of a temptation to several of our families. On the Protestant side Jane Grey's younger and more foolish sisters played with the fire of their family's claim and got burned. And since Catherine Grey surreptitiously married Somerset's son, the Earl of Hertford, the Seymours fell under a renewed cloud as well.

On the other side, the Howards, who had regained their titles and estates under Mary, lost them all again when a scheme was floated for the fourth duke to marry Mary, Queen of Scots the year after her arrival in England. He was executed in 1572. Norfolk himself remained staunchly Protestant. But his son Philip, Earl of Arundel in right of his mother, converted to Rome; while his brother, Lord Henry Howard, more cautiously inclined that way. This ensured the exclusion of the main line of the family from power for the remainder of Elizabeth's reign.

Finally, the Talbots, Earls of Shrewsbury, who so far had steered clear of involvement in high politics, found themselves caught up, when George, the sixth earl, was appointed custodian of Mary, Queen of Scots. The resulting strain helped wreck his marriage to the strong-willed Bess of Hardwick; still worse, his stepdaughter by Bess married the Earl of Lennox, the uncle of James VI of Scotland and grandson of Margaret Tudor. That brought the Talbots into the charmed and fateful circle round the throne, where, as the poet Sir Thomas Wyatt wrote under Henry VIII, 'lightning strikes'.

In contrast, two other families gained hugely from Elizabeth's accession: it made the Cecils and remade the Dudleys. The Cecils were different from the other Tudor dynasties and had no ties of intermarriage with them. Not only were they not gentle, they were not even English but Welsh. William Cecil made up for these defects of background by his own academic brilliance and by the fact that his father, though in a modest capacity, was employed in the inner Royal Household. William had had a meteoric career under Somerset, becoming Secretary of State. He had also got to know Elizabeth then and seems immediately to have won her trust. Even before her accession he was advising her on the future shape of her Council; when she became Queen her first official appointment was to restore him to his office of Secretary. Unusually, she responded to his oath of office with an affirmation of her own: both kept their word.

Robert Dudley, the man with whom Cecil's career was to be so closely intertwined, was of a totally different stamp. He was third son of the Duke of Northumberland, and a soldier not a scholar. He was given a different sort of job as well, as Master of the Horse, and had a different relationship with the Queen, first as her half-acknowledged suitor, then as a surrogate consort . Cecil, despite being made Lord Treasurer and Baron Burghley in 1572, went out of his way not to affect nobility: he rode a mule side-saddle; wore clerical black, and built the conspicuously unmilitary Italianate palace of Burghley as his main house. In contrast, the Earl of Leicester, as he became in 1564, gloried in his nobility to the point to which others (looking at the attainder of his father and grandfather) came to doubt it (p. 157). He turned the mastership of the horse into a substitute earl marshalship; he was portrayed either in lavish court dress or in armour, and he made his principal seat at Kenilworth Castle. His very title, which had been Simon de Montfort's, breathed high medieval romance - and the high political claims of the medieval peerage.

Any tendencies in that direction were, however, kept under check by his genuine regard for Elizabeth, which she reciprocated. And the very contrast between Leicester and Burghley helped their co-operation, which, after the uncertain first decade of the reign, was reasonably smooth. It was to be different with the two men who were, in various ways, seen as Leicester's heirs. Leicester, to his bitter regret, had no children (pp. 166-7); nor did his elder brother Ambrose, created Earl of Warwick in 1561. This left the offspring of his sister Mary as the hope of the house. Mary had married Sir Henry Sidney, of a rising gentry family. Their eldest son was the famous Sir Philip Sidney, poet and would-be Protestant hero. His proudest boast was that he was a 'duke's daughter's son'. Philip, having spent a life as heir to two earls, was cheated of the succession by his own death at Zutphen. His brother Robert, who was eventually given the Dudley titles of Viscount Lisle and Earl of Leicester by James I, lacked Philip's fire. This left Leicester's stepson, Robert Devereux, Earl of Essex, to pick up his political mantle. Essex also married Sir Philip Sidney's widow, again as a conscious gesture of succession.

The Devereux, like the Dudleys, owed their noble blood and grand titles to female descent. And they too had realized their claims through shrewd politics: they had got the viscountcy of Hereford in 1550 for backing Warwick against Somerset, and the earldom of Essex in 1572 for supporting Cecil against Norfolk. Robert Devereux, the second Earl, inherited the grandeur without the shrewdness. On Leicester's death in 1588, he succeeded him as both royal favourite and (as Master of the Horse) military factotum (p. 275); he followed Sidney as prophet of war against Spain, and after the death of his father-in-law Sir Francis Walsingham he took over his role as gatherer of foreign intelligence (though the work was largely done by Essex's clients, the brilliant brothers Anthony and Francis Bacon).

Finally, in 1597 he was made Earl Marshal. Partly this was to restore his standing against his rival, Lord Howard of Effingham, the Lord Admiral (p. 280). Effingham had been created Earl of Nottingham, which gave him precedence over Essex. But, since by the Act of Precedence the Earl Marshal ranked above the Lord Admiral, Essex's new appointment propelled him into first place once more. But Essex also wanted the office because he was going back to a deeper stream of antiquarian lore than the Act of 1539. The Act in any case was half-defunct: Elizabeth had changed the rules again by not creating peers and by leaving most of the great offices of state unfilled. It was cheap;

Rivals in image (2): left, Elizabeth I in triumph, wheeled in procession on a mobile throne under a canopy borne by four gentlemen; right, the Earl of Essex riding to his fall in Thomas Cockson's 1600 engraving showing him in an imperial pose and with the inscription 'God's Elect'.

it avoided quarrels over precedence, and it was a sensible tactic for a female ruler who had to deal with a peerage of male chauvinist pigs. On the other hand, Elizabeth's economy with honour reopened the question of crown-noble relations which Henry VIII's generous settlement of 1539 appeared to have solved. This was dangerous: Essex's antiquarian researchers told him that Earl Marshals had ranked higher than seventh among the great officers, and had done much more than be useful at coronations.

Essex aspired to test his powers, real and potential, in war. In their various ways, Leicester, Sidney, and Walsingham had all been frustrated by the long peace with Spain of the first decades of the reign; in contrast, the open warfare of the 1590s gave Essex rope, and rope enough to hang himself. The Cadiz Expedition of 1596 was a triumph; the Islands Voyage of 1597 was a military success but a financial disaster, while his expeditionary force to Ireland in 1599 was a catastrophe.

Worse than his military record, however, was his open defiance of the Queen. Leicester loved her; Essex came near to despising her. Instead of courting her, he courted 'popularity' (p. 281-3). Like Surrey before him, he set himself up in rivalry with his sovereign: there was a clash of images, as his engraved portrait, ultimately derived from the equestrian statue of the Emperor Marcus Aurelius and inscribed 'God's Elect', was circulated in London; and there was a clash of arms as the earl, in desperation, engaged in open rebellion in 1601. The earl was executed on 25 February 1601.

The reign of Elizabeth has been seen as 'The Crisis of the Aristocracy', with Essex's rebellion as the final futile (if not farcical) gesture. But Essex's son, the third Earl, was to lead the parliamentary armies to victory over Charles I only forty years later. His platform, of religion, chivalry and hereditary great office, was the same as his father's and as Surrey's, and his propaganda was similar too. Tudor government was strong, but it did not break the power of the nobility. It only channelled it in new directions, which still clothed themselves in the old language. In our last letter, written only a few months after Elizabeth's death, Lord Cecil recognizes ruefully that, after the interval of female rule, things were back to normal (p. 283). And it was to be a normality that left much less room for his like and much more for an increasingly self-confident and assertive nobility.

War and Glory under a Young King

THE HOWARDS

The Howards' rise to the upper heights of the peerage from their relatively small estates in a windswept corner of north-east Norfolk took place in the fifteenth century. For two centuries they had produced a worthy crop of distinguished lawyers and soldiers; the subsequent career of the family was founded on the marriage of Sir Robert Howard to the elder daughter of Thomas Mowbray, Duke of Norfolk, in about 1420. Robert's son John prospered in the service of the Yorkist kings: he was ennobled by Edward IV and granted the dukedom of Norfolk, which had rather dubiously been granted to Richard, the younger of the Princes, following his child-marriage to Anne, the last Mowbray heiress. Richard III made himself king on 25 June 1483 and, on 28 June, he created John Howard Duke of Norfolk. This fixes the most likely date for the murder of the two brothers.

John Howard, Duke of Norfolk's loyalty to Richard III, however, also brought him disaster.

He was killed at the battle of Bosworth which destroyed Richard and brought Henry Tudor to the throne as Henry VII, and now the family fortunes faced shipwreck. It took several decades before the King allowed the Howards to reassemble their estates, while they proved their loyalty by hard work in his service. Norfolk's son, Thomas, Earl of Surrey, spent a decade in the North from 1489 acting as the King's Lieutenant, and succeeded in gaining the King's trust, becoming a senior member of his Council. The patience and caution which characterized his whole career were rewarded by the complete restoration of his father's estates in Henry VII's will, of which he was made an executor; and the succession of a young, energetic King brought new opportunities for advantage, for his son Edward became a great royal favourite.

Naturally, the political game was not straightforward in its outcome. Surrey found that Henry VIII's favour was increasingly given to

Thomas Wolsey, whose busy administrative efficiency could be used to feed the King's appetite for war; while Sir Edward was killed at sea and his brother Thomas did not command the King's affection. However, once more a battle transformed the Howards' fortunes. Left behind in England while Henry set off to seek military glory in France, the Howards found the country facing an invasion from Scotland. It was they who directed the campaign which culminated in the battle of Flodden; where the death of one king had lost them a dukedom, the death of King James IV of Scotland regained it for them.

Surrey was now second Howard Duke of Norfolk, while his son Thomas gained his title of Surrey. Although in his last years the second Duke felt that enough was enough and retired to his Suffolk estates to avoid clashing with Wolsey, his son was not so reticent when he succeeded to the ducal title in 1524; he would become one of the major forces during three vicious and often confusing decades of Henry VIII's reign.

In the spring of 1509 Henry VII lay uneasy on his deathbed, aged beyond his fifty-two years by a long struggle to take and hold the throne. In many ways he had been a successful ruler, but he feared for the fate of his soul at the hands of a wrathful and distant God, and he feared for the fate of the kingdom in the hands of his inexperienced seventeen-year-old son. On 21 April he died, and one of the country's most respected clergymen, John Fisher, Bishop of Rochester, preached the sermon that appears on the following page at his funeral.

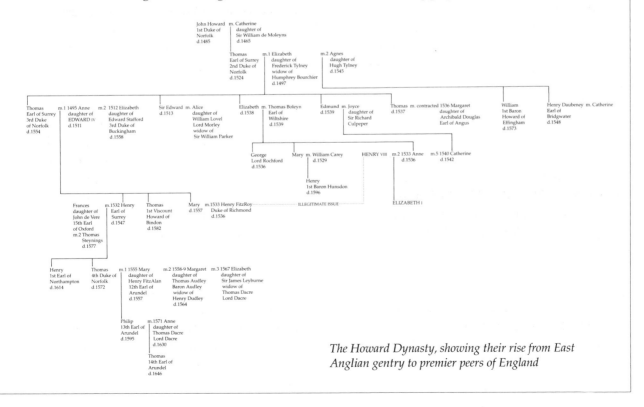

The Howard Dynasty, showing their rise from East Anglian gentry to premier peers of England

Bishop Fisher of Rochester: 11 May 1509
sermon at the funeral of Henry VII

... His politic wisdom in governance it was singular, his wit always quick
and ready, his reason pithy and substantial, his memory fresh and holding,
his experience notable, his counsels fortunate and taken by wise
deliberation, his speech gracious in diverse languages, his person goodly
and amiable, his natural complexion of the purest mixture, his issue fair
and in good number. Leagues and confederacies he had with all Christian
princes, his mighty power was dread everywhere, not only within his
realm but without also, his people were to him in as humble subjection as
ever they were to king, his land many a day in peace and tranquillity.
His prosperity in battle against his enemies was marvellous, his dealing in
time of perils and dangers was cold and sober, with great hardiness. If any
treason were conspired against him, it came out wonderfully. His treasure
and riches were incomparable, his buildings most goodly and after the
newest cast, all of pleasure. But what is all this now? A smoke that soon
vanisheth, and a shadow soon passing away ...

   At the beginning of Lent last passed he called unto him his confessor ...
After his confession made with all diligence and great repentance,
he promised three things: that is to say, a true reformation of all them that
were officers and ministers of his laws, to the intent that justice from
henceforward truly and indifferently might be executed in all causes;
another that the promotions of the Church that were of his disposition
should from henceforth be disposed to able men such as were virtuous and
well learned; third, that as touching the dangers and jeopardies of his laws
for things done in times past, he would grant a pardon generally unto all
his people ... And many a time unto his secret servants he said that if it
pleased God to send him life, they should see him a new changed man ...

   He received ... the sacrament of penance with a marvellous compassion
and flow of tears, that at some time he wept and sobbed by the space of
three quarters of an hour. The sacrament of the altar he received at mid-
Lent, and again upon Easter Day with so great reverence that all that were
present were astonished thereat ... The image of the crucifix many a time
that day [21 April] full devoutly he did behold with great reverence,
lifting up his head as he might, holding up his hands before it, and often
embracing it in his arms and with great devotion kissing it, and beating oft
his breast ...

   He ... that is wrapped indeed in the very sorrows and pains of death,
he feeleth much grievance, specially if his body be delicate, and he of
tender and sensible nature as was this noble King ... Ah, King Henry,
King Henry! If thou wert alive again, many one that is here present would
now pretend a full great pity and tenderness upon thee ...

In truth, few were sorry to see the old King dead. His determination to control his subjects and to make the monarchy financially strong led him to unpopular measures which verged on tyranny and alienated nobles, merchants and clergy alike. It made perfect sense for the new King - and Henry's surviving Councillors - to put all this aside and begin his reign on a wave of public acclaim. Thomas More put it in terms reminiscent of the Church's great liturgical hymns of joy at Easter.

Thomas More: poem on the coronation of Henry VIII   1509

If ever there was a day, England, if ever there was a time for you to give thanks to those above, this is that happy day ... for this day consecrates a young man who is the everlasting glory of our age, and makes him your King, a king worthy not just to rule a single people, but single-handed to rule the entire world, a king who will wipe the tears from every eye and banish our long distress with joy ...

Now the people, liberated, run before their king with bright faces ... Now the nobility, long since at the mercy of the dregs of the population ... lifts its head and rejoices in such a king - and with good reason.
Now, the merchant, previously deterred by numerous taxes, once again ploughs seas grown unfamiliar. Now laws previously powerless, or even bent to unjust ends, have happily regained their proper force ... No longer is it a criminal offence to own honestly acquired property ... No longer does fear hiss whispered secrets in one's ear ...

Among a thousand noble companions, the King stands out the tallest, and his strength fits his majestic body. His hand is as skilled as his heart is bold ... There is fiery power in his eyes, beauty in his face, and the colour of twin roses in his cheeks ...

Our Prince has provided promptly on his first day such benefits as few rulers have granted even in extreme old age. He has immediately arrested and imprisoned anyone who had harmed the realm by plots. Whoever was an informer is closely fettered and confined ... If any excessive duties were required of the merchants, he lightened their burden. And the long-scorned nobility recovered the ancient rights of nobles on our Prince's first day. He now gives to good men the honours and public offices which used to be sold to evil men ... The entire population used to be in debt to the king, on many counts, and this especially was the evil they feared; but our King, though, had he wished, might have inspired fear by this means and gathered immense riches thereby, has forgiven everyone's debts ...

Sir Edward Howard, second son of the second Duke, and his great friend Sir Thomas Knyvett, were leaders among the small group of martially minded young men who surrounded the King in his early years. After Knyvett was killed in battle with the French in 1512, Howard vowed that 'he would never see the King in the face' until he had revenged his friend's death; and he was indeed himself killed in an attack on the French fleet at Brest. His deed was a typical piece of noble bravado, spectacular but pointless: rather like the King's French wars in general.

Sir Edward Echingham, Captain of the Fleet,   5 May 1513
to [?Thomas Wolsey]
Plymouth

Sir, for to write unto you the news of these parts, they be so dolorous that unneth [scarcely] I can write them for sorrow ...

Upon St. Mark's day ... my L[ord Ad]miral [Sir Edward Howard] appointed four captains and himself for to board the [galleys ...] there could no ship com[e near] them for lack of water, for the said French galleys lay in a bay [under] two rocks, and on both sides of the galleys was made bulwarks [which] lay full of ordnance, that no boat nor vessel could come unto th[em] but that they must come between the bulwarks, the which [shot] so thick with guns and crossbows that the quarrels [crossbow arrows] and g[unstones] came together as thick as had it been hailstones. For all this my Lord would needs board the galleys his own s[elf], for there could no man counsel him the contrary. And at t[he] hour above written he boarded the galley that Preyer John [Pregent de Bidoux, Knight of St John, admiral of the French galleys] w[as] in, and as soon as he was aboard of Preyer John's galley, he le[apt] out of his own galley unto the forecastle of Preyer John's ga[lley], and Sharon the Spaniard [John de Sharon, captain in the English fleet] with him, with sixteen other persons; Sir, [by] advice of my Lord Admiral and Sharon they had cast their anchor into [————] of the French galley, and fastened the cable unto the capstan, for this c[ause:] if it had happened any of the galleys to have been on fire that they might have veered [sheered] the cable and have fallen off.

But Sir, howsoever it was, the Frenchmen did hew asunder the cable, or else some of our mariners in our galley let slip the cable when my Lord Admiral [leapt] into the French galley, and all for fear of the ordnance that w[as shot from] the galleys and from the land; and so they left this m[y] lord in the ha]nds of his enemies, where, as by divers men's saying, [he was killed wi]th morris pikes [pikes taking their name from their supposed Moorish origin]. Sir, there was a mariner that [saw it bef]all, the which is wounded in eighteen places ...

The Lord Admiral and the Navy

Henri Grâce à Dieu *or* Great Harry. *Laid down in 1512 for Henry VIII, it was given a major refit in 1540. It was the first four-masted ship launched in England and could carry 349 soldiers, 301 sailors and 50 gunners.*

The defence of England, her continental ambitions, and her growing trading interests throughout the known world made the Navy of prime importance. No one appreciated this better than Henry VIII. As early as 1514 the 1000-ton *Harry Grâce à Dieu* was launched as his flagship, and the Corporation of Trinity House for pilots was founded. Henry spent some of the profits from the dissolution of the monasteries on upgrading a royal fleet as the nucleus of the national defences, to be augmented by merchant and fishing vessels in times of emergency. (Three-quarters of the fleet that met the Armada came from such sources.) This was money wisely spent, despite the loss of the pride of the fleet, the *Mary Rose*, which sank in 1545. Henry laid the foundations of dockyards at Chatham and Portsmouth, and towards the end of his reign set up a Navy Board ('the principal office of the Navy') under the Lord High Admiral, which in its essentials served the Navy until the time of William IV.

The post of Lord Admiral grew in prestige, being held at the end of Henry's reign by Lord Lisle, later Duke of Northumberland, and from the accession of Edward VI by Lord Seymour, brother of Protector Somerset. From 1550 two Lord Admirals saw out the century between them: Lord Clinton, later Earl of Lincoln and Charles, Lord Howard of Effingham,

later Earl of Nottingham, who led the fleet that defeated the Armada.

The key to English naval supremacy lay in replacing what were essentially floating castles, designed to grapple with an enemy, and letting soldiers do the real fighting. The new ships - galleons with an average length three times that of their beam, relatively low in the water, carrying guns able to deliver pulverizing broadsides and manoeuvrable enough to do so repeatedly - were themselves capable of overpowering other vessels. Although the Navy retained oared galleys for use when there was no wind, and also developed light, fast pinnaces, the galleons were the heart of the fleet.

The archetypal late Elizabethan galleon was the middle-sized *Revenge* of about 500 tons, chosen by Drake as his flagship in 1588, and all but unsinkable as the Spanish found in the Azores in 1591. Thomas Hawkins, who was appointed Treasurer of the Navy in 1577 - with other 'principal officers' like Sir William Winter, Drake and the master-shipwrights Matthew Baker and Peter Pett - was largely responsible for the provision of a modern, efficiently run naval force when England most needed it.

Overleaf: The embarcation of Henry VIII at Dover, probably for his second meeting with Francis I of France in 1532.

Besides the poignant memory of Sir Edward Howard's death, the one event which assured the Howards' triumphant return to favour was Surrey's overwhelming defeat of the Scots at Flodden. For this victory he was rewarded with his restoration to the dukedom of Norfolk and a permanent addition to the family coat of arms with an inset of the Scottish lion chopped in half, with an arrow stuck down its throat! Catherine of Aragon wrote an exultant letter about the battle to the King, then absent on his rather less spectacular campaign in France. There is an unexpected note of triumphant ferocity in her letter to her husband, which reminds us that she was the descendant of Spanish dynasties for whom warfare was a way of life.

Queen Catherine of Aragon to Henry VIII   16 September 1513
Woburn

Sir, my Lord Howard hath sent me a letter open to your Grace with one of mine, by the which ye shall see at length the great victory that Our Lord hath sent your subjects in your absence, and for this cause it is no need herein to trouble your Grace with long writing; but to my thinking, this battle hath been to your Grace and all your realm the greatest honour that could be, and more than ye should win all the crown of France: thanked be God of it. And I am sure your Grace forgetteth not to do this, which shall be cause to send you many more such great victories, as I trust he shall do. My husband, for hastiness with Rouge Croix, I could not send your Grace the piece of the King of Scots' coat which John Glynn now bringeth. In this your Grace shall see how I can keep my promise, sending you for your banners a King's coat. I thought to send himself unto you, but our Englishmen's hearts would not suffer it. It should have been better for him to have been in peace than to have this reward. All that God sendeth is for the best. My Lord of Surrey, my Henry, will fain know your pleasure in the burying of the King of Scots' body, for he hath written to me so, with the next messenger your Grace's pleasure may be herein known. And with this I make an end, praying God to send you home shortly, for without this, no joy here can be accomplished. And for the same I pray, and now go to Our Lady at Walsingham that I promised so long ago to see. At Woburn, the 16th day of September,
 Your humble wife and true servant,
 Katherine.
I send your grace herein a bill found in a Scottish man's purse of such things as the French King sent to the said King of Scots to make war against you, beseeching you to send Matthew hither as soon as this messenger cometh to bring me tidings from your Grace.

The Coronation of Henry VIII

The joint coronation of Henry VIII and Catherine of Aragon on Midsummer Day 1509 from the celebratory pamphlet. The intertwined rose and pomegranate symbolize the union of the dynasties of England and Spain.

Though his father died on 21 April 1509, Henry VIII was not crowned for more than two months. The delay was unusual, but perhaps it was thought best to wait until Henry was very nearly eighteen years old. There was no harm in doing so, for after the tense and secretive few days following his father's death, during which his succession was assured and political stability established, an effective challenge to Henry's rule was most unlikely. There was to be a double coronation, because on 10 May Henry had married Catherine of Aragon, allegedly in fulfilment of his father's death-bed wish.

By tradition the great lords of the realm played prominent parts in the ceremony, and the ancient noble offices of Steward and Constable of England (which were no longer granted for life, or still less hereditarily, because of fears that the holders might exploit them to political ends) were allocated for the day to Edward Stafford, third Duke of Buckingham, the senior lay peer. Thomas Howard, Earl of Surrey, was temporarily appointed Marshal of England, and on 20 June he presided over the Court of Claims, at which those who claimed the hereditary privilege of performing certain duties at the coronation had to prove their case.

On Saturday 23 June, Henry and Catherine processed from the Tower through London to Westminster, accompanied by richly dressed bishops, noblemen, knights and royal household servants. The route was hung with tapestry and cloth of gold, and the city livery companies lined the streets to honour their sovereign. On Sunday morning King and Queen walked from Westminster Palace to the Abbey, along a carpet of striped cloth which was unceremoniously 'cut and spoiled by the rude and common people' (as the chronicler Hall put it) once the royal party disappeared inside the Abbey. Henry swore the coronation oath to uphold the law and protect the Church; he and Catherine were anointed and crowned by Archbishop William Warham; the congregation shouted their assent when Warham asked them if they took Henry for their king, and the peers did homage for their lands.

The banquet followed, at which the King's hereditary champion rode into the hall in full armour, threw his gauntlet to the ground, and challenged anyone who denied Henry's title to the throne. Lastly there were celebratory jousts. Henry VIII's reign had been formally launched on its magnificent way, and with it the burgeoning careers of his greatest noble servants, the two Thomas Howards and the upstart Charles Brandon.

'The Estate of Nobility': Robes, Ranks, Creation

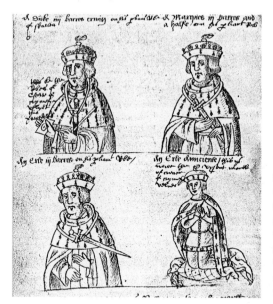

The uniform of honour: a Tudor drawing showing the different robes and coronets of a duke (with a rod in his hand), a marquess, an earl and a viscount. Even the angle of the sword worn round the neck varies from the vertical of the duke to the near horizontal of the earl.

In an age which set great store by defining certain groups by means of clothing which no one else was entitled to wear, the Tudor peerage would stand out clearly in their splendid robes of state on any formal occasion. The nobility was a group defined by its special relationship to the monarch: peers were those who received a personal summons to Parliament. During the fifteenth century, this personal summons gradually came to be seen as a prescriptive right, capable of being passed in hereditary succession - although, not surprisingly, the monarch guarded jealously its right to create new peerages without restriction. Quite apart from the need to reward good servants and show how generous the Crown could be, the creations were necessary to replace natural wastage among families; the average extinction rate among the nobility from the fourteenth to the sixteenth centuries was more than a quarter in every twenty-five years. Henry VIII was as generous with the creation of peerages as his father had been mean; Elizabeth returned to meanness, provoking further lavish creation of honours by her successor James I.

The strains of the Reformation, and the weight of legislation which it entailed, also influenced the Crown in ennoblements; with the House of Lords now a separate body within Parliament, the monarch might also have to consider how to influence the weight of opinion within the House. When the conflict with the Church was beginning to shape up in 1529, Henry took the highly unusual step of creating seven new barons and promoting three secular peers, thus at a stroke giving the secular peerage an absolute majority over the spiritual lords. Under Edward VI the system was hijacked to reward those great men who were prepared to accept the decidedly dubious adaptation of old King Henry's death-bed wishes in the interests of the Protestant clique around the Protector Somerset.

Promotions formed part of the system of honours alongside creations because there were various steps on the ladder of nobility, from barons at the bottom of the pile (also the most numerous category) through diminishing numbers of viscounts, earls and marquesses up to the exalted rank of duke. Naturally, each rank had its own variations on the peerage's robes of state, complete with the details of the coronet to which each was entitled: a uniform of honour. Precedence within the grades was also as important as the order of seating within an old-fashioned classroom, because in this world it denoted formal nearness to or distance from the King: the source of power, wealth and position.

Surrey was created Duke of Norfolk on 2 February 1514. At the same time Sir Charles Brandon, who had been Henry VIII's deputy commander in the French campaign was made Duke of Suffolk. The creation of two dukes in a single day was quite exceptional even by the standards of the English court. There was the bonus of a captive French Duke to show off to the King's subjects. For the nobility it represented the highpoint of their new position of influence with the young King, having done what they were supposed to do best: fight the King's wars. The surviving account, probably by a herald, shows that the nobility's interest in attending put strains on stage management.

Description of the creation of Surrey and of Lisle   2 February 1514
as Dukes of Norfolk and of Suffolk

In the year of our Lord 1513 [1514], the 5th year of our sovereign Lord King Henry VIII on Candlemas Day [2 February], the King being at Lambeth, were create these estates following: that is to say, the Earl of Surrey, Sir Thomas Howard senior, Earl Marshal and Treasurer of England, create Duke of Norfolk; the Viscount Lisle, Sir Charles Brandon, late Marshal of the King's Army, was create Duke of Suffolk; the Lord Howard, Sir Thomas Howard the younger, Lord Admiral of England, was create Earl of Surrey; the Lord Herbert, Sir Charles Somerset, Lord Chamberlain, was create Earl of Worcester, in manner as ensueth:

First, after the King and the Queen had offered and other lords and ladies as accustomed, the said Lords went in to two chambers that was prepared for them: that is to say, one chamber for the dukes, another chamber for the earls; which were in a gallery at the great chamber end, where they did on their robes of estate. And when the high mass was done, the King came to the said great chamber and there stood under his cloth of estate, not being crowned, accompanied with the great part of the nobles of his realm, and also the Duke of Longueville of France which was prisoner [captured at the battle of the Spurs, 1513]. The Queen and the ladies stood there as they might see all the order of their creations.
The press was somewhat great, notwithstanding the doors were straitly kept; yet the number of noble men because of the parliament time was so great] ...

The King and his Favourite Courtier

THE RISE OF CHARLES BRANDON, DUKE OF SUFFOLK

Wedding portrait of Mary Tudor and Charles Brandon, Duke of Suffolk. The bride wears black, as widow of Louis XII of France, and sports some of her magnificent French jewels. Henry VIII took most of these in the tough financial settlement he exacted for agreeing to the shot-gun marriage of his sister and favourite.

Charles Brandon was without doubt the most successful courtier of the Tudor age. In five years he rose from esquire to duke, and, more remarkable still, he survived another thirty-one years at Henry VIII's Court, to leave his family amongst the greatest in the realm at his death. The secret of his success lay neither in outstanding abilities nor in ruthless ambition, but in charm, a vital attribute in an age of personal politics. On embassy or in command of Henry's armies, he relied not on an understanding of the complexities of diplomacy or on any great technical skill in generalship, but on his ability to deal with people. As a royal Councillor he displayed no specialized knowledge of finance or the law, but showed common sense and an ability to work with others. Above all, he won and exercised influence at Court and in the country at large because he was one of the King's closest friends.

Brandon's family background prepared him for a career at Court. Though the Brandons were recent county gentry in 1485 (their ancestors had been merchants trading from East Anglian ports), they did well out of backing Henry Tudor against Richard III. Brandon's father died

at Bosworth, but his uncle Thomas became one of Henry's leading courtiers, holding the post of Master of the Horse, in charge of the royal stable, which Brandon would hold under Henry VIII. A place at Court was found for Brandon, who emerged as one of Henry VIII's favourites in the years following his accession as King. Henry granted him offices and titles - Viscount Lisle in 1513, Duke of Suffolk in 1514 - and made him his second-in-command when he invaded France in 1513. Brandon's influence with the King and his rapid elevation to the highest rank of the nobility made others envious and alarmed, and they had their chance to decry him when he gambled recklessly on Henry's favour by marrying the King's sister Mary, the widowed Queen of France, without permission in 1515.

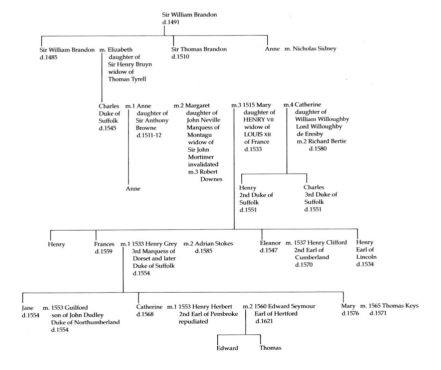

The Brandon dynasty: Charles Brandon's marital history was almost as complex as Henry VIII's and no more productive. Within a generation the inheritance had passed through the female line to first the Greys and then the Seymours.

At Henry VII's court Charles Brandon soon demonstrated his aptitude for two of the most absorbing activities of the early Tudor courtier, jousting and courtly love. The first stood him in good stead once the chivalrous enthusiast Henry VIII was on the throne, but the second led Brandon into a tangle which two of his contemporaries recalled nearly fifty years later when giving evidence in a court case concerning the legitimacy of Brandon's daughter Anne.

Deposition of Walter Devereux, Viscount Hereford   1552

... This deponent saith he was a page, waiting on the lords' cups in the Court in Henry VII's time, at which time the said duke [of Suffolk] was a sewer [waiter] for the board's end ... and by that occasion they did often dine and sup together, which gave cause of much familiarity ... He knew Anne Browne ... waiting on Queen Elizabeth, at which time waited also Mistress Margaret Wootton and Mistress Anne Green, those at that time being called the three gentlewomen of honour ...

He saith that he knew the said Duke of Suffolk was in love and resorted much to the company of the said Anne Browne in the said King Henry VII's time, but how long before the death of the said king he doth not certainly remember ... He remembreth well that the said duke had one daughter by the same Anne Browne, before any matrimony solemnized, whose name was Anne ... This deponent saith that he doth well remember that the said duke and Anne Browne were married in the time of King Henry VIII, at a church in London called St Michael's church in Cornhill, where this deponent gave her at the church door, the said Anne Browne being then great with child, whereof she was shortly after delivered ... There was present at this marriage Sir John Russell, knight, now Earl of Bedford, Sir William Sidney, knight, Sir Griffith Don, knight, and one Guyot a Burgundian, Dorothy Yaxley and Margaret, late wife to one Vernon. The said duke's gown was then of velvet russet faced with martens joined with beaver ...

Deposition of Thomas, third Duke of Norfolk   1552

He saith that he knew Charles Brandon ever since he was of the age of 8 or 10 ... He saith that the said Duke of Suffolk did keep the said Anne Browne as his concubine before he was married to her in King Henry VII's days, but how long he kept her so this deponent doth not now remember ...

Jousts and Revels

Trumpeters summon the jousters to the Westminster Tournament, 1511.

Henry VIII's court inherited from his father's a lively tradition of jousting, dancing and court entertainments. But after 1509 the expenditure lavished on such revels and the attention paid to them by ambassadors and other observers increased dramatically. This was because the new King took part in masques and tournaments at which his ageing, sickly and half-blind father had been merely a spectator. Henry's participation showed off his own skill, strength and grace, but it also showed off the favour of the courtiers whom he chose to accompany him. The rise of the Duke of Suffolk, for instance, can be clearly traced through the outfits provided for him to wear in court festivities, which increasingly matched those worn by Henry himself, with their rich and costly materials spangled with gold and silver. From 1512 until 1516 Suffolk was the King's regular partner in tournaments; thereafter Henry decided that only Suffolk was an opponent fit to counterpoint his own skill, and they led opposing teams in the major court jousts until 1524, when Suffolk nearly killed the King and swore never to run against him again.

Tournaments could be dangerous - Henry had another nasty fall in 1536 - but they were no longer the barely restrained private wars they had been in the twelfth century. Most frequently, jousters ran at each other down opposite sides of a wooden barrier, aiming to shatter their lance on their opponent or, exceptionally, unseat him. Though the lances were by no means frail, a firm strike at full speed on a thickly armoured breastplate usually splintered them impressively; surviving score-sheets show that lances broken on the opponent's head (marked by a stroke through the upper line) or glancing blows (marked by strokes which did not break the lines) were less common than lances broken on the body (a stroke through the lower line). Hitting the right target repeatedly was difficult, and on bad days many knights missed each other completely. But Henry and Suffolk do seem to have been able tilters, and they usually acquitted themselves well against French competition, though nobles from the Netherlands, the great centre of a late flowering of chivalry, rather showed up all the English at Margaret of Austria's court in 1513.

The ladies of the court could only watch in the tiltyard, but they danced with the King and his favourites in masques or disguisings, which were often part of elaborate entertainments including allegorical pageants, short plays, musical interludes and indoor mock-tournaments where the combatants, ladies included, bombarded each other with fruit and sweets. All this revelry reflected the carefree and open-handed spirit of Henry's early years as king, but it waned significantly as he grew older and his reign more sombre; only during Elizabeth I's reign did the court regain some of the gaiety of Henry's golden youth.

Overleaf: Henry VIII jousting before Catherine of Aragon at the Westminster Tournament held to celebrate the birth of his short-lived son in 1511. Henry, shown breaking his lance on his opponent's helmet, won the prize.

Between Brandon's first involvement with Anne Browne and their public marriage he had married her widowed aunt, sold some of her lands to meet the expenses of life at Court, and then, overwhelmed by scruples, had this second marriage annulled and returned to Anne, who died not long afterwards. At the time, this scandal did little to hold back Brandon's career, but years later his murky marital history would come back to haunt his descendants.

By late 1513 Brandon had emerged from the circle of courtiers around Henry VIII to acknowledged supremacy as the King's closest friend - a fact soon confirmed by his creation as Duke of Suffolk. When Henry visited the Regent of the Netherlands, Margaret of Austria, during his campaign in France in the autumn of 1513. Brandon turned his charm on her - though whether in real hope of marriage to Europe's most eligible young dowager, or merely as part of the courtly game of flirtation, we shall never know.

Margaret of Austria to Sir Richard Wingfield   [May 1514]
Louvain

... Ye may know, my lord the ambassador, that after some days having been at Tournai, knowing from day to day the great love and trust that the King bare and had to the personage which is no need to name [Suffolk]; also with the virtue and grace of his person, the which me seemed that I have not much seen gentleman to approach it; also considering the desire the which always he showed me that he had to do me service; all these things considered by me, I have always forced me to do unto him all honour and pleasure, the which to me seemed to be well agreeable unto the King his good master. Who, as I may imagine, seeing the good cheer and will the which I bare him, with the love which he beareth unto him, by many times spake unto me for to know if this good will ... might stretch unto some effect of promise of marriage ... Wherunto many times I answered ... the several reasons wherefore it was not to me possible ... I think not to again never to put me where I have had so much of unhap and misfortune ...

[Suffolk] said ... that he should never do thing, were it of marriage, or to take lady nor mistress, without my commandment, but would continue all his life my right humble servant ... I cannot tell if the king, which was truchman [interpreter], because of the love which he beareth him, might have taken it more forward for to interpret more his desire ... One night at Tournai, being at the banquet, after the banquet [Suffolk] put himself upon his knees before me, and in speaking and him playing, he drew from my finger the ring, and put it upon his, and since showed it me, and I took to laugh, and to him said that he was a thief, and that I thought not that the King had with him led thieves out of his country ...

The whole business became an acute embarrassment for Margaret when betting opened in London on whether she would marry Suffolk, and Henry had to hush the matter up. It did nothing to dent his friendship for Suffolk, which revolved most visibly around the sports they both loved: hunting, tennis, and the joust. Suffolk's letters home from his first embassy to France, which included a grand tournament to celebrate the marriage of Henry's sister Mary and King Louis XII, give a glimpse of his relationship with Henry. In the original spelling (erratic even for the early sixteenth century) they also suggest that Suffolk did not have the sort of educational polish that would grace later Tudor courtiers.

Duke of Suffolk to Henry VIII   14 November 1514
Paris

Please it Your Grace, this letter shall be to advertise Your Grace as near as I can of my Lord Chamberlain's and your ambassadors' demeanour, the which, I assure Your Grace, has been to your honour; and, Sir, I beseech Your Grace in my most humblest wise to give them thanks for the great goodness that I have found in them, specially for your causes, and also for the good fellowship that I have found in them for my part; and, Sir, as for news I cannot write you more than they can show Your Grace.

Sir, I see the time now that, if it were possible, I would rather than all that I have in the world that you might be with me unknown, for I think you should lose none honour, and I should have a better stay [jousting partner] than I can find in France, as knows God, who send Your Grace your most noble heart's desire. Written at Paris the 14 day of November with the hand of your most bounden servant,
Charles Suffolk

plysset your gras thys lettar schall by to awartes your grace as near as i cane of me lord chambarlayn and your inbassetoures dymenour the wyche i insuar your grace has by to your honnour and sr i bysche your grace in me most youmbyllest wyes to gyef thym thankyes for the gryth goodnes yt i have found in thym spysseall for your causses and all soo for the good fyllowschype yt i have found in thym for me par and sr as for nues i cannot wryth you mor thyn thay cane schaw your gras sr i sce the thyem nhow yt yf et war possebbyll i wold radar than hall yt i have in the warld yt you myth by wyet me anknowne for i thynke you schold lyes non honnor and i schold have a byettar stye thyn i cane fyend in france as knowes god who send your grace your most nobyll hartys dyssear wretton at pares the xiiij day of nowyembar wyet the hand of your most bounden sarwant
charlys suffolk

Marriage and the Law of Matrimony

In the sixteenth century it was remarkably easy to marry. The mere exchange of vows between a couple over the age of consent - twelve for girls, fourteen for boys - without any public ceremony or even the presence of witnesses, constituted a valid marriage in the eyes of the Church courts. Even a promise to marry in the future, followed by consummation, made a binding contract. The authorities pressed all couples to marry publicly at a church with a priest's blessing, but failure to do so did not invalidate a marriage in law. This made it easy to assert or deny the existence of clandestine marriages, or marriages by promise and consummation like that which the young Charles Brandon was said to have contracted with Anne Browne.

Because the descent of property depended on the legitimacy of offspring, the stakes involved in establishing whether or not couples were married could be very high. Among the landowning classes, marriages were usually arranged by parents for financial or political reasons, but this did not always make them loveless. Widows or widowers seem to have enjoyed a freer choice of partner, one indulged by Catherine Parr and Catherine, Duchess of Suffolk.

Early in the century the great loophole in marriage law was the problem of consanguinity. Marriages with fairly distant relations, both by blood and marriage, and even with relations by godparenthood were banned - though dispensations could be obtained to permit many such unions to go ahead. Brandon managed to extricate himself from his marriage to Anne Browne's aunt partly by showing that her first husband was related to his grandmother. Yet it was unclear which of these limitations were merely decreed by the Church and could therefore be dispensed with, and which were directly instituted by God and thus irrevocable.

When Henry VIII became convinced that only divine disapproval of his marriage could account for its failure to provide a satisfactory heir, an understandable conclusion in the light of the Tudors' stress on the support of God's providence for their dynasty, he found a biblical curse - Leviticus 20:21, 'If a man shall take his brother's wife, it is an impurity ... they shall be childless' - which seemed to fit his marriage to Catherine of Aragon, the widow of his elder brother Prince Arthur. The pope who had granted a dispensation for their marriage had acted beyond his powers, concluded the King, and his successor should annul the match.

Henry's case was a field day for theologians, canon lawyers and students of the biblical languages. But neither Wolsey nor his successors could secure compliance at Rome. It was the radical solution of England's withdrawal from the jurisdiction of Rome under Henry's imperial supremacy over the Church that won the day. In 1533 the King got his new wife, but the struggle for the divorce had isolated England in European politics, broken the careers of Wolsey and More, and set Henry, Cranmer and Cromwell on the road to Reformation.

Catherine of Aragon as a young woman. Her marriage to Henry showed how easy it was to get round the laws of matrimony in the right circumstances; her divorce, how difficult it was in the wrong ones.

France and the Valois

The Valois Court: Henry III (and poodle) at the wedding ball of the royal favourite Joyeuse in 1581.

In the second half of the fifteenth century the Valois kings re-established France as the strongest monarchy in Europe. A reliable tax system, a powerful standing army, sophisticated artillery and plentiful supplies of Swiss mercenaries enabled them to recover peripheral provinces - Normandy, Picardy, Gascony,Provence, Brittany and half of Burgundy and Artois - from the English or semi-independent dukes, and then to pursue their claims to Naples and Milan. But the ambitions of Charles VIII, Louis XII, Francis I and Henry II led them into sixty-five years of intermittent conflict with the native Italian rulers (including the Pope), the kings of Spain (who claimed Naples) and the Holy Roman Emperors (who claimed the overlordship of Milan). For Francis and Henry this was an exhausting contest with Charles V, Holy Roman Emperor, King of Spain, ruler of the Netherlands, and heir to the Burgundian dukes' rivalry with France. Peace was made in 1559,

confirming Spanish hegemony in Italy but ratifying French conquests on the northern and eastern fringes of the kingdom.

While jousting at the tournament to celebrate peace, Henry II was mortally wounded by a splinter from a lance. Three of his sons followed him on the throne, but the youth of Francis II and Charles IX and the fecklessness of the poodle-fancier Henry III made the monarchy unable to control a developing domestic crisis. The social and economic strains of war combined with the political and social disruption caused by the growth of the French Calvinist churches to set off a series of civil wars between 1562 and 1598. England and Spain intervened to support the Protestant and Catholic parties, and the wars ended only when the Protestant leader Henry of Navarre succeeded the assassinated Henry VIII as king, converted to Catholicism but decreed toleration for Protestants under the Edict of Nantes.

Princess Mary's marriage to King Louis did not last long. The aged bridegroom died on New Year's Day 1515, and Mary determined not to continue with a run of diplomatic marriages like those which had left Margaret of Austria so unhappy. When Suffolk arrived in Paris to take her home, they agreed to ask Henry for permission to marry on their return to England, which he granted. But Mary was still afraid that Henry might change his mind and find her another husband as ghastly as Louis. She insisted that 'she had rather to be torn in pieces ... and with that she wept.' 'Sir,' added Suffolk in explaining to Henry, 'I never saw woman so weep.' She then pressed Suffolk to marry her at once, adding urgency with the warning 'Look never after this day to have the same proffer again.' They married, in secret, in Paris, and then worked out how to break the news to Henry. At first they relied on the rising chief minister, Thomas Wolsey, Archbishop of York, to handle things with the King.

Duke of Suffolk to Thomas Wolsey   5 March 1515
Paris

My Lord, I recommend me to you, and so it is that I wit that you have been ... the helper of me to that I am now (next God and my master), and therefore I will never hide none thing from you, trusting that you will help me now as you have done always. My lord, so it is that when I came to Paris I heard many things which put me in great fear, and so did the queen both; and the queen would never let me be in rest till I had granted her to be married. And so, to be plain with you, I have married her heartily, and have lain with her, in so much I fear me lest that she be with child. My lord, I am not in a little sorrow if the King should know it, and that his Grace should be displeased with me. For I assure you that I had rather have died than he should be miscontent ... Let me not be undone now, the which I fear me shall be, without the only help of you. My lord, think not that ever you shall make any [friend] that shall be more obliged to you ...

   I beseech you to instruct me in all the haste possible ... Now, my Lord, [you] know all, and in you is all my trust. Beseeching you now of your assured help, and that I may have answer from you of this and all my other writings as shortly as may be possible, for I assure you that I have as heavy a heart as any man living, and shall have till I may hear good [tidings] from you ... At Paris the 5 day of March by your most assured,
   Charles Suffolk

Suffolk's concern was fully justified. Henry was furious, not so much because of the marriage as because of its circumstances, which suggested to the world that his own sister and his leading courtier neither trusted his word nor cared much about flouting his authority. In particular he was upset that Suffolk, 'the man in all the world he loved and trusted best', had broken a promise made to the King that if he and Mary did agree to marry, they would not do so until their return. Despite Wolsey's efforts, those jealous of Brandon's startling rise - in particular the Howards - inflamed the King's anger, and on the way back to Calais Suffolk found himself appealing for his life.

Duke of Suffolk to Henry VIII   22 April 1515
Montreuil

Most gracious sovereign Lord, so it is that I am informed divers ways that all your whole council, my lord of York [Wolsey] excepted, with many other, are clearly determined to tempt Your Grace that I may either be put to death or be put in prison, and so to be destroyed. Alas, Sir, I may say that I have a hard fortune, seeing that there was never none of them in trouble but I was glad to help them to my power, and that Your Grace knows best. And now that I am in this none little trouble and sorrow, now they are ready to help to destroy me. But, Sir, I can no more, but God forgive them whatsoever comes on me, for I am determined.

   For, Sir, Your Grace is he that is my sovereign lord and master, and he that has brought me up of nought, and I am your subject and servant, and he that has offended Your Grace in breaking my promise that I made Your Grace touching the queen your sister. For the which I, with most humble heart, I will yield myself unto Your Grace's hands to do with my poor body your gracious pleasure, not fearing the malice of them. For I know Your Grace of such nature that it cannot lie in their power to cause you to destroy me for their malice. But what punishment I have, I shall thank God and Your Grace of it, and think that I have well deserved it, both to God and Your Grace. As knows Our Lord, who send Your Grace your most honourable heart's desire with long life, and me, most sorrowful wretch, your gracious favour, what sorrow soever I endure therefor. At Montreuil, the 22 day of April, by your most humble subject and servant ...

Henry could not find it in his heart to destroy his best friend. They paid for his forgiveness with a slice of Mary's dower revenues, but they survived. Charles Brandon's courtliness had made him not only a duke, but the husband of a queen.

The Chief Minister and the Nobles

THE DUKES OF NORFOLK AND SUFFOLK 1514-1526

Pride. Thomas Wolsey as Cardinal Minister. As a cardinal Wolsey took precedence of all peers; as the King's chief councillor and favourite he had more power.

Fall. Left, the loss of political power as Wolsey surrenders (on the second time of asking) the Chancellorship to the Dukes of Norfolk and Suffolk; right, the loss of property as his treasures are displayed for seizure by the King (who viewed them with Anne Boleyn).

In the first five years of Henry VIII's reign a third man rose to power, in parallel with Brandon and the Howards. Thomas Wolsey, a cleric of humble birth, combined administrative ability with political adroitness. The first gave him a crucial role in Henry's first French war, organizing supplies, finances, and at length the entire war effort. The second enabled him to combine this administrative supremacy, which he retained at the coming of peace in 1514, with an influence over the King and a dominance among the Councillors. His rise in the Church paralleled that in the State, as he became Archbishop of York in 1514, a cardinal in 1515, and papal legate, with sweeping powers over the English Church, in 1518. Wolsey succeeded because he gave Henry what he wanted: power over the Church and his subjects, a reputation for justice and social reform at home, and a prominence on the European political stage. In the years around 1520 and the famous meeting with the French at the Field of Cloth of Gold, Wolsey made his King the glorious arbiter of European peace; when the peace broke down, Wolsey did his best to make Henry a mighty conqueror in France. There was a part in all this for Norfolk, Surrey and Suffolk, but it was strictly limited. Wolsey and the King usually made policy between them and consulted others only about how to carry it out. Yet when the policy failed, as it did in 1525 when tax-payers refused point blank to fund yet another campaign in France, the great nobles were needed to keep the countryside under control, and Wolsey had to pay rather more heed to their views. In the early years of Henry's reign Wolsey acted as court agent for the veteran statesman Richard Fox, Bishop of Winchester, who emerged as Surrey's main competitor for leadership of the new King's Council. While doing so, he developed an expertise in dealing with the King and with rivals for power which would serve him well once he became chief minister.

Thomas Wolsey to Bishop Fox of Winchester   30 September 1511
Windsor

... Yesterday I ... showed unto his Grace how much honour and also furtherance of all his affairs in time to come should ensue to him, if that by his commendation some cardinal might attain to be pope; and, seeing that the emperor was effectually intending the preferment of the Cardinal Adrian, which in manner is as the king's bounden subject, with his gracious help the matter should be much the sooner brought to pass.
I found his grace very conformable and agreeable to my saying. Howbeit, I durst not further wade with his grace ... I trust that ye will take my doing (which proceeded of good will, thinking that it was for the best) in good part.

My Lord, in communication at the large, I have felt how that my lord chamberlain and [my Lord] of Durham be much inclined to the Cardinal of St George, and in all their talk they cannot speak too much honour of him, dispraising the Cardinal Adrian afore. If your lordship were here, this matter would be soon brought to your purpose. And, my lord, for divers urgent causes it is thought very expedient that ye should repair unto the King, for all his great matters be deferred unto your coming, which is daily looked for and desired of all those that would the King's causes should proceed in a good train ...

My Lord Treasurer [Surrey], at his last coming to the King, which was this day sevennight [a week ago], had such manner and countenance showed unto him that on the morrow he departed home again, and as yet is not returned to the court. With little help now he might be utterly, as touching lodging in the same, excluded; whereof, in my poor judgment, no little good should ensue ...

Mr. Howard [Sir Edward] marvellously incenseth the king against the Scots; by whose wanton means his grace spendeth much money, and is more disposed to war than peace. Your presence shall be very necessary to repress this appetite...

At Windsor in haste, the last day of September, with the rude hand of your loving and humble priest...
Thomas Wolsey

By 1514 Wolsey was working closely with Suffolk, for both were natural competitors of the Howards. They committed themselves to a policy of peace and alliance with France, and sealed it with a marriage between Henry's sister Mary and King Louis XII. But Mary was upset when Louis sent home most of her English servants soon after their wedding, a step in which Surrey, who had escorted her to France, acquiesced. Suffolk, on his way across the Channel for secret talks with Louis and the grand tournament at Mary's coronation, was quick to suspect a plot against Wolsey and himself, and with characteristic verve dashed off a letter so fast that the Charles of his signature ran into the Suffolk.

Duke of Suffolk to Thomas Wolsey   20 October 1514
Dover

My Lord, I recommend me unto you. And so it is that [I] met with Dannet at Canterbury, and he has shown me divers news, the which he will tell you at his coming. My Lord you shall well perceive by the handling of these matters what my Lord of Norfolk and his son mean, and, as I take it, they have been the chief causers that the Queen's servants be put from her, because they were of your choosing and not of theirs ... My Lord, if the Queen should not be well entreated she may blame you and me, and so it shall be laid in our necks by them that be the causer, and love neither you nor me. My Lord, I pray you let me have your mind what you think I may do in this, and how I shall order myself in it, for I will do nothing but as you shall advertise.

   My Lord, at the writing of this letter I came to my ship, and I trust by the help of God to be at Boulogne by noon, and so tomorrow on to Paris with all my harness [armour], and my horses shall come fair and softly after. My Lord, I make the more haste because I would be loth to be returned again. For, my Lord, now I am over, if the Frenchmen would forsake their challenge (as I think they will not for shame), yet I may do the King's other business, and come the sooner home. Wherefor, my Lord, I beseech you, hold your hand fast that I be not sent for back; for I am sure that the father and the son would not for no good I should speak with the French king, but so I trust to do. And I doubt not but I know all their drifts ... Written at Dover the 20 day of October by yours assured,
   Charlesfolk

Lodgings at Court

Henry VIII dining, alone and under a cloth of estate in his Privy Chamber. The royal apartments were on the first floor; directly underneath were lodged the leading servants of the Privy Chamber (in 1526 two shared a bed). In the 1540s all councillors were given lodgings as well, though even the greatest rarely had more than two rooms.

The Royal Household was the core of the Court. Tudor monarchs felt the same tension as their late medieval predecessors and Stuart successors between the desirability of maintaining a large and splendid Household and the cost that it involved. But at the same time every courtier craved the prestige, financial benefits and potential for access to the monarch provided by a place on the establishment of the Household.

Cost-cutting ministers like Wolsey, Cromwell and Burghley paid close attention to the financial implications of expansions and contractions of the Household, both of the actual staff of royal servants and of those great men and women with the privilege of 'bouge of court', the right to lodgings and supplies of food, drink and firewood in the royal palaces. There were further limitations on the number of servants that courtiers of different rank might maintain while at Court, and on the numbers each might take to diplomatic occasions like the Field of Cloth of Gold.

Such matters had political implications too. Those without assured lodgings - including the great majority of the peerage - had to ask royal permission to come up to Court, and it might be refused as a mark of disfavour or suspicion, as well as from simpler motives such as the royal fear of plague. Those whose right to lodgings was abrogated - as Wolsey hoped Surrey's might be in 1511 - would find the expense of long stays at Court crippling, and would thus be less active about the monarch and almost certainly less influential in politics and government.

Their loss of privilege might in itself constitute a strong hint that their continual presence was no longer desired, just as the regular provision of lodgings for the Gentlemen of the Privy Chamber and the members of the Privy Council in the 1540s reflected the institutional maturity of the household department responsible for the monarch's private service and of the attendant council with its clearly defined membership. For the individual gentlemen and councillors, the title to rooms near the King's own suites in the grand new palaces at Whitehall and Hampton Court was itself a token of power in a personal monarchy. John Skelton chose well when he entitled his poem on the opportunities, perils and temptations of court life 'The Bouge of Court'.

Wolsey took an increasingly tight grip on government and politics in the years that followed, and Suffolk's desperate need for help over his marriage to Mary made him less the cardinal's colleague than his client. In similar though less spectacular fashion many of the nobility found themselves dependent on the new minister's goodwill in their dealings with the King. Yet Wolsey's relations with lay noblemen were often uneasy, for some of them regarded him as a pompous upstart and many of his policies seemed to threaten their power. He also did nothing to allay Henry's periodic fears of conspiracies by nobles against the Tudors, like those of 1518 which were stoked by rumours from abroad, and caused the King to restrict the number of retainers that noblemen brought to Court at Easter (a move which equally helped to reduce Henry's worries about catching the plague). The cardinal's conspicuous zeal for Henry's security of course also increased the King's confidence in Wolsey's management of national affairs.

Richard Pace to Thomas Wolsey   3 April 1518
Abingdon

Please it Your Grace, the King's highness hath this morning received Your Grace's letters, with all other letters and instructions annexed unto the same with singular great diligence (to his grace's great contentation) ... His Highness doth give unto Your Grace most hearty thanks for the final clause of your letters, touching great personages, and doth right well perceive hereby, and most lovingly accept, the especial regard that Your Grace hath to the surety of his Grace's person. And his highness doth signify unto Your Grace that he hath not been negligent herein himself; but at such time as his Grace had perfect knowledge of the coming of the said great personages unto him, his Grace did secretly provide that they should be advertised by their own servants resident in the Court, as well of the strait [restricted] lodging here as of the penury [shortage] of horsemeat [fodder], and for these respects to bring with them but a very small company. And Sir Henry Marney [the captain of the guard] is executor of this the King's pleasure and commandment, and doth look thereunto both wisely and faithfully, as well within this town as nigh thereunto ...

His Highness doth see so great scarceness of victuals, and especially of horsemeat, here, that he cannot here continue ... Wherefor his highness desires Your Grace to provide for to have perfect knowledge if there be any manner of infection of the great sickness in London, or in any of his Grace's palaces nigh thereunto, and to advertise his grace of the same. This day arrived here the Duke of Buckingham. My lord, I did read to the King's grace every word of Your Grace's letters directed unto myself, and his Grace said that he had good cause to approve your wisdom ...

In foreign affairs Wolsey offered Henry the prominence in European politics which the King craved. From 1518, when the cardinal negotiated a general European peace pact in London, King and minister presided over a brittle *Pax Anglicana*. Its high point was the meeting between Henry and King Francis I of France at the Field of Cloth of Gold in June 1520, and the associated interviews between Henry and the Emperor Charles V. The brevity of the international concord they celebrated made them a good subject for a sermon on the fleeting nature of worldly glory.

Bishop Fisher, sermon on the Field of Cloth of Gold   1520

I doubt not but ye have heard of many goodly sights which were shown of late beyond the sea, with much joy and pleasure worldly. Was it not a great thing, within so short a space to see three great princes of this world - I mean the Emperor, and the King our master, and the French king; and each of these three in so great honour, showing their royalty, showing their riches, showing their power, with each of their noblesse [nobility] appointed and apparelled in rich clothes, in silks, velvets, cloths of gold, and such other precious raiments. To see three right excellent queens at once together, and of three great realms: that one, the noble Queen our mistress, the very example of virtue and nobleness to all women; and the French queen; and the third Queen Mary, sometime wife unto Louis, French king, sister to our sovereign lord, a right excellent and fair lady; and every of them accompanied with so many other fair ladies in sumptuous and gorgeous apparel. Such dancings, such harmonies, such dalliance, and so many pleasant pastimes ... so delicate wines, so precious meats, such and so many noble men of arms, so rich and goodly tents, such joustings, such tourneys, and such feats of war ... Nevertheless, these great sights have a far difference from the joys of heaven ...

The pleasures whereof I spake, had many interruptions. For that little while that we were there, sometimes there was such dust, and therewithal so great winds, that all the air was full of dust. The gowns of velvet and of cloth of gold were full of dust, the rich trappers of horses were full of dust, hats, caps, gowns were full of dust, the hair and faces of men were full of dust, and, briefly to speak, horse and man were so encumbered with dust, that scantly one might see another. The winds blew down many tents, shook sore the houses that were builded for pleasure, and let [prevented] divers of them to be builded. Sometimes again we had rains and thunders so unmeasurably that no man might stir forth to see no pleasures. Sometimes, when men would longer have disported them at the jousts, came the night and darkness upon them, and interrupted their pleasure. In heaven is no such interruptions ...

The Field of Cloth of Gold

In 1520 Henry VIII met Francis I of France at the Field of Cloth of Gold.

But the serious business was transacted in two meetings with Emperor Charles V.

International politics in the age of Henry VIII was mostly a matter of personal relations between sovereign princes. They fought wars to win inheritances and battles to win honour, and made peace by marrying off their children. This made meetings between monarchs even more significant than modern summit conferences.

Excitement therefore mingled with tension as Henry rode out on 7 June 1520 from the English outpost of Guines, a satellite fortress of Calais, to meet Francis I of France, England's traditional enemy. With Henry was Wolsey, the architect of the peace among the European powers of which this encounter was the greatest celebration; and each king was accompanied by the flower of his nobility. Fortunately Henry and Francis got on quite well, vying to outdo one another in generosity, politeness, and demonstrations of their mutual trust. There was only one awkward moment in the seventeen days that followed, when Henry was thrown heavily to the ground during a wrestling match with Francis.

Friendly but intense and extravagant competition was the keynote of the meeting. The centrepiece of the English encampment was a prefabricated palace with a shining expanse of glass windows, and fountains that ran with wine. (In the storms that marred the festivities it fared much better than the enormous golden tents inhabited by the French dignitaries.) Both entourages shimmered with jewels, silks and the cloth of gold which gave the event its name. The banquets excelled in exoticism and sheer scale: the English contingent of some six thousand contributed about forty thousand gallons of wine and over fourteen thousand gallons of beer and ale. There were splendid tournaments, a grand mass at which the choirs of both royal chapels sang, and frequent masques and dances.

As a diplomatic exercise it was largely futile. Before and after the meeting, Henry and Wolsey held more business-like conferences with Francis's rival, the Emperor Charles V; there they laid the basis for an alliance with him against the French, to be concluded should his differences with Francis prove irreconcilable - as they soon did. Within months of the revellers' dispersal, John Fisher used the Field of Cloth of Gold as an illustration of the impermanence and unreliability of the things of the world.

Overleaf: The Field of Cloth of Gold. In the foreground Henry's procession (left) and his temporary palace (right); in the middle distance, the meeting of the Kings, and, top left, the firework dragon let off before the blessing of the meeting.

All too soon Europe was at war again, and Wolsey could maintain the King's prestige only by joining in. For Suffolk and the Howards this brought once again the trials and opportunities of military command. Surrey led inconclusive raids on France in 1522, but in autumn 1523 he was on the northern border, facing a Scottish invasion led by the pro-French Duke of Albany, and grumbling about the distaste of younger courtiers for the rigours of soldiering.

Earl of Surrey to Cardinal Wolsey   8 October 1523
Newcastle upon Tyne

... I have advertisements that the duke [of Albany] prepareth all that he can to invade this realm with the light of this next new moon, and by his words does right little esteem the power of England ... And notwithstanding that the weather hath been here so foul, with marvellous great rain divers days, and most specially yesterday with rain and this day with snow, so that the opinion of many wise men is it shall be very difficult for the said duke to carry any great ordnance (unless it be to Berwick), yet forasmuch as he might do infinite hurt in overrunning the country unless he were resisted, I shall cause all my said power to come forwards, and to be here at the day prefixed ...

God knoweth, if the poorest gentleman in the king's house were here, and I at London and were advertised of these news, I would not fail to kneel upon my knees before the King's grace, to have licence to come hither in post to be at the day of battle. And if young noblemen and gentlemen be not desirous and willing to be at such journeys, and to take the pain and give the adventure [run the risks] - and the king's Highness well contented with those that will do so, and not regarding others that will be but dancers, dicers and carders - his Grace shall not be well served when he would be. For men without experience shall do small service, and experience of war will not be had without it be sought for, and the adventure given.

Of likelihood no man living shall ever live to see the Scots attempt to invade this realm with the power of Scotland if they may be well resisted now. And by many ways I am advertised that the Duke of Albany is a marvellous wilful man, and will believe no man's counsel, but will have his own opinion followed ... He is so passionate that [if] he ... hear anything contrarious to his mind and pleasure, his accustomed manner is to take his bonnet suddenly off his head, and to throw it in the fire, and no man dare take it out, but let it to be brent ... at his last being in Scotland he did burn above a dozen bonnets after that manner. And if he be such a man, by God's grace we shall speed the better with him ...

War and the Nobility

 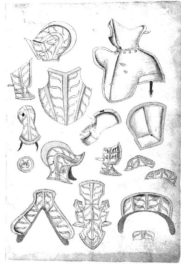

Design for a suit of armour for the Duke of Norfolk with, right, the specialized pieces intended for different forms of combat, mounted and on foot. Norfolk only wore armour in battle once, in 1560, when as Earl Marshal he was supreme commander against Scotland (but with a lower ranking professional under him to do the serious business).

During the first half of the sixteenth century, service to the Crown in war remained the primary justification for the nobility's wealth and status. Armies in the 1510s, 1520s, 1540s and 1550s were largely raised by noblemen from their tenants and servants. Military ability and the successful commanding of armies still accounted both for the prestige of existing noble families (the Howards in particular) and for many new creations, from Edward Stanley, Lord Mounteagle (who obtained his barony for his part in the victory at Flodden) to the rise of Edward Seymour, John Dudley and William Herbert in the 1540s.

Apart from a handful of baronies awarded for service against Wyatt's Rebellion in 1554, the situation changed dramatically after the mid-century. None of Elizabeth I's very small number of new peers obtained his creation for purely military service, and the number of peers who were active military commanders was also limited, even during the long war with Spain between 1585 and 1604. The exception that proves the rule was the promotion of Lord Howard of Effingham, the victorious commander against the Armada, to the Earldom of Nottingham in 1597.

The absence of 'fighting lords' was due in part to the increased sophistication of warfare after 1540, which led to the emergence of a new type of semi-professional officer first encountered in the garrisons of Calais, Boulogne, Berwick-upon-Tweed, Scotland and Ireland. It was from their ranks that the captains for the forces Queen Elizabeth raised were drawn. A few of them were peers by inheritance, and a greater number younger sons of peers - Sir John Norris, the leading officer of the early Netherlands campaigns, was a son of the recently ennobled Lord Norris of Rycote, for example. Although many of those who survived the reign ultimately received peerages from James I, none received more than a knighthood from Elizabeth. The second Earl of Essex attempted to revive the military role of the nobility at the end of Elizabeth's reign, but her suspicion of a 'military faction' was one of the reasons for his fall.

The nobility did, however, retain a major influence over the militia. The office of lord-lieutenant delegated to them the primary responsibility for its mustering and training. However, this was really an aspect of their wider role in local government. 'Seeing the wars' was still considered important for a nobleman's education, but governing was increasingly being seen as his social function.

Overleaf: The Battle of the Spurs, the highlight of the English war against France in 1513, preceded (in the foreground) by the meeting between Henry VIII and his ally, the Emperor Maximilian. Almost every available noble accompanied Henry VIII in this campaign.

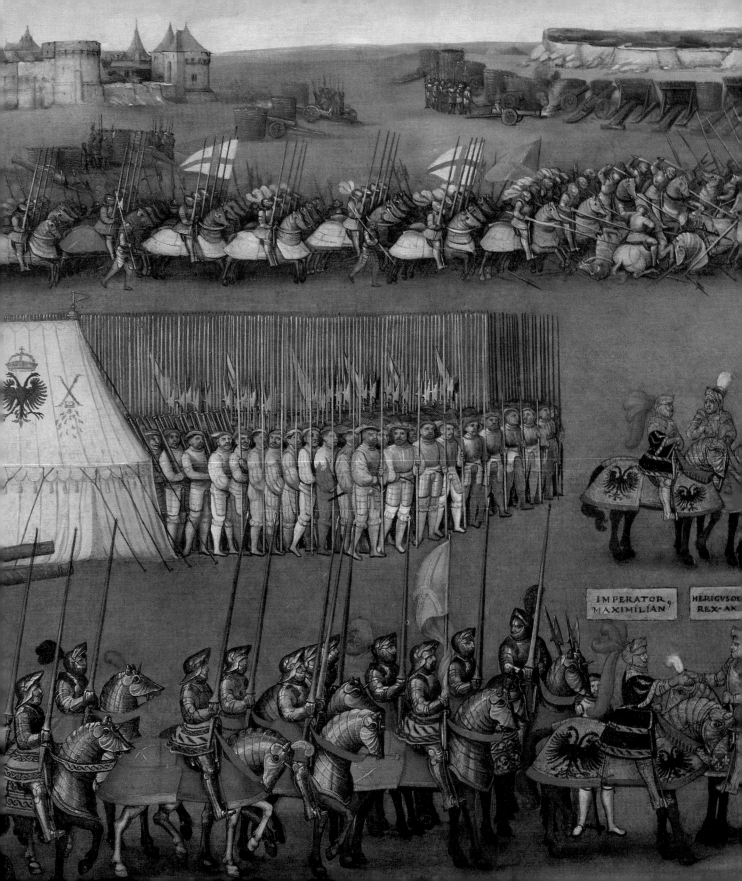

IMPERATOR
MAXIMILIAN

HERIGVSOE
REX·AN

Meanwhile Suffolk was marching deep into France, trying to link up with a rebel French nobleman, the Duke of Bourbon. Bourbon's revolt crumbled, and Suffolk's dispirited and disease-ridden men had to retreat in appalling weather which cruelly exposed the difference between the few professional soldiers, like Elis Gruffydd, a Welshman who later made a career in the Calais garrison, and the mass of raw recruits, who eventually mutinied.

Elis Gruffydd, *Chronicle*   November 1523

... Some said it was too much for them to be lying there on the earth under hedges and bushes dying of cold, another said that he wanted to be home, in bed with his wife, which was a more comfortable place for his head than here ... And yet they had no reason to complain, except of their own sluggishness and slovenliness. For there was no lack of food, or drink, or wood for fire or making huts, and plenty of straw to roof them and to lie on, if they had only fetched it ...

At last on Wednesday night there rose a noise and shouting amongst the host and especially around the tents of the duke, and some of the soldiers said they would tarry there no longer, and that they would go home willy nilly the next day ... Against this some of their comrades said ... that what they were discussing was no less than treason ... To this these obstinate senseless men answered that it was no worse being hanged in England than dying of cold in France. My master, Sir Robert Wingfield, heard all this noise and talking, and made me get out of my bed, where I was as snug as a small pig, to listen to the talk, and to take note of those men who were making this noise ...

And as soon as day came, they began to talk about their journey to England all through the host, and then they shouted out loud 'Home! Home!'... The sensible men got up and went each to his company, to pacify the unruly ones with fair words and promises that they should take their journey back to England the next morning ... and after the people had been quieted, the duke and his captains went into council to decide which way they should next take ... And so the host marched against the freezing wind throughout that day ... which was one of the worst and hardest days for frost that the oldest man in the army had ever seen, and there were many men who were over sixty years of age. This day, if people can be believed, many men on horse and on foot died from sheer cold. Others said that some had lost the use of their limbs from the force of the frost wind. And others said that they had lost the use of their waterpipes, and could not pass any water that way until they had got fire and warm water to thaw them ...

Henry's ambition and Wolsey's efficiency were a dangerous mixture, and by 1525 the country had been taxed hard to pay for wars which seemed to achieve little. The attempt to levy a large 'Amicable Grant' to pay for the King to invade France in person met with general refusal, and provoked a rebellion in the county of Suffolk which the two East Anglian dukes worked together to suppress. Even as the rebels submitted, Howard and Suffolk were worried that Wolsey and the King did not appreciate the strength of feeling against the project, and might try to press on with it: they demanded a Council meeting at Court with the King (a comparatively rare event during Wolsey's ascendancy) so that they could make their views plain.

Dukes of Norfolk and of Suffolk to Cardinal Wolsey   12 May 1525
Lavenham

Please it Your Grace to be advertised that continually more and more knowledge doth come to us, that the confederacy with the evil disposed persons of this town extended to many places, not only in this shire and in Essex, but in Cambridgeshire, the town and university of Cambridge, and divers other countries ... It was time to stop this matter, and now is time convenient to take such order that it be not renewed ...

And if Your Grace shall determine either to have practice to be made for the moiety [half the original demand] with such as have not granted, or else a general practice for such sum as they will grant of their benevolent and loving minds, then we beseech Your Grace to be contented that we attempt neither of the same until the time we have first spoken with the King's highness and Your Grace, to declare and show more of that we have heard and seen than we can write. And assured Your Grace may be that we will not depart hence unless that we see no matter of likelihood of no new business to arise after our departure; and yet we shall put such order in both shires that if any such should chance, all the power of the King's servants and ours shall be ready to withstand the same, and chieftains appointed to lead therein; and we with all possible diligence to return. And assuredly, all things well considered that we hear and see, we think we never saw the time so needful for the king's highness to call his council unto him, to debate and determine what is best to be done ... Written at Lavenham, the 12th day of May, at noon.

After the writing of these premises [the above] divers offenders be come unto us out of sundry towns, and this afternoon many more will come, as well from Sudbury and Melford as from other towns, to submit themselves in like manner as they of Lavenham have done.

Yours most bounden,   Yours assured,
T. Norfolk   Charles Suffolk

Divorce and Reformation in the Reign of King Henry

THE DUKES OF NORFOLK AND SUFFOLK 1527-1537

The Amicable Grant was abandoned, and Wolsey made peace with France. The cardinal's climb-down over the scheme was temporarily embarrassing, but seems to have done his position as chief minister no lasting damage. Even the changes he made to the Council's working arrangements, to provide more important Councillors at Court around the King, had little practical political impact. The fatal challenge to Wolsey's supremacy after 1525 would arise from a new and unforeseen problem, that of the King's divorce.

By early 1527 Wolsey faced the greatest test of his career, in trying to secure a papal annulment of Henry's marriage to Catherine of Aragon. The cardinal applied all his skill in diplomacy and ecclesiastical politics to meet Henry's wish, but progress was slow. Frustration set Henry on edge, and he began to doubt Wolsey's commitment to his cause. Serious reverses in the summer of 1529 gave Wolsey's rivals for power the chance to urge Henry to dispose of his

minister, and in the autumn the cardinal was dismissed from the chancellorship. Norfolk and Suffolk led the new ministry, while Sir Thomas More replaced Wolsey as Lord Chancellor, and Anne Boleyn, the queen-to-be, exercised considerable influence with Henry behind the scenes, working with her father and other relations. Tensions in the new regime soon became evident. More opposed the King's divorce and the assertion of royal dominance over the English Church which accompanied the moves to achieve it, and he wanted to intensify the persecution of the slowly spreading Protestant movement; the Boleyns wanted an urgent divorce and protected Protestants. More lost the struggle and resigned the chancellorship in May 1532, to be executed three years later for his continued opposition to the King. Suffolk, Anne's uncle Norfolk, and even her father the Earl of Wiltshire found Anne more belligerently independent-minded than they might have hoped, and Norfolk and

The Act in Restraint of Appeals, from the collection of acts printed at the end of the parliamentary session of 1553. By forbidding appeals to Rome, the act allowed the divorce to be settled in England by Archbishop Cranmer.

Suffolk also had their differences. Meanwhile Thomas Cromwell, Wolsey's private secretary who had risen in the cardinal's service and personal household, gradually took over the daily work of government and the political influence that went with it.

Anne at last married Henry in January 1533, was crowned queen in June, and gave birth to a daughter, the future Queen Elizabeth I, in September. But religious conservatives were loth to accept her or to countenance Elizabeth's displacement of Catherine's daughter Mary in the line of succession to Henry. Anne's own aggressive involvement in politics helped to make her the object of hostile plots at court, to which her failure to provide the King with a son made her dangerously vulnerable; in spring 1536 she was supplanted in Henry's affections by Jane Seymour, and destroyed in the most rapid and bloody political crisis of the century.

Neither Anne's fall nor the Pilgrimage of Grace (a vast rebellion in the North) stopped the Reformation, which proceeded apace under Cromwell's direction. The monasteries were dissolved; Protestant preachers received support from Cromwell and Archbishop Cranmer; new doctrinal formularies were issued which seemed to draw England closer to the continental Protestants, and the struggle between the old and new faiths divided communities all over the country.

While Norfolk did his best to suppress what he saw as heresy in East Anglia, Suffolk was more ambivalent, and happily appointed both conservatives and reformists to church livings. In 1537 the King ordered him to reside in Lincolnshire to ensure the county's obedience after its involvement in the Pilgrimage, and by 1539 he had exchanged nearly all his estates in Norfolk and Suffolk for Crown lands, mostly taken from the monasteries, in Lincolnshire. When combined with the local inheritance of his new wife, Catherine Willoughby (whom he had married in 1534), these grants made him by far the most powerful man in the county. In the years up to his death in 1545 they enabled him to dominate Lincolnshire in a way that he had never been able to achieve in the counties of Suffolk or Norfolk.

No single minister replaced Wolsey. Instead, as the Emperor Charles V's ambassador reported, Norfolk, Suffolk and Sir Thomas More, the new Lord Chancellor, together led the Council. Norfolk was the regime's figurehead, but until Wolsey's death in November 1530 he was insecure in his position, and extremely worried that the cardinal might yet stage a comeback.

Eustace Chapuys to Charles V   6 February 1530
London

... The duke [of Norfolk] asked ... Master Russell [Sir John Russell] if he thought the cardinal still hoped or dreamed of returning to favour. The said Master Russell replied that the duke must know well enough that the courage and ambition of the said cardinal would never let him stand back if he saw the chance to take over affairs, and that that might well happen if some business arose in which the King needed his advice concerning the matters he used to conduct. Then the said duke began to swear vehemently that rather than suffer that, he would eat him up alive ...

   Brian Tuke ... told me of the King's determination to manage his own affairs, for which purpose he has named several Councillors, so that he should not be deprived of a Council when my Lord of Norfolk, the Chancellor and others are detained here by judicial business and cannot be in the country with the King. He has therefore had the Estates General [Parliament] pass an act that, in the absence of the others, the president of his council attendant on his person shall have authority to decide matters as if the Chancellor, the Great Treasurer of England, and other officers of justice had been involved. To this office the Duke of Suffolk has been appointed ...

As Wolsey's successors fell out among themselves in the early 1530s, the two dukes became increasingly alienated from each other. The situation was partly caused by conflict between their followers in East Anglia, which led to the murder of Suffolk's servant Sir William Pennington by Howard's clients, the Southwell brothers, in the sanctuary at Westminster Abbey during April 1532. This was the sort of incident that raised the spectre of the disruptive noble feuds of the fifteenth century and embarrassed the peers involved, especially when Cromwell repeated to the King rumours that Suffolk's servants were plotting a revenge killing.

Duke of Suffolk to Thomas Cromwell   20 July 1532
Ewelme

In my hearty wise I commend me unto you. So it is that within these 5 or 6 days past, I sent my servant John Cavendish unto the Court, where amongst other things my lord of Norfolk showed unto my said servant that one Threshwell and a servant of mine old Lady of Norfolk should show you that they heard a servant of mine say that divers of my servants should make and take their oaths upon a book to myself, that if ever they might see or meet with Southwell at any time during their lives, they would ['slay him although it were in the King's chamber or at the high altar' struck out] be revenged. Wherof my Lord of Norfolk, as he showed my said servant, would never have spoken any word, supposing it, as it is, untrue, if ye had not shown it unto the King's grace before he knew thereof.

And much I marvel ye would do so, showing no better knowledge thereof, taking you so faithfully for my friend as I do. Trusting also though such information was made unto you, ye would have thought if any such thing should have been done before my face (albeit it had been by the best in my house), remembering my promise made unto the King's highness therein, which God to record and witness I never intend to violate, I would either have sent my said servant or servants unto the King's highness with their words and sayings, or else I would have so ordered them that Southwell and others should have been out of dread of them. Assuring you there was never no such oath made before me nor in none other place to my knowledge; praying you therefore, as my trust is in you, ye will so call upon them which made this information unto you that I may have knowledge which of my servants showed them thereof. I cannot be quiet until I have tried it to the uttermost ... At my manor of Ewelme, the 20 day of July, Yours,
    Charles Suffolk

Great Offices of State

The ability of the Crown to appoint freely to office in Court and Council was a major issue of the medieval constitution. By the sixteenth century the Crown's power over most household offices was unquestioned. But the Great Offices of State retained a certain independence. Historically there were five: the Steward, Constable, Marshal, Chamberlain and Butler of England. Each had at one stage or another been claimed by inheritance as a dignity 'incident to' one of the greater peerages. By Henry VIII's reign, the Steward and the Constable had reverted to the Crown, the latter after the execution of the third Duke of Buckingham in 1521. The Earl Marshalcy had been claimed by the Dukes of Norfolk, but their rights had been forfeited after Bosworth Field, and the office was granted to the sixteenth-century Howard Dukes for life only. The Earls of Oxford also lost the Great Chamberlaincy after 1526, but the earl was allowed to resume it in 1553 as an hereditary right by Mary, the most traditionalist of all the Tudors. Thus only the Great Butlership remained in unbroken hereditary tenure (in the hands of the Earls of Arundel) throughout the sixteenth century. But this office was mostly ceremonial and carried (unlike the rest) no seat on the Council.

Henry VIII increased the number of Great Offices of State, a process concluded by the Act of Precedence of 1539. These now included the Lord Chancellor, Lord High Treasurer, Lord President of Council (created in 1529), Lord Privy Seal, Lord High Admiral and (until it was demoted after Thomas Cromwell's resignation from the office) the Principal Secretary of State.

Most of these offices were to be held by members of the nobility, with the exceptions of the Lord Chancellorship (which went to a senior churchman or lawyer) and the Secretaryship.

The new Offices of State were also granted for life, and admitted to no claims of inheritance, thus maintaining the King's control. However, there was also a tradition, reflected in Thomas Starkey's *Dialogue between Pole and Lupset* in the 1530s and later in Essex's investigations into the Earl Marshalcy at the end of the century, that the older offices provided the nobility with a formal independent power. They would thus act as barriers to royal despotism, and their holders could, in theory, summon Parliament in the case of an emergency. The medieval theories of aristocratic constitutionalism, so important in the following century, were not entirely extinct under the Tudors.

Striking testimony to this is a manuscript written for either the third or fourth Duke of Norfolk as Earl Marshal. It contains English translations of two of the main 'baronial' treatises of the Middle Ages: 'The Form and Manner of the Keeping of the Parliament of England' and the 'Treatise' on the marshalship itself. 'The Form and Manner' was a potent mixture of fact, partisanship and creative fiction.

At least as explosive were the claims made by the other 'Treatise' for the marshalship. It opens with the Marshal's role at the coronation (which is still pre-eminent). First come the straightforward claims to perquisites; then a sudden shift of gear to the Marshal's constitutional status: 'The Earl Marshal ought to have the King's horse with all the harness that is on him, and the Queen's palfrey, when they light at the place where they shall be crowned. The Earl ought to be always next the King at his coronation and ought to hold his crown in his hand. And when time is he shall set the crown on the King's head and sustain it by the flower that is before. Because that he is Marshal both in peace and war ought in time of peace to keep the peace and do every man right, and in other things that appertain to the King and to the Court and twelve miles compass about it. And in time of war [he] ought to have the forward of the host.'

The authority cited for all this is the powers of 'Gilbert de Strogell', Marshal of England under Henry II. No such person existed; while the crown was actually placed on the King's head by a bishop (usually the Archbishop of Canterbury).

But there was reality too. Gilbert was Marshal to Henry I (not Henry II), and the office did pass by marriage into the family of the Earls of Pembroke ('Strogoil'). Subsequently, through other female descendants, it came to the Howards. And it was the first Duke of Norfolk who carried the crown at Richard III's coronation; while the third Duke successfully cited the 'Treatise' to claim command of the vanguard against the Pilgrimage of Grace in 1536. Old claims never die; in an aristocracy they scarcely even fade away.

Symbols of office: Holbein's portrait of the third Duke of Norfolk with the Earl Marshal's baton and the Lord Treasurer's stave.

Suffolk's troubles did not end there. Early in 1533 Norfolk, in preparation for his niece Anne's coronation as queen, pressed Suffolk to give up the office of Earl Marshal, the nation's arbiter in matters of honour and chivalry. The office had long been held by the Howards' Mowbray ancestors, but Henry VIII had earlier granted it to Suffolk. His surrender of a dignity which carried such prestige was a sign of his political isolation, and Cromwell's efforts to reassure him can have been little comfort.

Thomas Cromwell to Duke of Suffolk　　　　　　　　April 1533
London

After my most humble recommendations, it may please Your Grace to understand that the King's highness hath been assuredly advertised how that Your Grace is content to surrender your patent of the office of the earl marshal into his hands. Wherupon his Majesty hath granted the same unto my Lord of Norfolk's grace, whose ancestors of long time had the same until now of late. And his Highness is content that Your Grace in the lieu and place thereof shall have his letters patent of the justiceship of the forests on this side [of the river] Trent, for term of your life.

　　Assuring Your Grace, his Highness doth not only repute much honour in Your Grace for that ye so kindly will depart with the said office of marshalship unto my said Lord of Norfolk, but also his Majesty supposeth and perfectly perceiveth that Your Grace hath much more estimation and zeal to nourish kindness and love between my said Lord of Norfolk and you, than ye have to that or any other office. Which undoubtedly is highly to his gracious contentation, to see and perceive two so great and honourable personages his subjects so lovingly and friendly the one to love the other. Wherefor, as he that always reckoneth himself bounden unto Your Grace, and being also very joyous to perceive how pleasantly the king's Highness taketh in good part and repute your honourable and most gentle demeanours in this and all other your proceedings, [I] thought I could no less do than to advertise you thereof ... Beseeching Your Grace to pardon my bold and rude writing, which I am moved unto for the poor good will I bear Your Grace, as knoweth the Holy Trinity, who preserve Your Grace in long life, good health, with the increase of much honour, at London the ... day of April.

Part of Suffolk's discomfiture sprang from his ill-concealed sympathy for Catherine of Aragon, whom Henry delighted in humiliating even after he had pressed ahead with his new marriage. She refused to be cowed, and resisted the King's attempts to change her title to Princess Dowager (as widow of his brother Arthur, Prince of Wales), to cut down her household, and to move her to unhealthy residences in the fens.

Duke of Suffolk, Robert, first Earl of Sussex,   19 December 1533
Sir William Paulet and Richard Sampson
to Henry VIII
Buckden

Please it Your Highness, upon Wednesday last past, after dinner, we, according to your commandment, showed and declared your most gracious pleasure to the Princess Dowager, in her great chamber, all manner servants of the house then there being, to hear what should be said. Whereunto the said princess, persisting in her great stomach and obstinacy, made answer with an open voice, saying that she knew herself for your queen and true wife ...

   And for as much as she, wilfully, and against all humanity and reason, continueth still in this opinion, saying that, although Your Grace have appointed her to remove to Somersham, she [neither] may, nor will, in any wise follow Your Grace's pleasure therein, unless we should bind her with ropes, and violently enforce her thereunto; saying, also, that she will not take the service of these men, sworn to her as Princess Dowager, but as the service of men that have the keeping of her; and for as much as she persisteth in this obstinacy, and so will continue, as we surely think; and for that also, by her wilfulness, she may feign herself sick, and keep her bed, or keep her bed in health, and will not put on her clothes, or otherwise order herself, by some imagination that we now cannot call to remembrance; which extremities were not remembered at the making of our instructions, by reason whereof, your pleasure is not set forth in our said instructions, what order should be taken with her, being in any such extremities; we most humbly beseech Your Highness, the premises considered, to send unto us your express pleasure how, and in what manner, Your Grace will have the same ordered ...
   By your most humble subjects and servants,
   Charles Suffolk   Robt Sussex
   Richard Sampson   William Paulet

The Earl Marshal

'Treatise' on the Earl Marshalcy: a copy made for the third and fourth Dukes of Norfolk. The Earl Marshal appears in the illuminated initial, with his attendant heralds. The manuscript is mock-antique, but incorporates regulations made in 1526 and so was intended for practical use.

The Earl Marshalcy was one of the five historic Great Offices of State. In the fifteenth century it had been claimed as descending with the dukedom of Norfolk in tail male, but the first Howard Duke forfeited his rights to the office along with his peerage after Bosworth Field. It was granted to the second, third and fourth Howard Dukes for life only, and was not restored to the family as an hereditary office until 1672. After the execution of the fourth Duke of Norfolk in 1572, it was granted to the sixth Earl of Shrewsbury for life; following his death in 1590 it was obtained by the second Earl of Essex in 1597.

The Earl Marshal had originally been the subordinate of the Constable of England and he shared that office's claim to deputise for the king in the command of his armies. He also presided over the College of Arms and the High Court of Chivalry. Not only did he appoint or promote the heralds at arms, but (in theory) he had the power to vet claims

to arms or titles and to adjudicate disputes - though in cases involving major titles the Crown usually intervened. There is some evidence that the Howard Dukes adopted a conservative policy towards the granting of arms. Shrewsbury's guardianship of Mary, Queen of Scots made him very much an absentee, and the College was supervised by his deputy, the Earl of Leicester. Their policy towards claims and grants appears to have been more liberal.

The Earl Marshal also shared the Constable of England's role in aristocratic constitutionalism. As the king's deputy he was supposed to possess the power to summon Parliament in an emergency. The potential functions of the Marshalcy were explored most keenly by Essex, who inspired considerable research into its history. What his ultimate aims were is still not clear, but such an approach to so potentially dangerous an office did not calm Elizabeth's fears about his ambitions.

Anne Boleyn and her Family

The Boleyns have been misplaced by popular memory amid the subtleties of Tudor status. They have often been seen as *nouveaux riches* because Anne Boleyn's great-grandfather Geoffrey Boleyn had made his fortune as a mercer in London, becoming Mayor for 1457-8. But this is rather hard on a family who had become well established in the upper reaches of the Norfolk gentry a half-century before Anne's birth. Moreover Boleyn had married one of the daughters and co-heiresses of a noblemen, an example followed by first his son and then his grandson, Anne's father Thomas.

Thomas Boleyn's wife was sister to the third Duke of Norfolk, and it was probably the Howard link which made it easy for Boleyn to enter court circles. By the death of Henry VII he was well ensconced in court office as an Esquire of the Body to the King, and could compare with anyone in courtly pastimes. He was also a competent administrator, while his frequent employment on embassies abroad was a recognition of his diplomatic talents. This continental perspective led him to send Anne abroad to spend seven years in service in the household of Queen Claude, wife of Francis I of France. This long training was a clear investment in education for a place at the English court, and soon after her return to England in 1521 she was to be seen in Court.

Anne was probably twenty-five in 1526, when the thirty-six-year-old King became attracted to her. Her years at Court up to then are obscure, although as a charming and accomplished young woman she seems to have attracted two distinguished suitors: the heir to the earldom of Northumberland and the courtier poet Sir Thomas Wyatt. Wyatt, however, found himself overtaken by a dangerous rival: the King himself. Henry had enjoyed an affair with Anne's elder and more racy sister Mary Carey during these years but his involvement with Anne was on a different level. By 1526 all the indications are that the King had decided to divorce Catherine of Aragon.

Proof of his love was his painful effort in writing letters to her, several of which survive: Henry loathed the mechanics of letter-writing. Clearly Anne was a lady to be reckoned with: high-spirited, sharp-tongued, musical and with an eye for works of art of beauty and style. Proof of her exceptional personality was her refusal to sleep with the King until she was assured of a crown herself. It is likely that by 1527 they were informally betrothed; by August the King was approaching the Pope about the divorce, and he soon began to shower gifts on his new love.

No one could have expected that the divorce would be so complicated and prolonged that it would be six years before a marriage could take place. In the meantime, Anne's family realized many of their courtly ambitions. Her father, a viscount since 1525, in 1529 gained a double triumph by being granted not only a senior Irish title, the earldom of Ormonde, to which his father's marriage gave him a connection, but also the earldom of Wiltshire; her brother then succeeded as Viscount Rochford and won a place in the King's Privy Chamber. In the same way, her death would prove their undoing; disgrace for Wiltshire and trumped-up scandal and death for Rochford.

Anne Boleyn. Her dark eyes helped begin her affair with Henry and her 'little neck' helped the headsman end it.

Norfolk, on the other hand, was firmly identified with the King's new marriage to his niece, Anne Boleyn. All was not plain sailing, however. As Queen, Anne Boleyn pursued as active a political role as she had done on her way to the throne. Norfolk confronted her more than once, perhaps over competition for royal patronage for their followers, perhaps over their very different religious loyalties. Yet the significance of such quarrels is hard to judge when the only evidence for them comes from third-hand gossip sent home by the Spanish ambassador, who fell eagerly on any hints that all was not going well for the hated 'King's woman', who had displaced Catherine of Aragon.

Eustace Chapuys to Charles V   1 January 1535
London

... The Earl of Northumberland is far from pleased with this King and his ministers, as I learned two days ago from the physician of the said Northumberland, in whom his said master confided about the grievances and wrongs that he had suffered, for which those who mistreated him would soon have cause to repent ... And afterwards the said Northumberland began to complain of the arrogance and wickedness of this king's woman, saying, among other things, that lately she used more insulting language to the said Norfolk than one would to a dog, such that he was obliged to leave the room, and, though he found in the hall only someone to whom he no longer bore affection, nonetheless his anger made him forget that, and moved him to unburden himself to the said personage, and heap abuse on the said lady. One of the least offensive things he called her was 'great whore'...

Anne and her family did have allies at Court, some of whom paid tribute to her with the romantic admiration conventionally lavished on great ladies by male courtiers - the forerunner of the pining of Elizabeth I's gallants for a gentle glance from the Virgin Queen. It was the ambiguities inherent in this game of courtly love that served to destroy Anne. On 2 May 1536 she was taken to the Tower, accused of adultery with a number of courtiers on the basis of their unguarded expressions of affection for her: these men included Henry Norris, the chief Gentleman of the King's Privy Chamber, Francis Weston, another of the King's closest servants, and a court musician, Mark Smeaton, the only supposed lover who actually confessed.

Sir William Kingston to Thomas Cromwell   [2] May 1536
Tower of London

This is to advertise you, upon my Lord of Norfolk and the King's Council departing from the Tower, I went before the Queen into her lodging. And then she said unto me, 'Master Kingston, shall I go into a dungeon?' 'No, Madam, you shall go into your lodging that you lay in at your coronation.' 'It is too good for me' she said, 'Jesu, have mercy on me', and kneeled down weeping a great pace [while], and in the same sorrow fell into a great laughing, and she hath done so many times since. And then she desired me to move the King's highness that she might have the sacrament in the closet by her chamber, that she might pray for mercy. 'For I am as clear from the company of man, as for sin', said she, 'as I am clear from you, and am the King's true wedded wife'.

And then she said 'Master Kingston, do you know wherefor I am here', and I said 'Nay'... 'I hear say', said she, 'that I should be accused with three men, and I can say no more but nay, without [unless] I should open my body', and therewith opened her gown, saying 'O Norris, thou hast accused me, thou art in the Tower with me, and thou and I shall die together; and Mark, thou art here too'... Then she said 'Master Kingston, shall I die without justice?', and I said the poorest subject the king hath, had justice, and therewith she laughed ...

Sir, since the making of this letter the queen spoke of Weston, that she had spoken to him because he did love her kinswoman Mistress Shelton, and that she said he loved not his wife. And he made answer to her again, that he loved one in her house better than them both. She asked him 'Who is that?', to which he answered that 'It is yourself'. And then she defied him.

William Kingston

The poet Sir Thomas Wyatt, an admirer of Anne before she caught the King's eye, was among those arrested during the crisis, but unlike those whom Anne mentioned he was not tried. He watched the executions of his friends from the Tower of London's Bell Tower. This shattering experience taught him the danger of involvement in high politics: *circa Regna tonat*, thunder rolls around the throne.

Sir Thomas Wyatt (after Seneca), on the events of May 1536

V. Innocentia [Innocence]
Veritas Viat Fides [Truth Wyatt Faith]
Circumdederunt me inimici mei [My enemies have surrounded me]

Who list [wishes] his wealth and ease retain
Himself let him unknown contain
Press not too fast in at that gate
Where the return stands by disdain,
For sure, *circa Regna tonat*.

The high mountains are blasted oft
When the low valley is mild and soft.
Fortune with Health stands at debate.
The fall is grievous from aloft.
And sure, *circa Regna tonat*.

These bloody days have broken my heart.
My lust, my youth did them depart,
And blind desire of estate.
Who hastes to climb seeks to revert.
Of truth, *circa Regna tonat*.

The Bell Tower showed me such sight
That in my head sticks day and night.
There did I learn out of a grate,
For all favour, glory or might,
That yet *circa Regna tonat*.

By proof, I say, there did I learn:
Wit helpeth not defence too yern [eager],
Of innocency to plead or prate.
Bear low, therefore, give God the stern,
For sure, *circa Regna tonat*.

Poetry and Politics

The poetry of Tudor courtiers, like Sir Thomas Wyatt the elder and the Earl of Surrey, has been both sentimentalized and probed for private indiscretions, processes that began within the sixteenth century. *Tottel's Miscellany* of 1557, in which many of their works were first printed, accentuated Wyatt's supposed relationship with Anne Boleyn. Thomas Nashe and Michael Drayton, later in the century, gave currency to the idea of Surrey as the languishing lover of 'fair Geraldine' (Elizabeth, daughter of the tenth Earl of Kildare), though he perhaps wrote only one sonnet for her when she may well have been no older than nine.

At the same time the sincerity and value of their poetry has been questioned because so much of it is translated either from Italian or Latin originals. So the application of Wyatt's 'Who so list to hunt, I know where is an hind' to Anne Boleyn has been questioned because even its most pungent lines ('*Noli me tangere* [Do not touch me] for Caesar's I am') can be traced back to Petrarch.

All of this misses the point. Their poetry is autobiographical, in the sense that it vividly reflects the intolerable tensions of political life at Court (Surrey, after all, did die on the block, and Wyatt was lucky to avoid such a fate), though it is discreet enough to make it unwise to try to reconstruct specific events or relationships from it. The fact that a poem was a translation was a matter of discretion in itself, distancing the poet from the views expressed. Wyatt, for instance, commented on the death of his friend and patron Thomas Cromwell by translating from Petrarch 'The pillar perished is whereto I lent', while his satires on court life, addressed to his friends John Poyntz and Sir Francis Bryan, are adapted from Horace or Alamanni.

The wit and poignancy lie in the aptness of the work to English conditions, not its strict originality. Even Surrey's translations from a classic like Virgil's *Aeneid* were subtly pointed; he focused on Book 2, an apocalyptic vision of the fall of Troy, and Book 4, the tale of Aeneas's love and desertion of Dido, and her suicide: tales of imperial destiny, and the conflicts between love and duty, which echoed the concerns of a great court.

The pose of the Petrarchan lover, the ardent suitor forever disdained by his mistress, may or may not

Henry VIII reading the Psalms in his Bedchamber. Surrey hailed Sir Thomas Wyatt's Psalm translations as his greatest verse.

be literally true, but it certainly mirrors the life of the courtier dependent upon a capricious monarch. It is impossible to say whether Wyatt's haunting 'They flee from me that sometime did me seek' more aptly registers rejection by a mistress or by the king. The metaphorical fusion of monarch and mistress naturally intensified with a woman on the throne, the nub of the mythology of Elizabeth I as Gloriana. The most sustained contribution from a senior courtier is Sir Walter Ralegh's enigmatic 'Book of the Ocean to Cynthia', punning on his own name (ocean=water=Walter) and saluting the Queen as the virgin huntress. Others, like Sir Philip Sidney, exploited these conventions more obliquely to comment on their political roles.

Anne's fall did not halt the King's dissolution of the nation's smaller monasteries, and individuals, including Norfolk and Suffolk, joined in the rush to strip the Church of its landed wealth. But in the autumn of 1536 they had to cope with the consequences: the Pilgrimage of Grace, the largest rebellion in Tudor England. The first outbreak was in Lincolnshire; Henry sent Suffolk to suppress it, but that was easier said than done.

Duke of Suffolk to Henry VIII   9 October 1536
Huntingdon 'In haste haste haste'

Please it Your Highness, this Monday the 9th day of this month at 6 of the clock in the morning, I arrived at Your Grace's town of Huntingdon, with 24 or 30 of mine own servants ... trusting to have found here in readiness both ordnance and artillery, and some convenient number of men to have put in experience [in effect] the staying of these traitors at Stamford according to Your Highness's commandment. And at my coming, I found neither ordnance, artillery, neither no number of men to do anything with. And ... I hear in these parts ... that the men which shall be gathered here be in a manner naked, without harness [armour] or weapons, by reason whereof they be evil willing to come out. Most humbly beseeching Your Grace that ordnance and artillery may be sent hither with all speed possible, and if it might please Your Highness to send down a thousand or two of harness, it should comfort the hearts of the people very much; and also that Your Grace will provide that as many horsemen as may be thought requisite may be sent for, and to resort to these parts, assuring Your Highness after my opinion it is ordnance and horsemen that must do this feat. And in case Your Highness should put this in hazard of a battle, considering these traitors are well horsed and harnessed, and also of so great a number as they say they be of, it may be doubted what the success thereof should be ... Most humbly desiring Your Grace to send money necessary for those men ...

   It is said in these parts that these traitors intendeth to be at Stamford this night, where Sir William Parr and others be already with their companies, to whom I have written my letters that in case they with such number as they have, and such as I have, may be able to stop these traitors there, I shall not fail to repair unto them with all speed possible for the stoppage of the same there, according to Your Grace's commandment. And in case they shall advertise me that our puissance [force] at this time is not sufficient to stay them there, then that the said Sir William Parr and others with him, and also the said Sir Francis Bryan with his band and company, shall come and resort hither unto me with all speed, where upon any good likelihood that we may be able to stop them we shall do our best here ...

To Suffolk's great relief, the Lincolnshire rebels did not march on London but concentrated at Lincoln. When he duly gathered his horsemen and artillery at Stamford, and the fourth Earl of Shrewsbury collected another army in Nottinghamshire, the insurgents dispersed and Suffolk was able to occupy Lincolnshire. The Pilgrims in Yorkshire, Lancashire and the counties further north took longer to appease, but by spring 1537 the crisis was past. Suffolk's role in the suppression of the uprisings did much to regain him the King's favour after the difficulties of the past few years. Like Norfolk and other noblemen he was generously rewarded for his service with lands from the dissolved monasteries, which helped to establish him as the most powerful man in Lincolnshire. Less tangible, but no less important, was the renewed warmth in his relationship with Henry, a warmth which would last to the end of Suffolk's life.

Henry VIII to Duke of Suffolk   12 December 1536

Right trusty and entirely well beloved cousin, we greet you well, and have ... received your sundry letters ... declaring your most entire and fervent love and zeal towards us and the advancement of our affairs, with the great desire you have not only to serve us in the same with the force of your body and person, but also with the employment of your whole substance, if the case should so require. The overture whereof, albeit we trust we shall not need to accept, for that we have certain affiance [trust] in God that the matter shall shortly take end ... yet we do no less thankfully receive the good will thereof, declaring your noble and most loyal and assured heart towards us, than if we should therewith also take presently all the whole benefit and commodity of that which is offered if the same were ten times so much. Surely, cousin, you have in no part deceived our expectation of you, but in this (and your faithful service otherwise) given us as much cause to rejoice of our favour and goodness heretofore extended unto you as of any like thing that we have done since our reign [began]. And doubt you not but, God granting us life, we shall so remember this time towards you that you shall have good cause to say you serve a master that will not put the faithful service and gratuity [gratitude] of his servant in oblivion ...

The Pilgrimage of Grace

By autumn 1536 cataclysmic changes were penetrating every area of England. The smaller monasteries were being dissolved; the clergy were paying new taxes, and were being examined for their fitness to keep their jobs; a number of saints' days had been abolished, and new statements of faith had been produced which omitted many traditional beliefs; the laity were paying taxes in peacetime, and had been largely deprived (by the 'statute of uses') of control over the descent of their lands; the Queen had just been executed, and a layman of obscure birth, Thomas Cromwell, was in direct and subversive control of the Church.

These startling events gave rise to rumours of worse to come: the abolition of many parish churches, a tax on the eating of white bread, Cromwell's marriage to Princess Mary and accession as king, and so on. In October, false news that royal commissioners were coming to take away the plate and vestments from their parish churches prompted riots in the Lincolnshire towns of Louth, Horncastle and Caistor. Within days Lincolnshire was up in arms from Lincoln to the Humber, and in the next three weeks most of Yorkshire, Lancashire, Cumberland, Westmorland, Northumberland and County Durham joined the revolt.

The behaviour and specific grievances of the rebels varied from region to region, and so did the involvement of the local nobility and gentry, whose attitude ranged from enthusiastic and belligerent leadership, through reluctant acceptance of their duty to keep the common rebels in check and negotiate with the King, to diehard loyalty to Henry and armed opposition to the risings. The more sophisticated rebels doubtless hoped to stimulate political change at Court, in order to overthrow Cromwell and restore the conservative impetus of the attack on Anne Boleyn. Some commoners were working off grudges against their landlords. But the aim that united all those involved was defence of the old religion.

Lincolnshire bore the full weight of the government's first response, and its rebels dispersed when faced by armies under the Duke of Suffolk and the fourth Earl of Shrewsbury, but the more northerly insurgents advanced in strength to confront Shrewsbury and Norfolk across the River Don. There was a truce while Henry considered the demands of the pilgrims, as they called themselves, for the reversal of many policies and the removal of Cromwell and the Protestant-inclined bishops. Henry played for time, but the Pilgrimage did not crumble: in December Norfolk had to promise the rebels a general pardon and a free Parliament at York to discuss their grievances.

The leaders were satisfied and sent their forces home, but in early 1537 Henry exploited renewed disorder in Yorkshire and Cumberland to have the leading pilgrims tried and executed. The York Parliament never met, Cromwell remained in power, the Council in the North was strengthened to increase royal control in the region, and in the next four years the great northern abbeys surrendered one by one.

The tower of St James's Church, Louth. Determination to protect its parish treasures sparked revolt in 1536.

The Henrician Reformation

Thomas Cranmer, Archbishop of Canterbury. Cranmer, believing both in Protestantism and in the right of King Henry (who was not Protestant) to determine doctrine, personified the tensions within the new Church of England.

The Reformation under Henry VIII combined three different but interconnected movements, in each of which influences from the Continent blended with home-grown traditions. First, and most distinctively English, was the assertion of royal supremacy over the Church, the repudiation of allegiance to Rome, the confiscation of much of the Church's wealth and the taxation of its remaining income for the Crown's benefit. Its initial stimulus was the need to enable the English Church to judge the King's divorce without papal interference. But further implementation of the supremacy depended on Henry's fascination with the idea that his 'imperial' jurisdiction could brook no alternative source of authority within the realm.

There was a fairly general consensus that Henry's authority should be used for some sort of reform of the Church. Improvements in the education and morality of the parish clergy, the conversion of some of the wealth to educational or social ends, and the encouragement of more thoughtful and less superstitious lay piety were fairly uncontroversial

objectives in themselves. But attempts to implement them raised the third and most disruptive factor in the equation. This was the spread of Protestant ideas both at the highest levels of government and the Church and among the populace.

The struggle for the supremacy and the divorce brought to power Queen Anne Boleyn, Thomas Cromwell, Archbishop Cranmer and other bishops who gave reform a Protestant tinge. The monasteries were at length dissolved, many images and shrines were destroyed, the Bible was printed in English, and by the end of the reign Cranmer was changing parts of the church service from Latin to the vernacular.

Yet alongside this was the King's own doctrinal conservatism, the hostility to change of many of the laity, and the readiness of many in authority to go along with the supremacy and to implement limited reforms, but to fight hard against thorough-going Protestantism. The result, by the time of Henry's death, was a strangely hybrid and fundamentally unstable Church of England.

In the struggle for England's religious future which continued through the remainder of Henry's reign and well beyond, powerful reformists used their influence to support local clergy and laity of their persuasion, but doctrinal conservatives fought back hard and could often claim the support of the silent majority. Great men of no very definite religious commitment, like Suffolk, and, in some ways, Henry himself, were caught in the middle, trying to please friends and followers on both sides and to avoid the disorder which could accompany violent disagreement.

Sir Thomas Tyrrell to Duke of Suffolk 12 June 1537

With most humble recommendations, please it Your Grace, my lord, to be advertised, that the vicar of Mendlesham, my neighbour, hath now at the feast of Pentecost last past brought home his woman and children into his vicarage, openly declaring how he is married unto her, and she is his lawful wife. This act by him done is in this country a monster, and many do grudge at it. But, for that he reporteth that the King's grace doth know he is married, men do refrain to do that their hearts would serve them to do; and as to our ordinary [bishop], he dare do nothing. I most lowly beseech Your Grace that I may know your pleasure what is best to be done for the reformation of his open crime, which is abominable in the judgement of the lay people. And his example unpunished shall be occasion for other carnal, evil disposed priests to do in like manner, which God defend [forbid], and preserve Your Grace in health, with long prosperous life, the joy future trusted upon not thereby in any wise minished. Written the 12th day of June,
   Your humble daily beadsman [someone who prays for you daily],
   poor Thomas Tyrrell

Whether in religious matters or secular, the local power of a great nobleman had to be exercised forcefully or it might wither away. This letter from Suffolk to the corporation of Lincoln, written in an ultimately unsuccessful attempt to impose one of his estate officers on the city as a magistrate, shows him touchily aware of how a lack of respect for his commands might impugn his authority in county society. Yet it also reveals what valuable help he could offer the city - in its campaign for the remission of the £80 fee-farm it paid annually to the dean and chapter of the cathedral - since he was an influential patron at Court and had the King's ear.

Duke of Suffolk to the mayor and aldermen of Lincoln   26 March 1545
'The Court'

After our hearty commendations; where you have been long suitors for the discharge of £80 yearly, ye shall understand that at this present the King's majesty's affairs be so weighty and of such importance, as yet no conclusion can be had therein to your expectation. But think not the contrary, when convenient opportunity may thereunto serve us, we will, according to our former letters, take so good an end as it shall be to your contentation, as well in that matter as also in all your reasonable requests hereafter to be made unto us.

   Yet we not a little marvel that you will say us nay in a request made unto you for John Dyon to be one of your justices of peace, who is a man of good learning, judgement and right meet [very suitable] for the same. Wherefor these shall be eftsoons [once again] to require you forthwith [immediately] to proceed to the election of him thereunto, or else to certify us in writing why you make denial thereof, by this bearer William Alynson, who hath right honestly and diligently applied your matter here very painfully. Thus fare you well, from the Court the 26th of March,
   Your friend,
   Charles Suffolk

In local politics as in Henry's Court and Council, Suffolk managed to gain and exercise power without making himself many obvious enemies, a significant and unusual feat. His important role as a military commander in Henry's last wars with France and Scotland won him further honour and royal favour, and when Suffolk died in August 1545 he left his sons, aged nine and seven, an enviable position at the head of the English peerage and in command of his adopted county.

'Vain, Proud, Foolish Boy'

THE EARL OF SURREY AND THE FALL OF THE HOWARDS

Henry Howard, Earl of Surrey, son and heir of the third Duke of Norfolk. The father always knew when to abase himself before the King; the son, poet, Protestant and passionate in all things, dared to stand up to him. He paid the price with his own head and his family's ruin.

A senior Tudor politician needed nimble footwork in the latter half of Henry's reign just to keep up with the King's matrimonial entanglements. Anne Boleyn fell, to be supplanted by Jane Seymour, whose tragic death (twelve days after giving birth to Henry's long-awaited heir, Prince Edward) set the King searching for a wife once more. The choice of Anne of Cleves proved a fatal blunder for Cromwell; yet once she had been pensioned off, the sexual adventures of her replacement, Catherine Howard, narrowly missed bringing a similar catastrophe for Norfolk. Only with Catherine Parr did Henry find some measure of tranquillity in his last years.

For the Howards, these were roller-coaster years indeed, as the third Duke saw his enemies tumble, two marriages of his nieces to Henry VIII, and his daughter Mary's marriage to Henry's illegitimate son, the Duke of Richmond. Yet he also saw Mary left a widow by Richmond's early death and his two nieces go to the scaffold, while despite his bewildered and genuine protestations of his lifelong loyal service to the King, he found that the folly of his son Henry, titular Earl of Surrey, destroyed everything that he and the second Duke had painstakingly built up. The Howards' fifteenth-century marriage alliances which had brought them such fortune also made them dangerously

The tomb in Framlingham church of Thomas, third Duke of Norfolk and his second wife Elizabeth Stafford (who, separated from her husband in life, is buried in Lambeth).

close in blood to the throne, and it was pride in this blood which brought the family down through Surrey's heraldic display.

It was not just a dangerous inheritance which brought troubles, as Surrey's antics showed. Lord Thomas Howard manufactured disaster for himself by his marriage to the King's niece, and Catherine Howard's death was the result of her own adolescent folly. Moreover, the Howard family was dangerously disunited. The third Duke's second marriage to Elizabeth Stafford, daughter of the last Duke of Buckingham, turned out disastrously. After a few years the duke took a mistress, Elizabeth Holland, and his wife broke conventions by publicly expressing her objections to this arrangement.

Her son Surrey and daughter Mary had little sympathy for her in the quarrel, but Mary had her own reasons for resentment against her father. He gave her no backing in her efforts to get adequate maintenance from the King after the Duke of Richmond's death, and persistent shortage of money made her a bitter woman; she would be ready to co-operate in her brother's destruction in 1546. Norfolk himself was indecently ready to abandon those members of his family who seemed doomed to destruction in the wake of the Catherine Howard catastrophe.

The third Duke was as cold as any stereotype of a modern business tycoon. From the Tower in 1546, he reeled off a long list of those powerful men and women who had hated him and sought to destroy him. Nor did the serfs on his estates mourn his passing in 1547. The duke's son Surrey, on the other hand, remains a more attractive figure, a poet of high ability and an unusual combination of scholar and soldier.

Despite the threat of a rival dynasty of Seymours, the death of Queen Jane seems genuinely to have affected Norfolk, no doubt because of the King's deep grief.

Duke of Norfolk to Lord Cromwell   24 October 1537

My good Lord, I pray you to be here tomorrow early to comfort our good master, for as for our mistress, there is no likelihood of her life (the more pity), and I fear she shall not be on live at the time ye shall read this.
At eight at night, with the hand of your sorrowful friend.
   T. Norfolk

Duke of Norfolk and Sir William Paulet   1 November 1537
to Lord Cromwell
Hampton Court

These noblemen, we trust, will be ready to give attendance at Hampton Court, and so to Windsor:-
   My Lords of Norfolk, Suffolk, Marquess [of] Dorset, Marquess [of] Exeter, the Earls of Surrey, Oxford, Rutland, Wiltshire, Sussex, Hertford, Southampton, the Lord Privy Seal [Cromwell], the Lord Chamberlain [William, first Lord Sandys], if your Lordship have passed letters for them, as we trust you have ...
   At the interment of Queen Elizabeth [of York, mother of Henry VIII] were 7 marquesses and earls, 16 barons, 60 knights, and 40 squires, besides the ordinary of the King's house, which is more than we be certain of. Therefore we have named more persons hereafter, that you may choose them and others at the King's pleasure. Please it your lordship to write speedily that they may be ready to set forwards with the corpse Friday morning, 9th day of November, which is the uttermost day of our appointment. If you require longer time we cannot set forward till the Monday after, and must know the certainty of this. The Earl of Surrey and the Lord Chamberlain are sent for; the residue to be sent for are contained in the schedule enclosed.

In July 1536 Lord Thomas Howard, youngest brother to the third Duke of Norfolk, was sent to the Tower for making a secret marriage contract with Lady Margaret Douglas. Lord Thomas was attainted by Act of Parliament, dying in prison, and Lady Margaret Douglas was committed to the Tower. The poet Earl of Surrey recalls his uncle's tragedy while renouncing his love for Anne Seymour (née Stanhhope), Countess of Hertford.

Earl of Surrey, on the death of his uncle and the renunciation of his love

Each beast can choose his fere [mate] according to his mind,
And eke can shew a friendly cheer, like to their beastly kind.
A Lion [crest of the Howards] saw I late, as white as any snow,
Which seemed well to lead the race, his port the same did show.
Upon the gentle beast to gaze it liked me,
For still methought he seemed well, of noble blood to be.
And as he pranced before, still seeking for a make [mate],
As who would say 'There is none here, I trow will me forsake',
I might perceive a Wolf [crest of Stanhopes] as white as whale's bone;
A fairer beast, a fresher hue, beheld I never none;
Save that her looks were fierce, and forward eke her grace:
Toward the which, this gentle beast gan him advance apace.
And with a beck full low he bowed at her feet,
In humble wise, as who would say, 'I am too far unmeet'.
But such a scornful cheer, wherewith she him rewarded
Was never seen, I trow, the like, to such as well deserved! ...
'Lion' she said, 'if thou hadst known my mind befor'n,
Thou hadst not spent thy travail thus, nor all thy pain forlorn ...'
... And unto her thus gan he say, when he was past his rage:
'Cruel! you do me wrong, to set me thus so light;
Without desert for my good will to shew me such despite.
How can ye thus intreat a Lion of the race
That with his paws a crowned King [James IV] devoured in the place
Whose nature is to prey upon no simple food,
As long as he may suck the flesh, and drink of noble blood.
If you be fair and fresh, am I not of your hue?
And for my vaunt, I dare well say, my blood is not untrue.
For you yourself doth know, it is not long ago,
Sith that for love one of the race did end his life in woe,
In Tower both strong and high; for his assured truth;
Whereas in tears he spent his breath, alas! the more the ruth.
This gentle beast so died, whom nothing could remove,
But willingly to seek his death for loss of his true love ...

Jane Seymour

The Seymour family were gentry with noble connections not unlike the family of Anne Boleyn. Like Anne, Jane was brought up to serve royalty, entering the service of Catherine of Aragon in 1529 as the divorce battle reached its height; subsequently she served Queen Anne.

However, as Anne showed herself unable to make the transition from headstrong lover to submissive wife, her conservative enemies saw their chance; they created the Seymour marriage, choosing Jane as their passive instrument. She was the exact opposite of Anne in her demureness and lack of intellectual fire. So Jane was brought to the King's attention, and tutored in what to say and do: in particular, as the King rose to the bait, to take a leaf out of Anne's book and refuse anything less than an offer of marriage.

By January 1536 the scheme was bearing fruit, as an anxious Cromwell realized: after Anne, he was bound to be the chief target of the conservatives. Yet Anne and he were increasingly at odds. Anne was furious with him for reopening negotiations with the Emperor Charles V now that Catherine of Aragon was dead, and the connection between his diplomacy and Anne's position in the King's affections was clear: Cromwell's efforts accelerated in the month that Anne miscarried of a son. Cromwell therefore siezed the chance to take over the Seymour scheme from the conservatives, and (typically) made a more thorough and ruthless job of it.

The King's mind was poisoned: for Henry, always paranoid about his failure to produce a male heir, the miscarriage was easily made to suggest the monstrous crime of incest, and so the miscarriage became the excuse for a bizarre series of allegations about the Queen's virtue, extending through adultery as far as incest with her brother. Anne was destroyed, and the Seymour marriage took place only eleven days after her execution, on 30 May 1536.

Cromwell had triumphed, and the defeat of the Pilgrimage of Grace at the end of the year sealed his success, enabling him to rid the court of those conservatives marked out for their support of the Princess Mary. What a bizarre alliance the marriage plot had become! Despite the subsequent Protestant stance of her brothers, Jane mirrored the opinions of her conservative sponsors, arguing for the retention of the monasteries, and even trying to get the King to restore Mary to the succession. In this, as in so much else, she was an abrupt change of flavour for Henry from Queen Anne; Sir John Russell commented when writing to Lord Lisle: 'the King hath come out of hell into heaven, for the gentleness in this, and the cursedness and the unhappiness of the other.'

The longed-for prince was born on 12 October 1537, and named Edward; at last the King had a legitimate male heir. But joy was short-lived: by 23 October the Queen was dead, killed by the after-effects of the Caeserian section which had ensured the safe delivery of her son. The shock and grief of the Court was genuine; and once more the King was a widower.

Jane Seymour, Henry VIII's third Queen. Her motto was the self-effacing 'Bound to obey and serve'.

Badges and Retinues

The south porch of Lavenham Church. The church was rebuilt to celebrate the restoration under the Tudors of the De Veres, Earls of Oxford, and is decorated with their badges: the boar (verres in Latin) in the spandrels of the arch, and the mullet or star at the base of the flanking buttresses. Their coat-of-arms appears in the shields over the doorway.

In a widely illiterate society, badges and insignia were an even more potent form of identification than they are today. Great men and women marked everything connected with them with their badge, usually a simple motif derived from their inherited coat of arms. The Duke of Suffolk set his crowned lion's head along the bridge at Westhorpe. The de Vere Earls of Oxford put their five-pointed star on churches throughout the area of their influence in Essex and Suffolk. A nobleman's servants wore his livery of coats or caps decorated with his badge: they were a sign that the lord's protection extended to his men, and that they acted with his authority.

The problems inherent in the giving of livery had vexed the Crown since the late fourteenth century. Noblemen or gentlemen bent on violence might recruit an armed band by indiscriminate distribution of their badge; those who wore the badge of a powerful magnate, with or without his permission, might abuse his authority to tyrannize their neighbours. Henry VII tightened the legal constraints on the distribution of livery and the associated practice of retaining, whereby peers and knights contracted with less powerful gentry to pay them annuities, or merely offer them protection or 'good lordship', in return for their allegiance in military service and local politics.

Early Tudor England did not see private warfare on the scale of the mid-fifteenth century, and the work of Henry VII, Wolsey and Cromwell to impose royal justice and royal authority on the greatest noblemen and the most remote areas of the kingdom took clear though gradual effect. Yet the rival affinities of local magnates retained the ability to disrupt county government, and the Crown's reliance on the nobility to raise troops prevented any comprehensive challenge to the power of the badge and the great man it represented.

Lady Margaret Douglas was not one to cry over spilt milk; knowing that she was in mortal danger, she made it clear to the Council in a letter to Cromwell in 1537 that she had abandoned Lord Thomas Howard. She was a born survivor; she later married the Scottish Earl of Lennox, fought long and hard to get her son Lord Darnley married to Mary Queen of Scots, and died in 1578 with the satisfaction of seeing Darnley's son and her grandson on the Scottish throne as King James VI. It was thus through James that Lady Margaret's Stuart descendants also won the English throne.

Lady Margaret Douglas to Lord Cromwell   1537

My Lord, what cause have I to give you thanks, and how much bound am I unto you, that by your means hath gotten me, as I trust, the King's grace his favour again, and besides that that it pleaseth you to write and to give me knowledge wherein I might have his Grace's displeasure again, which I pray our Lord sooner to send me death than that; and I assure you, my Lord, I will never do that thing willingly that should offend his Grace. And my Lord, whereas it is informed you that I do charge the house with a greater number than is convenient, I assure you I have but two more than I had in the Court, which indeed were my Lord Thomas' servants; and the cause that I took them for was for the poverty that I saw them in, and for no cause else. But seeing, my Lord, that it is your pleasure that I shall keep none that did belong unto my Lord Thomas, I will put them from me. And I beseech you not to think that any fancy doth remain in me touching him; but that all my study and care is how to please the King's grace and to continue in his favour. And my Lord, where it is your pleasure that I shall keep but a few here with me, I trust ye will think that I can have no fewer than I have; for I have but a gentleman and a groom that keeps my apparel, and another that keeps my chamber, and a chaplain that was with me always in the Court. Now my Lord, I beseech you that I may know your pleasure if you would that I should keep any fewer. Howbeit, my Lord, my servants hath put the house to small charge, for they have nothing but the reversion of my board; nor I do call for nothing but that that is given me; howbeit I am very well intreated. And my Lord, as for resort, I promise you I have none, except it be gentlewomen that comes to see me, nor never had since I came hither; for if any resort of men had come it should neither have become me to have seen them, nor yet to have kept them company, being a maid as I am. Now my Lord, I beseech you to be so good as to get my poor servants their wages; and thus I pray our Lord to preserve you both soul and body,
    by her that has her trust in you,
    Margaret Douglas

Lord Thomas Howard's death rid the Henrician regime of an embarrassment, and all that remained was to dispose of his body, as is shown in this brutally dismissive letter from the King's new brother-in-law, the Earl of Hertford.

Earl of Hertford to Lord Cromwell   1537

My Lord, I have showed the King's highness of my Lord Thomas's death as Master Wriothesley [Thomas Wriothesley, later Earl of Southampton] desired me, as also my lady his mother's request for the burying of him. His Grace is content she hath him according to your advice, so that she bury him without pomp,
    Your Lordship's loving friend,
    E. Hertford

Cromwell had to endure the Duchess of Norfolk's breathless style in a series of letters. She was inconsistent in her abuse of her husband's mistress, Bess Holland, citing among other characteristics her low birth. Her attempt at a pun on 'Hertfordshire' is indeed the lowest form of wit.

Elizabeth, Duchess of Norfolk to Lord Cromwell   26 June 1537
Redbourne

... The cause of my writing unto you is, that I may know whether I shall have a better living or not ... which my Lord my husband hath forgotten now he hath so much wealth and honours, and is so far in doting love with that quean [whore] ... He knoweth it is spoken of far and near, to his great dishonour and shame; and he chose me for love, and I am younger than he by twenty years, and he hath put me away four years and a quarter at this midsummer; and [I] hath lived always like a good woman, as it is not unknown ... He hath taken away all my jewels and my apparel, and kept me four years and more like a prisoner ... Another cause: he set his women to bind me till blood come out at my fingers' ends, and pinnacled me, and sat on my breast till I spit blood; and he never punished them: and all this was done for Bess Holland's sake ... I live in Hertfordshire and have but ... 50 pounds a quarter, and keep twenty persons daily, besides other great charges, which I have rehearsed before. I livebetter cheap in London than I do here. It may well be called 'Her fourth shire' [share or period] ...

The duke had his side of the story, which he indignantly recounted to Cromwell. After this mutual abuse, it is strange to see effigies of the duke and duchess lying side by side in splendid tranquillity on their great tomb at Framlingham in Suffolk, but the tomb is a fitting symbol of the sham that their marriage became: in reality the Duchess lies on her own, far away in Lambeth parish church in south London.

Duke of Norfolk to Lord Cromwell   c. 1537
Buntingford

My very good Lord, it is come to my knowledge that my wilful wife is come to London, and hath been with you intending to come to me to London. My Lord, I assure you as long as I live I will never come in her company, unto the time she hath first written to me that she hath untruly slandered me in writing and saying that when she had be in childbed of my daughter of Richmond two nights and a day, I should draw her out of her bed by the hair of her head about the house, and with my dagger give her a wound in the head. My good Lord, if I prove not by witness, and that with many honest persons, that she had the scar in her head fifteen months before she was delivered of my said daughter, and that the same was cut by a surgeon of London for a swelling she had in her head, of drawing two teeth, never trust my word after; reporting to your good lordship whether I shall play the fool or no, to put me in her danger, that so falsely will slander me, and so wilfully stick thereby. Surely I think there is no man on live [alive] that would handle a woman in childbed of that sort, nor for my part would not so have done for all that I am worth.

Finally, my Lord, I require you to send to her in no wise to come where I am, for the same shall not only put me to more trouble than I have (whereof I have no need), but might give me occasion to handle her otherwise than I have done yet. Yet if she first write to me, confessing her false slander, and thereupon sue to the King's highness to make an end, I will never refuse to do that his Majesty shall command me to do; but before, assuredly never ...

Thomas Cromwell

Thomas Cromwell, Wolsey's former servant and successor as chief minister. Unlike Wolsey, his lowly origins were not disguised by the ecclesiastical rank. This and the sharp ideological conflicts of the Reformation made his relations with the nobility far more difficult than Wolsey's and they exulted in his fall.

A self-made man, Thomas Cromwell left his humble origins in Putney to live by his wits in Italy and the Netherlands, and gained experience in the cloth trade. He then returned to London to marry into a merchant family, set up in business, and study and practise the law. By 1524 he had entered Wolsey's administrative service. He stood by his master at his fall, but also took the chance to build a new career in the King's service, aligning himself with the Boleyns, and specializing in parliamentary management.

In 1532 Cromwell provoked and manipulated a confrontation between the Commons and the Convocation of the Clergy, to break the opposition to the implementation of Henry's supreme headship of the Church. In this crisis Cromwell demonstrated two of his characteristic skills, the ability to manage the King and the political struggles around him with bold but unshowy deftness, and the ability to use Parliament to promote and secure political and governmental change. He gradually recreated Wolsey's position as chief minister, taking an influential part in the distribution of royal patronage, building up an income that oustripped those of the greatest noblemen, and accumulating many offices and honours.

Cromwell's character and achievements were intensely controversial in his own day, and they remain so. To his most extreme opponents he was an amoral, Machiavellian politician who exercised satanic influence on Henry, tempting him to despoil the Church with promises of untold wealth and power. To his Protestant admirers he was God's agent in guiding Henry into the Reformation. He was no great original thinker, but he ably welded together others' ideas and implemented changes forcefully, but with the administrative assiduity and political sense to avoid arousing insurmountable opposition.

Cromwell has been seen as the architect of a 'Tudor revolution in government'; while many historians would deny that his achievements merit the label, he unquestionably ranks among the greatest statesmen and politicians of the Tudor age.

The Howards' problems were not only domestic. Jane Seymour had died in 1537, but the fact that she had given the King his longed-for heir guaranteed her family's future power. The sudden rise of the Seymours was bound to be awkward for such an ambitious family as the Howards, however correctly Norfolk himself behaved. Matters were made much worse by the Earl of Surrey's passion for the Countess of Hertford, although Surrey found himself rebuffed. In 1537 the tension between Hertford and Surrey exploded - it is conjectured - when Hertford accused him of having favoured the rebels in the Pilgrimage of Grace. Surrey hit him in the face, and was rewarded with a brief imprisonment at Windsor Castle. This produced one of his most beautiful poems, as he reflected on earlier, happier days spent in the company of the young Duke of Richmond: a picture of an ideal court, where the whole game of courtly love could be played out with all the glitter of a modern soap-opera.

Earl of Surrey, imprisoned at Windsor, recalls past times   1537

So cruel prison how could betide, alas!
   As proud Windsor? where I in lust and joy,
   With a King's son my childish years did pass,
   In greater feast than Priam's sons of Troy.
Where each sweet place returns a taste full sour.
   The large green courts, where we were wont to hove,
   With eyes cast up into the Maiden's Tower,
   And easy sighs, such as folk draw in love.
The stately seats, the ladies bright of hue;
   The dances short, long tales of great delight;
   With words and looks, that tigers could but rue,
   Where each of us did plead the other's right.
The palme-play [tennis court], where, despoiled [stripped] for the game,
   With dazed eyes oft we by gleams of love,
   Have miss'd the ball, and got sight of our dame,
   To bait her eyes, which kept the leads above ...
And with this thought, the blood forsakes the face;
   The tears berain my cheeks of deadly hue;
   The which, as soon as sobbing sighs, alas!
   Up-supped have, thus I my plaint renew:
'O place of bliss! Renewer of my woes!
   Give me account, where is my noble fere [Duke of Richmond]
   Whom in thy walls thou didst each night enclose?
   - To other lief [dear], but unto me most dear.'
... And with remembrance of the greater grief,
To banish the less, I find my chief relief.

In the destruction of Cromwell, however, the Seymours seem to have worked closely with the Howards. The minister's position had been weakened by his sponsorship of the King's marriage in January 1540 with Anne of Cleves, whom Henry loathed at sight; the *coup de grace* was the revelation of his protection of religious radicals at Calais, which Norfolk and Hertford jointly brought to the King's notice. In June 1540 he was arrested in the Council Chamber. The French ambassador reports the scene. Particularly striking is his account of Norfolk's antipathy towards Cromwell: the duke wanted him to be downgraded from the peerage and treated, as he had been born - as a shearman (a labourer in the wool trade). This would have enabled him to be executed with the full horrors of hanging, drawing and quartering, instead of by beheading which was customarily granted to noblemen.

Charles de Marillac to Anne de Montmorency   23 June 1540
London

Monseigneur, if our posts had made as good speed as the courier of this King does, you would have heard straight away of the taking of Mr. Cromwell ... To begin with the day that he was taken in the King's House at Westminster and in the Council Chamber: as soon as the Captain of the Tower who had charge of making him prisoner told him of the order which he had from his master the King to make him prisoner, the said Cromwell, roused to fury, took his bonnet and having ripped it from his head, threw it in rage to the ground; saying to the Duke of Norfolk and the others of the Privy Council there assembled that this was the reward for the good services which he had done to the said Lord King, and that he challenged their consciences to affirm their accusation that he was a traitor ... The Duke of Norfolk reproached him with various villainies which he had committed, and tore from him him the Order of St. George which he wore at his collar; the Admiral [William Fitzwilliam, Earl of Southampton] (to show him that he was as a great an enemy to him in adversity as he had been thought a friend in prosperity) relieved him of the Garter - and through a door which looks over the water, without further ado the said Cromwell was put in a boat and taken to the Tower ...

    And my said Lord [the King] has caused public proclamation that none should any more call him Lord Privy Seal nor by any other estate or lordship, but only Thomas Cromwell, shearman; stripping him of all the privileges and prerogatives of nobility which he had granted him ... From this, Monseigneur, it is thought that the said Cromwell will not be tried according to the custom of the peers of this realm nor later executed with their customary beheading, but will be hurdled like a commoner and then hanged and quartered as a traitor ...

Sports and Pastimes

Court life was intended to be fun. Indeed, it was dangerous for the monarch if it was not, for boredom in a society of aggressive adult males with over-sized egos spells trouble. Ways also had to be found to contain the flirting of the young and unmarried (let alone that of the married), so that courtships could remain decorous while still retaining their savour. Entertainment needed therefore to be well provided for, and much of it had to be highly organized.

There always had to be something to do if a nobleman found himself unoccupied, even if it was as quiet an activity as a game of chess. For the young who wanted to show off their good looks and bodies, there needed to be plenty of sports to impress the audience; as Surrey's poem shows, the court for real tennis could be highly charged with sexual excitement. All royal residences of any consequence were equipped with a tennis court during the sixteenth century - Whitehall and Hampton Court had both closed (roofed) and open courts. Other energetic pastimes like hunting and jousting also required their buildings: lodges in the parks for spectators of the hunt, and tiltyards and grandstands for the tournament. For those inclined to show off with less expenditure of energy, bowling alleys were built, and from at least the time of Henry VII galleries were also provided for the simple pleasure of taking an indoor stroll when it was raining or cold. For the more intellectually inclined, pictures - usually portraits - adorned the walls of the palaces, and there was also the royal library containing books and manuscripts at Whitehall. Also, accomplishment in music and poetry was highly valued, as was the ability to dance.

Besides spontaneous entertainment, there were set-piece events to be staged. Standards had been set European-wide in the fifteenth century by the high-spending Burgundian court, which had carried to a pitch of refinement the ancient message that all court ceremony and entertainment showed forth the ruler's position as leader of the realm. There were several forms, outdoors and indoors. In the open air, tournaments were dangerous sporting events, but also dramatic performances: the entry of the combatant knights and the audience's appreciation of the themes and characters which they had chosen for themselves was as important as the actual running of the lists. Indoors, 'disguisings' - mimes performed with the Court as spectator - were gradually expanded during the early sixteenth century with speeches and greater audience participation, so that the whole dramatic performance became fused with dance to unite the Court (actors and audience alike) in the presentation of a message.

The end-product was a court masque. In his younger days, Henry VIII took the leading role in these performances; in later years he seems to have felt that his newly revealed dignity as Supreme Head of the Church of England (and perhaps also his newly acquired paunch) made a more dignified and distant role appropriate. Yet this did not diminish the value of the entertainments. The insecure aristocratic regimes of Edward VI found them useful displays to hide their tensions and uncertainties and to publicize their new religious policy, and so devoted a great deal of energy to them. Mary busied her court officials in continuing the tradition, although always with an anxious eye on expense amid her constant financial worries; while Elizabeth delighted in both the drama and the propaganda possibilities of the masque. Throughout the century, drama and tournaments were not just for fun. For those equipped to unravel their meaning, they carried important messages about the monarch's intentions.

An Elizabethan gentleman with his hawk. The nobility were obsessed with hunting in all its forms and even the poet Sir Thomas Wyatt regarded reading and writing as something to do only when 'foul weather' stopped him enjoying killing things.

Anne of Cleves and the Fall of Cromwell

Anne of Cleves, Henry's fourth Queen. In the divorce proceedings, Henry described graphically his inability to consummate the marriage, but asserted that his virility was normally unimpaired. There are reasons for doubting the assurance.

Despite the real depth of his grief for Jane Seymour, Henry was determined to marry again: but whom should he choose? This time there was little talk of an English bride. The marriage was planned to be a step in the complex diplomatic webs which England was trying to create on the Continent in order to find a reliable ally. The choice of a foreign princess would also indicate whether Cromwell or the religious conservatives at Court were uppermost in the King's affections, so the domestic stakes were high. The first-rank powers were not in a mood to co-operate. No Habsburg or Valois princesses were made available, so a bride of the second rank would have to do.

Cromwell decided on the Lady Anne from Cleves, a duchy between the Netherlands and the German Empire. Cleves was not only strategically important in relation to the Empire, but also suited Cromwell's religious policies: Duke William of Cleves was inclined to Protestantism. Henry declared himself very satisfied with Holbein's portrait of the Lady Anne, but his first glimpse of Anne in the flesh in December 1539 was a disaster. He tried to wriggle out of the marriage, but Cromwell was playing for high stakes and held him to it, brushing aside the King's legal objections; in the end the wedding took place only three days late, on 6 January 1540.

However, Cromwell had badly miscalculated. Not only did Henry still detest his bride, but the shifting diplomatic scene meant that the Cleves alliance proved not to be the sole salvation of England amid the Continental powers. The King insisted on divorce, and Anne took a handsome settlement of English lands and retired to them to spend two decades of discreet and comfortable grass-widowhood. Often seen through Henry's eyes as a dull and lumpish 'Flanders mare', she deserves reconsideration for her skilful reaction to what might have been a personal disaster. The fact that she learnt tolerable English from scratch within a few weeks of her arrival also indicates that she was no fool.

Now Cromwell's opponents, particularly the third Duke of Norfolk, had their chance to unseat him. Cromwell fought back with all his accustomed political skill. At first he seemed to have ridden out his mistake in triumph, getting himself appointed as nominal head of the King's Privy Chamber and Lord Great Chamberlain. Finally he was granted the title of Earl of Essex. Then came the counter-attack.

Buoyed up by their successful sponsorship in Parliament in 1539 of the Act of Six Articles, with its stringent penalties against most standard Protestant beliefs, the conservatives pursued Cromwell's links with a Protestant group in the garrison at Calais. Cromwell nearly succeeded in deflecting this move by counter-revelations of papalist Catholic conspiracy in the town, but in the end the charge of heresy did the trick with a King whose confidence in Cromwell had been severely dented. With startling suddenness in June 1540, Cromwell was arrested and executed before the King could change his mind.

A terrified Cromwell wrote to the King from the Tower, prefacing and ending a long account of the whole Anne of Cleves fiasco with the most abject grovelling.

Cromwell to Henry VIII   30 June 1540
The Tower of London

Most merciful King, and most gracious sovereign Lord, may it please the same to be advertised that the last time it pleased your benign goodness to send unto me the Right Honourable Lord Chancellor, the Right Honourable Duke of Norfolk and the Lord Admiral, to examine and also to declare to me divers things from your Majesty, amongst the which one special thing they moved, and thereupon charged me, as I would answer before God at the dreadful day of judgement, and also upon the extreme danger and damnation of my soul and conscience, to say what I knew in the marriage and concerning the marriage between your Highness and the Queen. To the which I answered as I knew, declaring to them the particulars as nigh as I then could call to remembrance. Which when they had heard, they, in your Majesty's name, and upon like charge as they had given me before, commanded me to write to your Highness the truth, as much as I knew in that matter; which now I do ... [A long description of the Cleves marriage fiasco follows] ...

  If I have not, to the uttermost of my remembrance, said the truth, and the whole truth in this matter, God never help me ... beseeching Almighty God ... so he now will vouchsafe to counsel you, preserve you, maintain you, remedy you, relieve and defend you, as may be most to your honour, wealth, prosperity, health and comfort of your heart's desire. For the which, and for the long life and prosperous reign of your most royal Majesty, I shall during my life, and while I am here, pray to Almighty God, that he of his most abundant goodness will help, aid and comfort you, and after your continuance of Nestor's years, that that most noble imp, the Prince's Grace, your most dear son, may succeed you to reign long, prosperously, feliciously to God's pleasure: beseeching most humbly your Grace to pardon this my rude writing, and to consider that I am a most woeful prisoner, ready to take the death, when it shall please God and your Majesty; and yet the frail flesh inciteth me continually to call to your Grace for mercy and pardon for mine offences; and thus Christ save, preserve and keep you. Written at the Tower this Wednesday, the last of June, with the heavy heart and trembling hand of your Highness's most heavy and most miserable prisoner and poor slave,
Thomas Cromwell
Most gracious Prince, I cry for mercy, mercy, mercy!

Cromwell's fall had not put an end to mutual jealousies and suspicions within the King's Council, now finding its feet in its new form as the Privy Council; royal servants had to have a keen ear for the struggles of power. Richard Pate was a busy career diplomat on the Continent who had his own preoccupations; he was a religious conservative who soon after these two letters would desert the royal cause and flee to the Pope. First, he is seen keeping in touch with his fellow-conservative and patron the Duke of Norfolk; Cromwell's suspicions had been a problem, but now Cromwell had fallen. Yet later Pate also had to preface a despatch to the whole Council with a fulsome and convoluted apology for addressing previous letters to the Duke of Norfolk alone; he put some icing on the Council's cake with some flowery compliments at the end, which make an interesting comparison with Cromwell's desperate prayers to the King in the letter above of 30 June 1540.

Richard Pate to the Duke of Norfolk   27 June 1540
Bruges

Your Lordship shall understand that I cannot sufficiently rejoice to see this day that all things thus prosperously succeeding, it is my fortune to write you my letters, that ever hath been my singular good lord of my small deserts, notwithstanding your infinite goodness hath been never of my part forgotten, albeit the just occasion of my knowledge [acknowledgement] thereof by mine humble thanks was utterly taken away, partly for a jealousy I was had in concerning mine often letters written, in my first legacy [embassy], to you, as I conjectured by a dangerous [threatening] question moved to me, at my return from the Emperor, of him [Cromwell] that never loved neither you nor yours (now brought whither he is worthy), and partly by an advertisement of the same at my last departure out of England; for the which considerations I never durst resort to do my duty unto your Grace ...

Richard Pate to the Privy Council   4 October 1540

... whereas since Lord Cromwell's fall and death I have not justly, as I understand, executed mine office in directing my letters neither to the King nor yet to you all in general, it shall be your prudence and goodness to interpret the same to the best part, perceiving inespecially mine error not wilfully committed but as following my first instruction ...

The Privy Council

The Privy Council at Edward VI's accession. Unlike the old royal Council, which sat in a 'U'-shape round the walls of the Star Chamber, the Privy Council was small enough to meet round a table. Hence, by metonymy, it was called the 'Board'.

Who would wield power in England with a King always ready to shape the broad strokes of policy, but constitutionally disinclined to fill in the detail? Would it be a group of hard-working if often quarrelsome advisers, or a single strong minister? Henry VIII's thirty-eight years on the throne show the alternation of these two styles of government, with Wolsey and Cromwell representing rule by dominant minister for more than half the reign. In reaction to such concentrated power, when the King's second dominant minister was finally destroyed, a permanent Council was set up. It was designed to curb the pretensions of any future aspirant to Cromwell's powers in the interests of the nobility, who regarded themselves as the King's natural councillors.

There had, of course, long been a King's Council, a large and often ill-defined group from which a king gathered advisers who usually included most of the major nobility. In his efforts to monopolize the position of royal adviser, Wolsey had turned the Council's activities away from the execution of policy towards the efficient settling of legal disputes.

During Cromwell's years of power, various members of the Council can be distinguished as 'Privy' Councillors: a description which had long denoted those advisers who were particularly close to the King in delicate and important political decisions.

Little more than a month after Cromwell's fall, on 10 August 1540, the Privy Council was set up for the first time as a formal body, with clerk and minute book, and a small fixed membership. In Henry's last years, the active Councillors were even more select in number than the membership lists would suggest: while the King took only a fitful interest in aspects of policy which he felt to be of major importance, nine Privy Councillors holding the great offices of the realm in effect ran the country between them.

However, factional struggle was not ended by the new position of the Privy Council. Just as much as the immediate entourage around the King's private chambers, the Council board (the table at which Councillors sat) became a setting for continuing vicious conflict between, on the one hand, the conservative nobility and their ally Bishop Gardiner, and on the other Archbishop Cranmer, the Seymours and the various leading men who were pressing for Protestant religious change.

Underlying these revelations in high politics had been Henry VIII's fifth marriage to Catherine Howard. The King was besotted with her; she, however, soon fell for the youthful charms of Thomas Culpeper, Henry's former page. Her letter to him, painfully written out by a young woman not well versed in the art of expressing herself clearly or elegantly, is a pathetic piece of calf-love, all the more poignant because it is the one definite proof of Catherine's unfaithfulness after her marriage to the King; even then, it expresses the intention rather than the deed.

Queen Catherine Howard to Thomas Culpeper ?April 1541

Master Culpeper, I heartily recommend me unto you, praying you to send me word how that you do. It was showed me that you were sick, the which thing troubled me very much till such time that I hear from you, praying you to send me word how that you do, for I never longed so much for thing as I do to see you and to speak with you, the which I trust shall be shortly now. The which doth comfort me very much when I think of it, and when I think again that you shall depart from me again it makes my heart to die, to think what fortune I have that I cannot be always in your company. Yet my trust is alway in you that you will be as you have promised me, and in that hope I trust upon still, praying you then that you will come when my Lady Rochford is here, for then I shall be best at leisure to be at your commandment, thanking you for that you have promised me to be so good unto that poor fellow my man, which is one of the griefs that I do feel to depart from him, for then I do know no one that I dare trust to send to you, and therefore I pray you take him to be with you that I may sometime hear from you. One thing I pray you, to give me a horse for my man, for I have much ado to get one, and therefore I pray send me one by him, and in so doing I am as I said afore; and thus I take my leave of you, trusting to see you shortly again, and I would you was with me now that you might see what pain I take in writing to you,
      Yours as long as life endures,
      Katherine

Catherine's half-truths availed nothing; under the Council's relentless inquisitions, the whole truth, including Culpeper, came out. A wave of arrests followed, including many Howard family members. Norfolk was in a highly embarrassing position. He took the usual way out of cowering abjectly in front of the King and unloading much of the blame on the other members of the clan, for whom, in any case, he had little love.

Duke of Norfolk to Henry VIII   15 December 1541
Kenninghall

Most noble and gracious sovereign Lord, yesterday came to my knowledge that mine ungracious mother in law [stepmother], mine unhappy brother and his wife, with my lewd sister of Bridgewater, were committed to the Tower; which by long experience, knowing your accustomed equity and justice used to all your subjects, am sure is not done but for some their false and traitorous proceedings against your royal Majesty. Which, revolving in my mind, with also the most abominable deeds done by two of my nieces against your Highness, hath brought me into the greatest perplexity that ever poor wretch was in; fearing that your Majesty, having so often and by so many of my kin, been thus falsely and traitorously handled, might not only conceive a displeasure in your heart against me and all other of that kin, but also in manner abhor to hear speak of any of the same. Wherefore, most gracious sovereign Lord, prostrate at your feet, most humbly I beseech your Majesty to call to your remembrance that a great part of this matter is come to light by my declaration to your Majesty, according to my bounden duty, of the words spoken to me by my mother in law when your Highness sent me to Lambeth to search Dereham's coffers; without the which I think she had not be further examined, nor consequently her ungracious children. Which my true proceedings towards your Majesty considered, and also the small love my two false traitorous nieces and my mother in law have borne unto me, doth put me in some hope that your Highness will not conceive any displeasure in your most gentle heart against me; that (God knoweth) never did think thought which might be to your discontentation. Wherefore, eftsoons [a second time] prostrate at your royal feet, most humbly I beseech your Majesty that by such as it shall please you to command, I may be advertised plainly how your Highness doth weigh your favour towards me; assuring your Highness that unless I may know your Majesty to continue my good and gracious Lord, as ye were before their offences committed, I shall never desire to live in this world any longer, but shortly to finish this transitory life, as God knoweth; who send your Majesty the accomplishments of your most noble heart's desires ...

News that Queen Catherine 'lived most corruptly and sensually' was broken to Henry at the end of the summer progress of 1541. At first only her pre-marital, teenage indiscretions were known. And, in her first confession to the King, these were all that she admitted. Nothing she said could be construed in law as adultery against the King. The tactic was the work, in part, of a residual streak of Howard self-preservation; more important probably was her desperate desire to protect Culpeper.

Confession of Queen Catherine Howard   November 1541

I, your Grace's most sorrowful subject and most vile wretch in the world ... do only make my most humble submission and confession of my faults. And where no cause of mercy is given upon my part, yet of your most accustomed mercy extended unto all other men undeserved, most humbly of my hands and knees do desire one sparkle thereof to be extended unto me, although of all other creatures most unworthy either to be called your wife or subject. My sorrow I can by no writing express; nevertheless I trust your most benign nature will have some respect unto my youth, my ignorance, my frailness, my humble confession of my fault and plain declaration of the same, referring me wholly unto your Grace's pity and mercy. First at the flattering and fair persuasions of Mannock, being but a young girl, suffered him at sundry times to handle and touch the secret parts of my body, which neither became me with honesty to permit nor him to require. Also Francis Derham by many persuasions procured me to his vicious purpose, and obtained first to lie upon my bed with his doublet and hose, and after within the bed, and finally he lay with me naked and used me in such sort as a man doth his wife many and sundry times, but how often I know not; and our company ended almost a year before the King's majesty was married to my Lady Anne of Cleve and continued not past one quarter of a year or little above. Now the whole truth being declared unto your Majesty, I most humbly beseech the same to consider the subtle persuasions of young men and the ignorance and frailness of young women. I was so desirous to be taken unto your Grace's favour and so blinded with the desire of worldly glory that I could not nor had grace to consider how great a fault it was to conceal my former faults from your Majesty, considering that I intended ever during my life to be faithful and true unto your Majesty after, and nevertheless, the sorrow of my offences was ever before mine eyes, considering the infinite goodness of your Majesty towards me from time to time ever increasing and not diminishing. Now I refer the judgement of all mine offences with my life and death wholly unto your most benign and merciful grace: to be considered ... only by your infinite goodness, pity, compassion and mercy.

Catherine Howard

Miniature by Holbein, supposed to be of Catherine Howard. Feckless parents, indulgence and neglect as a teenager, and a healthy sexual appetite made her a disastrous choice as Henry VIII's fifth Queen.

The conservatives at Court quickly lined up Catherine Howard, another niece of the third Duke of Norfolk, to act as a replacement wife after the Anne of Cleves fiasco. Their choice had the necessary glamour to put Anne of Cleves in the shade, but proved a disastrous one in every other way.

Catherine was daughter to Lord Edmund Howard, a younger son of the victor of Flodden. A wild and spirited girl, she was spoilt by her step-grandmother, who brought her up, and she had no problem in plunging into a series of steamy teenage affairs.

Norfolk and Gardiner showed themselves possessed of scant common sense or remarkably inept political improvisation in introducing this particular racy seventeen-year-old to the emotionally bruised King. Henry was immediately attracted to her, and Catherine gleefully embraced her greatest conquest yet; she became his mistress immediately, and was rumoured to have become pregnant by early July 1540, as soon as the Cleves divorce had been finalized. The new royal marriage took place three weeks later, and by the beginning of August the King was acknowledging her as Queen.

Catherine soon got bored with her dauntingly large and moody husband, and she did not appreciate the crucial importance of curbing her love of a good time. Although she had dismissed Francis Dereham, a previous lover, on her arrival at Court, she had soon begun an affair with Thomas Culpeper. Feydeau farce

quickly turned to grim political reality: this was the opportunity the Protestant party had been waiting for. On 31 October 1541 Archbishop Cranmer took the lead as the man whom the King was most likely to hear out without an explosion. Cranmer handed the King a paper listing Catherine's affairs.

Henry, at first incredulous, burst into tears, but he was soon convinced. On 10 December 1541 Culpeper and Dereham were executed, followed by Catherine and her conniving cousin Lady Rochford on 12 February 1542; considering Lady Rochford's part in the death of her own husband and that of Anne Boleyn, there was a certain justice in her death at least. Otherwise the toll of the dead was surprisingly small compared with the Boleyn debacle: the Protestants were not strong enough to press home their advantage, and the Duke of Norfolk got away with nothing worse than temporary disgrace. Nevertheless, it meant that the Howards could not follow up the full advantage of Cromwell's fall.

The full emotional cost to the King will never be known, but some hints can be gleaned from the intensity of his reading in the following months. In particular, there is the sad witness of his printed copy of the *Book of Proverbs*, dateable to 1542. For the first five chapters, he covered the margins with notes in his usual fashion, but then he apparently gave up on the volume for ever, after marking the words 'My son, why wilt thou have pleasure in a harlot?'

Norfolk knew his King. Catherine and her lovers were executed; the offending members of her family were imprisoned, but Norfolk and his son Surrey soon returned to Henry VII's favour to fight his wars against France and Scotland in the 1540s. Here the Duke of Norfolk warns Surrey against encouraging Henry to keep, or still worse to extend, his French conquests. Surrey ignored the warning , as he did all good advice.

Duke of Norfolk to Earl of Surrey   27 September 1545
Windsor

With this ye shall receive your letter sent to me by this bearer, by the which I perceive ye find yourself grieved for that I declared to the King such things as Cavendish shewed to me: which I did by his desire, shewing the same as his behalf without speaking of you. And if he will say he desired not me to shew the King thereof, ye may ['know' omitted?] he saith untruly; for (the King hawking for a pheasant) he desired me as he went homeward to declare the same to his Highness. This is true; and he taken here not of the best sort. Ye may be sure I do not use my doings of any sort that may turn you to any displeasure. Have yourself in await, that ye animate not the King too much for the keeping of Boulogne; for whoso doth, at length shall get small thank. I have so handled the matter, that if any adventure be given to win the new fortress at Boulogne, ye shall have the charge thereof; and therefore look wisely what answer ye make to the letter from us of the Council concerning the enterprises contained in them.

Having written the premises, Mr. Paget desired me to write to you in no wise to animate the King to keep Boulogne. Upon what grounds he spake it, I know not; but I fear ye wrote something too much therein to somebody. And thus with God's blessing and mine, Fare ye well. From Windsor the 27th of September at night,

Your loving father,

T. Norfolk

As his father feared, Surrey's appetite for glory caused him to overreach himself. Made Governor of Boulogne, he suffered many losses in a skirmish against the French and was recalled. Smarting with indignation at his ignominious departure from France, Surrey wrote to Sir William Paget, the King's Secretary, about unfinished French business. This is vintage Surrey, touchy and as full of family pride as ever; the low-born Secretary cannot have enjoyed reading this piece of aristocratic self-assurance.

Earl of Surrey to Sir William Paget   14 July 1546

... And now you shall give me leave to come to mine own matters. Coming from Boulogne in such sort as you know, I left only two of my servants behind me: John Rossington and Thomas Copeland. To the said John, for his notable service, I gave the advantage of the play [?beach] in Boulogne; to Thomas, the profit of the passage; whom my Lord Grey put immediately out of service after my departure, notwithstanding the letters I obtained from you to him in their favour. And, upon a better consideration, John occupieth his room [place], and my Lord to his use occupieth the other's office of the passage, saying that I and my predecessors there should use the same to our gain (which I assure you upon mine honour is untrue) and that it should be parcel of the entertainment of the Deputy; which in Calais was never used, and is (me seemeth) too near [trivial] for a Deputy to grate [take control of] unless it were for some displeasure borne to me.

    Finally, Mr. Secretary, this is the only suit that I have made you for any thing touching Boulogne sith my departure; wherefore it may please you that if my Lord Grey will needs be passager, and that the office was no less worth to the said Thomas than fifty pounds a year, being placed there by a King's Lieutenant (which methinketh a great disorder that a Captain of Boulogne should displace for any private gain), yet at the least it may please you to require my Lord Grey to recompense him with a sum of money in recompense of that that he hath lost, and purchased so dearly with so many dangers of life; which my said lord of his liberality cannot refuse to do. And for answer that my said lord chargeth me to have returned the same to my private profit, in his so saying he can have none honour. For there be in Boulogne too many witnesses that Henry of Surrey was never for singular profit corrupted; nor never yet bribe closed his hand; which lesson I learned of my father, and wish to succeed him therein as in the rest ... And thus wishing you [to continue ever mor]e my friend till I deserve of [any fault of mine the con]trary, I pray to God send you [whatever good your o]wn heart desireth ...

Up to July 1546 the conservatives, led by Norfolk, seemed to be carrying all before them. Then in July the Earl of Hertford and Viscount Lisle returned to Court. Surrey's recall in disgrace from France was the first blow against the Howards; the second was the arrest of father and son. Pride indeed came before a fall. Their arrest was another example of the sudden turnarounds in fortune which were possible in the unstable political atmosphere of Henry's last years. The draft articles drawn up against the pair show that the dying Henry VIII was still very active in this move. Surrey's folly had aroused all his old fears of challenges to the succession. In the following memorandum the italic text represents anxious additions by the King in his own shaky hand to the charges about heraldry and the succession; he makes no alterations to the other articles. Indeed, it would be on the heraldic charges that Surrey was condemned. A quick trial was followed by execution on 19 January 1547.

Draft articles against the Duke of Surrey and his father   1546

If a man coming of *the collateral line to the heir of* the Crown who ought not to bear the arms of England but on the second quarter with the difference of *their* ancestor do *presume* to change his right place and bear them in the first quarter leaving out the difference of the ancestor, and in the lieu thereof use *the very place* only of the heir male apparent: *how this man's intent is to be judged and whether this* import any danger, peril or slander to the title of the Prince or very heir apparent, and how it weigheth in our laws.

  If a man *presume* to take into his arms an old coat of the Crown *which his ancestor never bare nor he of right ought to be* and use it without difference: whether it may be to the peril or slander of the very heir of the Crown [the King adds in the margin '[to the w]rong [or prej]udice [of the he]ir'] or be taken to tend to his disturbance in the same; and in what peril they be that consent that he should so do.

  If a man compassing *with himself to govern the realm do actually go about to rule the King* and should for that purpose advise his daughter or sister to become his harlot *thinking thereby to bring it to pass and so would rule both father and son as by this next article doth more appear: what this importeth.*

  If a man say these words: 'If the King die, who should have the rule of the Prince but my father or I?': what it importeth.

  The depraving of the King's Council.

  If a man shall say these words of a [man] or woman of the realm: 'If the K[ing] were dead, I should shortly shut him up': what it importeth ...

  If a subject presume without l[icence to] give arms to strangers: what it imp[orteth] ...

Heraldry and Pedigrees

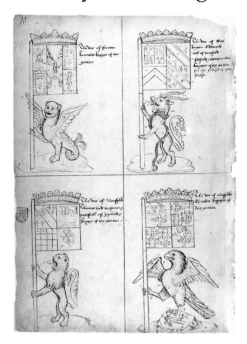

The pride of Heraldry: the banners, beasts and coronets of Henry VIII's three dukes of Buckingham, Norfolk and Suffolk and (top left) of his ally and sometime visitor, the duke of Ferrara.

For medieval and early modern Europe, heraldry was as much an élite international language as Latin; like Latin, it was universally understood and appreciated by those who mattered in society. Perhaps it had started as a means of identification in war, but it came to have many more uses than that. In a world where the lines of power were often the lines of personal relationships, the knowledge of heraldry and pedigrees was virtually a branch of political science. It was heraldry which brought down the Howard family in 1546; in the draft charges against Surrey, it is the technical intricacies of heraldry which top the list of Surrey's offences, and in the end it was only these heraldic charges of all the accusations which were used against the earl.

The centrality of heraldry and pedigree was not merely political. The economic changes which seemed so threatening in Tudor England created a general anxious search for stability, directed in particular around the family. The family gave an individual a stable place in the midst of change; a family pedigree was the expression of that stability, as well as an expression of a gentleman's right to a place in the circle of government. Expression of this is found in the increasingly elaborate heraldry on Tudor monuments, and in their frequent neurotic emphasis on the 'antiquity' of their subject's line.

Another symptom is the continued activity of the heralds in an age when their functions in warfare and diplomacy were becoming obsolete; instead of disappearing, the heralds formed a corporation. From the late fifteenth century, they undertook frequent visitations throughout the kingdom to certify coats of arms and determine family descent; visitation records still exist from the 1530s onwards.

Although their work was frequently inaccurate, the heralds played an important part in the growth of historical study. Their genealogical researches preserved much detail about churches which were suffering in the course of the Reformation; they also played the leading role in England's first society specifically devoted to preserving and seeking out evidence of the past, the Society of Antiquaries (founded about 1586). By the end of the century it was possible for a man to be appointed as herald specifically because of his reputation as an historian: the great William Camden, who rose to the heralds' supreme office as Garter King of Arms.

Howard Houses in the Tudor Age

All Tudor great families expressed their power in buildings; thus the fourth Duke of Norfolk eventually found himself with no fewer than six splendid houses. However, the Howards' remarkable powers of survival as a family have not been shared by either their Tudor or their later homes; for such prolific builders, their houses have suffered remarkable casualties over the centuries. From the sixteenth century only Charterhouse is substantially complete.

From their ancestors the Howards inherited a number of properties, both the relatively modest homes (for instance at Stoke by Nayland on the Essex-Suffolk border) which had been suitable for their needs as country gentlemen, and the more spectacular properties long associated with the title of Earl and Duke of Norfolk descended from the Bigods and Mowbrays. Greatest of these was the ancient castle at Framlingham in east Suffolk, to which the second Duke retired, and which was

Kenninghall Palace, Norfolk. The small surviving fragment of the residence built in 1505-25 for the Dukes of Norfolk. On the fall of the third duke in 1546 it was seized by the crown.

remodelled with an eye for introducing comfort without destroying its feudal magnificence. An outlying property at Chesworth in Sussex also received considerable updating, some of which can still be seen, and a few scraps of Tudor Howard domestication also remain at Castle Rising in north Norfolk, which the third Duke gained in 1544.

However, the biggest sixteenth-century enterprise for the family was Kenninghall, designed by the second and third Dukes to act as a central focus for their East Anglian estates. Kenninghall was built beside the site of an earlier house, but rightly earned the new name of a palace; now only one small range survives, and we know little of the appearance of the whole massive structure.

Similarly, the ducal palace in Norwich has entirely disappeared, and there is not a trace of the showy house which the Earl of Surrey built outside the same city and named with typical bravado Mount Surrey. Further costly plans by Surrey contributed to his downfall, as he quarrelled with the heralds about the heraldry which should adorn them, and were brought to an end by his execution.

When they were in or around the capital, the early Tudor dukes generally lodged at Court. But there are substantial remains of the fourth Duke of Norfolk's expensive alterations at the London Charterhouse. The Duke bought the former Carthusian priory in 1564 from Lord North, who had already converted it into a comfortable residence. The Duke built a minstrel's gallery in the hall, remodelled the great chamber, and made a gallery out of the old west cloister range.

As far as architectural style is concerned, the Howards were not behind other great aristocratic families in their patronage of continental classical change. Indeed, they were among the pioneers, with their sophisticated French-style tombs at Thetford and Framlingham. The Earl of Surrey's house outside Norwich may also have been in a classical style as advanced as anything put up by the evangelical-sympathizing mid-Tudor families. But his son seems to have been more conservative, to judge by the surviving work at the Charterhouse. It would take Thomas, fourteenth Earl of Arundel in the generation of Howards under James I, to reassert the Howards' interest in the up-to-date classicism of the Continent.

The preliminary investigations complete, Surrey and Norfolk were sent to the Tower on 12 December. That gave Henry VIII's agents about thirty-six hours to travel the hundred miles or so from London to Kenninghall and catch the Duke's family by surprise. The King's agents were a significant group: Gates and Southwell were among the architects of Surrey's fall, while Carew was brother-in-law to both Gates and the leading Protestant courtier and fellow-conspirator Sir Anthony Denny. Of the ill-assorted womenfolk whom they found, the Duchess of Richmond was characteristic of her generation of Howards in being ready to echo denunciations of her father and brother. But this is more understandable in the light of her bitterness about her poverty; her father and brother had refused to help her claim her dower from the King.

Sir Richard Southwell, John Gates   14 December 1546
and Wimond Carew to Henry VIII
Kenninghall

... we did declare our desire to speak with the Duchess of Richmond and Elizabeth Holland, both which we found at that time newly risen, and not ready. Nevertheless, having knowledge that we would speak with them, they came unto us without delay into the dining chamber, and so we imparted unto them the case and condition wherein the said duke and his son, without your great mercy, did stand. Wherewith, as we found the duchess a woman sore perplexed, trembling and like to fall down, so coming unto herself again, she was not, we assure your Majesty, forgetful of her duty, and did most humbly and reverently upon her knees, humble herself in all unto your Highness; saying that although nature constrained her sore to love her father, whom she hath ever thought to be a true and faithful subject, and also to desire the well doing of his son, her natural brother, whom she noteth to be a rash man, yet for her part, she would nor will hide or conceal any thing from your Majesty's knowledge ... hereupon we desired the sight of her chambers and coffers, of which presently she delivered us the keys, and assigned her woman to shew us not only her chamber, but so her coffers and closet, where hitherto we have found no writings worthy sending ... Thus, Sir, after a note taken of her chamber and all her things, we searched the said Elizabeth Holland, where we have found girdles, beads, buttons of gold, pearl and rings set with stones of divers sorts, whereof, with all other things, we make a book to be sent unto your Highness. And as we have begun here at this head house ... so have we presently and at one instant sent of our most discreet and trusty servants unto all other his houses in Norfolk and Suffolk, to stay that nothing shall be embezzled ... we most humbly beseech your Majesty to signify unto us whether you will have the whole household continue ...

Imprisoned in the Tower, where so many members of his family had preceded him, the aged Duke made a final plea for his life. His son was executed on 21 January 1547 but Norfolk was to cheat death yet again. But it was the King's own death, rather than any effort of his own, that saved him. Henry died on 28 January, and it was felt improper to associate the King's death with a further execution. It was, in any case, politically unnecessary, since there was no longer any chance that he would get a pardon from another twist in Henry's affections. In his letter, he rehearses the faithfulness to his King which had led him into so many unsavoury exploits, and gives a list of his enemies through his long career. The old duke's bitter diatribe can be seen as the culmination of a lifetime of mistrusting his contemporaries.

Duke of Norfolk to the Privy Council   December 1546
The Tower of London

... My good Lords, having made answer according to the truth of such questions as hath be asked me, most humbly I beseech you all to be mediators for me to his most excellent Majesty ... I think surely there is some false man, that have laid some great cause to my charge, or else I had not be sent hither ... My Lords, there was never gold tried better by fire and water than I have be, nor hath had greater enemies about my sovereign Lord than I have had, and yet (God be thanked) my truth hath ever tried me, as I doubt not it shall do in these causes ...

And whereas I have written that my truth hath be severely tried, and that I have had great enemies. First, the cardinal [Wolsey] did confess to me at Esher that he had gone about fourteen years to have destroyed me ... The Duke of Buckingham confessed openly at the bar (my father sitting as his judge) [1521] that of all men living he hated me most, thinking I was the man that had hurt him most to the King's majesty; 'which now', quoth he, 'I perceive the contrary' ...

What malice both my nieces that it pleased the King's highness to marry did bear unto me is not unknown to such ladies as kept them in this house ... Who tried out the falsehood of the Lord Darcy, Sir Robert Constable, Sir John Bulmer, Aske and many other, for which they suffered for [in the Pilgrimage of Grace]? But only I ... In all times past unto this time, I have shewed myself a most true man to my sovereign Lord. And sith [since] these things done in times past, I have received more profit of his Highness than ever I did afore. Alas! who can think that I, having be so long a true man, should now be false to his Majesty? I have received more profit than I have deserved; and a poor man as I am, yet I am his son's near kinsman. For whose sake should I be an untrue man to them? Alas, alas, my Lords, that ever it should be thought any untruth to be in me ...

Uncles to the King and Protectors of the Throne

THE SEYMOURS

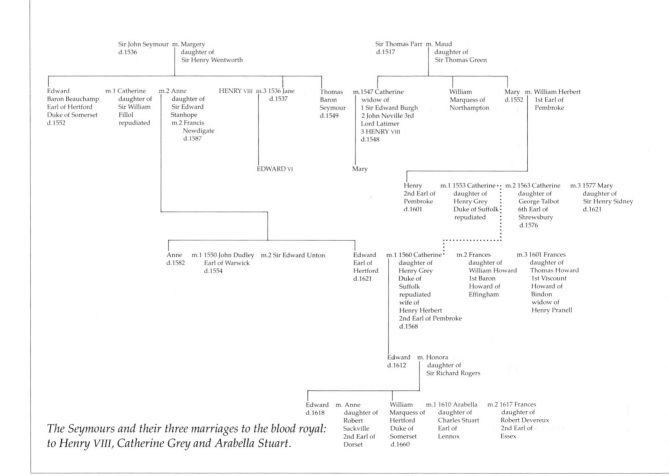

The Seymours and their three marriages to the blood royal: to Henry VIII, Catherine Grey and Arabella Stuart.

Through a series of judicious marriages and the investments of profits from public service, the Seymours had become one of the leading families in Wiltshire by the early sixteenth century. Of Sir John Seymour's ten children by Margery Wentworth four died young, but three others, whose lives and advancement were intertwined, became national figures.

The eldest surviving son Edward started his spectacular career as a page in the Household of Mary Tudor. But his steady progress took a dramatic upward turn when his sister Jane, a lady-in-waiting to two successive queens, Catherine of Aragon and Anne Boleyn, caught the attention of Henry VIII. So had other women before. What mattered this time was that Henry VIII's infatuation with Anne Boleyn had turned to dislike. Seymour promoted the dalliance, and even before Queen Anne's arrest he had been named a Gentleman of the Privy Chamber, from which post, so close to the King, he continued to encourage Henry's passion for his sister.

With Anne executed and Jane married to Henry VIII eleven days later on 30 May 1536, Seymour was ennobled as Viscount Beauchamp. Beauchamp was put on the Privy Council in 1537, and following the birth of Prince Edward he was raised to the earldom of Hertford.

The death of Queen Jane on 24 October 1537 was naturally a blow to the influence of the new Earl of Hertford. But his driving ambition and military skill ensured his survival in the closing years of Henry VIII's reign. Throughout the early 1540s Hertford succeeded in keeping the King's confidence when others, such as Norfolk and his son Surrey, failed to do so. A close relationship developed between Hertford and Secretary Paget, as did an understanding between him and Archbishop Cranmer. These two considerations were to prove decisive when in January 1547 Hertford's nephew, aged nine, succeeded to the throne as Edward VI. Hertford was one of the principal executors of Henry VIII's will, and in early 1547 he was appointed Lord Protector Somerset, the most important figure in the kingdom.

Somerset's rise to power and authority was mirrored to a lesser degree by his younger brother, Thomas. On his sister Jane's marriage to the King, Thomas Seymour succeeded to his brother Edward's place in the Privy Chamber. But beyond his naval interests and his activity as a courtier his real significance in the decade before Edward VI's accession was as a counter in the marriage market. He was deployed to promote the Seymour interest, with potential brides including two widows, the Duchess of Richmond and Catherine Parr. The chance to marry Catherine came with the death of Henry VIII, and the pair married secretly in May 1547. In his own eyes Seymour's marriage with the Queen dowager restored the balance between the two brothers.

By 1551, both brothers had been executed and the brief period of the Seymour ascendancy was over. Nevertheless, Somerset's widow and their children were to provide a source for scandal and gossip for the rest of the century. Somerset's wilful son, Edward, was imprisoned for marrying Lady Catherine Grey, younger sister of Lady Jane Grey. And the tradition of marital imbroglios continued into the next generation when, in 1602, another claimant to the throne, Arabella Stuart, proposed to Beauchamp's son Edward: eight years later Arabella married Edward's younger brother William.

The successful coup against the Howards was the political foundation of the Seymours' power: but it was Henry VIII's will that gave it constitutional legitimacy. Henry VIII had been empowered by statute to settle the succession to the English throne either by letters patent or by will signed with his 'gracious hand'. In fact, the will dated 30 December 1546 was only signed with a dry stamp by a clerk of the Council as Henry lay on his deathbed in January 1547. At most the King offered some sign of acknowledging it as his own. This document, drafted under the direction of the Earl of Hertford and Secretary Paget, provided for the welfare of the young Edward VI and for the government of the kingdom by Hertford. On being informed of Henry VIII's death by Paget, Hertford wrote back several hours later.

Earl of Hertford to Secretary Paget 29 January 1547
Hertford

This morning, between one and two, I received your letter. The first part thereof I like very well; marry, that the will should be not opened till a farther consultation, and that it might be well considered how much thereof were necessary to be published; for divers respects I think it not convenient to satisfy the world. In the meantime I think it sufficient, when you publish the King's death, in the places and times as you have appointed, to have the will presently with you, and to show that this is the will, naming unto them severally who be executors that the King did specially trust, and who be Councillors; the contents at the breaking up thereof, as before, shall be declared unto them on Wednesday in the morning at the Parliament House; and in the mean time we to meet and agree therein, as there may be no controversy hereafter. For the rest of your appointments, for the keeping of the Tower, and the King's person, it shall be well done you be not too hasty therein; and so I bid you heartily farewell. I have sent you the key of the will. From Hertford, the 29th of January between three and four in the morning.

Under the Protectorate of the Duke of Somerset the process of the Protestant Reformation in England accelerated. The monasteries and collegiate churches had disappeared and the Bible had been made available in English by 1547, but traditional medieval practices and services, including the Mass, had survived until then. Robert Parkyn, a curate at Adwick-le-Street in Yorkshire, kept a record of the changes in his commonplace book, which reveals not only a considerable distaste for Reform but also the speed and impact that these changes made, even in the North of England.

Robert Parkyn, commonplace book 1547-9

And in the first year of his reign was strict injunctions given to all the spiritualty of England, wherein specially was deposed all processions, and that none should be used, but only to kneel in the mid aisle of the church unto certain suffrages in English were sung or said on holy days.

Also in the beginning of the second year of his reign, Anno Domini 1548 on the Purification Day of Our Lady (viz Candlemas Day), there was no candles sanctified, born or holden in mens' hands, as before times laudably was accustomed, but utterly omitted.

In the beginning of Lent all such suffrages as pertained to the sanctifying of the ashes was omit & left undone & so no ashes was given to any person. In the same Lent all images, picture, tables, crucifixes, tabernacles, was utterly abolished ...

Item on Easter Day at morrow (being the first day of April), no mention was made of Jesus Christ's mighty resurrection, nor any procession that day before Mass nor at Evensong about the font, nor any other day in the week. And within 2 weeks after, all prebendaries, hospitals, chantries & free chapels within Yorkshire & other the King's dominions was given up by compulsion in to His Majesty's hands, with all manner of jewels, chalices, books, bells, vestments ...

Yea, & also the pixes hanging over the altars (wherein was remaining Christ's blessed body under form of bread) was despitefully cast away as things most abominable, and did not pass of the blessed Hosts therein contained but villainously despised them, uttering such words thereby as it did abhor true Christian ears for to hear, but only that Christ's mercy is so much, it was marvel that the earth did not open & swallow up such villainous persons as it did Dathan and Abiram. The said villainous persons denied that most blessed sacrament and so would have had no Mass used within this realm; yea, & stiffly affirmed that the Messiah was yet born, and so finally denied all sacraments, except matrimony, because it was first institute in paradise terrestry, affirming also that it was lawful for priests to marry women, using them as their wives, which was very pleasant to many.

Henry VIII's Will

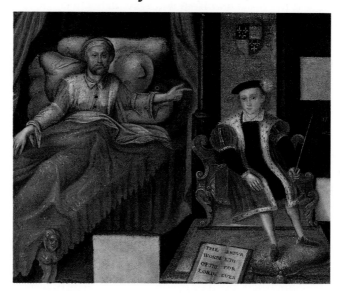

Henry VIII, alert and fully conscious on his death-bed, commends his son Edward to the protection of Edward Seymour, Duke of Somerset. The reality was more complicated.

Henry VIII was well practised in making wills and (like the rich and tyrannical of all ages) rather enjoyed changing them. Royal wills, however, had the special problem that there was nothing to compel the succeeding monarch to recongnize his predecessor's will. As so often, Henry VIII turned to Parliament to solve the difficulty, and the Second and Third Succession Acts gave statutory force to his 'last will made in writing and signed with your most gracious hand'. The Third Succession Act (1544) was passed with the imminent invasion of France in mind. And, to deal with the rather remote eventuality of his death in action, Henry indeed made a new will.

It was this will which Henry VIII decided to revise once more when he found himself on his real deathbed in December 1546. He had three considerations in mind. The first was to revise the composition of the Council (who would also be the executors of the will) following the fall of the Howards and Bishop Gardiner. The second was to distribute the Howard property. And the third was to determine whether his son's government should be run corporately by a Council or entrusted to a single Protector. Henry was not of course the only person to have strong views on these questions. It was Surrey's passionately asserted view that his father Norfolk should be Protector which had most damaged him.

While Surrey's opponents, who clustered round the Seymours, had their own fish to fry. The history of Henry's will is the story of the gulf between the King's intentions and theirs.

For Henry was determined to avoid a protectorate; Edward Seymour, Earl of Hertford and Prince Edward's maternal uncle, was equally set on becoming Protector. Negotiations dragged on for weeks with no agreement; nor was there a final conclusion on the distribution of land and titles either. The sudden worsening of the King's health forced Hertford to cut the Gordian knot. Sir William Paget, the King's Secretary and Hertford's ally, prepared a subtly amended version of the will. This provided for a Protectorate while seeming to exclude it; it also, by the 'unfulfilled gifts clause', allowed the King's executors a free hand in the distribution of honours and estates. Henry would not, and probably by this stage, could not sign it with his own hand as the Act required. Instead, it was signed with the stamp of the King's signature in the custody of Hertford's other principal ally, Sir Anthony Denny, Chief Gentleman of the Privy Chamber and antedated to 30 December.

Henry died on 28 January 1547. The machinery of the will worked like clockwork. Hertford was nominated Protector.

Once the machinery of the late King's will had been put smoothly in motion, Hertford was named Governor of his nephew Edward VI and Lord Protector on 31 January 1547, and then raised to the dukedom of Somerset in mid-February. This combination of appointment with ability, experience and ruthlessness left him politically unrivalled in England for over a year. The new duchess exalted in her new-found authority as well. However, her pride and tactlessness soon gained her enemies. It was a flattering sign of her position as wife to the Protector that the duchess received a letter from Princess Mary asking favours for two of the Princess's servants.

Princess Mary to Anne, Duchess of Somerset   24 April 1547
St. John's, Clerkenwell

My good Gossip,
    After my very hearty commendations to you, with like desire to hear of the amendment and increase of your good health, these shall be to put you in remembrance of mine old suit concerning Richard Wood, who was my mother's servant when you were one of her grace's maids, and, as you know by his supplication, hath sustained great loss, almost to his utter undoing, without any recompense for the same hitherto; which forced me to trouble you with this suit before this time, whereof (I thank you) I had a very good answer; desiring you now to renew the same matter to my lord your husband, for I consider that it is in manner impossible for him to remember all such matters, having such a heap of business as he hath.
    Wherefore I heartily require you to go forward in this suit till you have brought it to an honest end, for the poor man is not able to lie long in the city.
    And thus, my good Nann, I trouble you both with myself and all mine; thanking you with all my heart for your earnest gentleness towards me in all my suits hitherto, reckoning myself out of doubt of the continuance of the same. Wherefore once again I must trouble you with my poor George Brickhouse, who was an officer of my mother's wardrobe, of the beds, from the time of the King my father's coronation; whose only desire it is to be one of the knights of Windsor [the poor Knights of Windsor were a charitable foundation attached to the Order of the Garter] if all the rooms be not filled, and if they be, to have the next reversion; in the obtaining whereof, in mine opinion, you shall do a charitable deed, as knoweth Almighty God, who send you good health, and us shortly to meet, to his pleasure.
    Your loving friend during my life,
    Mary

The death of Henry VIII benefited Somerset's brother as well. He was able to renew his suit with Catherine Parr, whom he had hoped to marry as far back as 1543 when the King had intervened and made Catherine queen. As Queen dowager Catherine needed the consent of the Privy Council to remarry, but neither she nor Seymour sought conciliar permission, marrying clandestinely in early May. Although Catherine's sister Anne, her brother-in-law Sir William Herbert, and members of her household knew about the marriage, news of it was not revealed for several months. Shortly after their marriage, and after a meeting with Lady Herbert who had knowingly referred to it, Seymour wrote to Catherine.

Lord Seymour to Queen Catherine Parr   17 May 1547
St. James's Palace

After my humble commendations unto your Highness ...

 If I knew by what means I might gratify your Highness, for your goodness to me, showed at our last being together, it should not be slack to declare mine to you again. And to that intent, that I will be more bound unto your Highness, I do make my request, if it be not painful to your Highness, that once in three days I may receive three lines in a letter from you, and as many lines and letters more as shall seem good unto your Highness.

 Also, I shall humbly desire your Highness to give me one of your small pictures, if you have any left; who, with his silence, shall give me occasion to think on the friendly cheer that I shall receive when my suit shall be at an end. And thus, for fear of troubling your Highness with my long and rude letter, I take my leave of your Highness; wishing that my hap may be once so good, that I may declare so much by mouth at the same hour that this was written, which was twelve of the clock at night, this Tuesday, the 17th of May, at St. James's.

 From him whom you have bound to honour, love, and in all lawful things obey,

 T. Seymour

In August 1547 the Protector Somerset went on campaign in Scotland, leaving his younger brother as lieutenant of the South and one of the custodians of Edward VI. Resentful that he had not been given undivided custody of the King, Seymour thought about removing Edward VI into his own house, but on reflection he decided against this. Instead, he determined to secure his nephew's affections by providing him with money and by encouraging him to 'bear rule, as other kings do'. Seymour's attempts to manipulate the King were to prove unsuccessful, and Edward VI testified as to his uncle's misconduct.

Deposition of Edward VI concerning Somerset   January or February 1549

The Lord Admiral [Seymour] came to me at the last Parliament and desired me to write a thing for him. I asked him what, he said it was none ill. 'It is for the Queen mother.' I said, 'If it were good the lords would allow it; if it were ill, I would not write in it.' Then he said they would take it better part if I wrote. I desired him to let me alone. I asked [John] Cheke whether it were good to write and he said, 'No'. He said: 'Within this two year at least you must take upon you to be as you are, or ought to be, for you shall be able. And then you may give your men somewhat, for your uncle is old, and I trust will not live long.' I said, 'It were better for him to die before.' He said: 'You are a beggarly king. You have no money to play or to give.' I said that Mr. Stanhope had for me. Then he said he would give Fowler, and Fowler did give the money to divers men as I bid him, as to Master Cheke and the bookbinder and others. He told me these things often times. Fowler desired me to give thanks to my Lord Admiral for his gentleness to me and praised him to me very much.
    Edward Rex

In the month of September Anno Domini 1547 the Lord Admiral told me that my uncle being gone into Scotland should not pass the peace without loss of a great number of men or of himself and that he did spend much money in vain.
    After the return of my uncle, he said that I was too bashful in my matters and that I would not speak for myself. I said I was well enough. When he went to his country, he desired me not to believe men that would slander him till he came himself.
    Edward Rex

The Art of Miniatures

Miniature painting or limning, as it was known in the sixteenth century, was the unique contribution of England to the Renaissance. In its origins the art was a response to a demand from Henry VIII for images of members of the royal family during the 1520s, and miniatures were to remain almost exclusively a royal prerogative for half a century, although Hans Holbein would accept commissions from courtiers and others. With the careful management of Crown resources from the 1560s the monarch ceased to be a direct patron of the arts, and the responsibility transferred to the aristocracy. From his shop off Fleet Street in London in the 1570s Nicholas Hilliard accepted commissions from noble and gentle folk, and later on from merchants; Hilliard's pupil Isaac Oliver continued to work for the same clientele. The technique was derived from manuscript illumination, and it was a combination of drawing and watercolour painting on vellum mounted on a stiff backing - usually a playing card.

From the beginning miniatures were regarded as precious. They were put in ivory boxes with glass to protect them from dust and lids to prevent them from fading. Later, frames of stained ivory and ebony became popular. Queen Elizabeth kept her collection of miniatures in her bedchamber, each one wrapped up with a label bearing the name of the sitter. Some were given elaborate cases of gold and silver studded with jewels and patterned with enamels. Such miniatures were meant as gifts or rewards; and being designed as lockets, were intended as jewels to be worn either suspended by chains around the neck or waist, or else affixed to clothing or to a hat or plume. The possession of a miniature was a declaration of affinity through either kinship or alliance, or else of political or social dependence. When Lord Seymour asked for one of Catherine Parr's 'small pictures' he was not only declaring his love for Catherine but was also asserting his new relationship to the royal family. Initially miniatures depicted little more than head and shoulders, but with the introduction of cards greater than three inches in height full-scale figures, and even groups, became possible. The most famous of these later compositions is perhaps Hilliard's lyrical Young Man among Roses, almost certainly depicting Robert Devereux, second Earl of Essex. Others show aristocrats in the shimmering armour worn for the tournaments held on festivals and general entertainments at court. These allude to the mystery and mystique of nobility and courtiership. Puns, mottoes, birds, animals, flowers and landscapes also possessed a significance for the subject, the owner and the beholder, and gave miniatures a sanctity not fully understood since the Tudor period.

Hilliard's Queen Elizabeth with a lute, probably painted for her cousin Henry Carey.

The Gresley jewel, with Nicholas Hilliard's miniatures of Sir Thomas and Lady Gresley.

The Earl of Nottingham, painted by Hilliard's follower, Rowland Lockey.

Edward VI's Privy Chamber

Edward as Prince of Wales. Edward's chain incorporates the Prince's emblem of three feathers, while the fur lining suggest a date in the winter of 1546. It was during these last years of his father's reign that Edward formed his enduring friendships with the future intimates of his Privy Chamber.

During the reign of Edward VI the Privy Chamber underwent two dramatic transformations. By the time he came to the throne in 1547, the nine-year-old prince had had his own household for some years. Many of its officers were transferred to the new Royal Household, but this became very much absorbed into the Protector Somerset's own. Such blatant control of the King fuelled the growing concern among other Councillors over Somerset's autocratic pretensions. In his attempt to unseat his brother, Lord Admiral Seymour tried to exploit Edward's possible resentment at his 'dependence'.

Somerset's fall in 1549 and the new regime of the Duke of Northumberland saw a major revival of the Privy Chamber. Just as he refused the title Lord Protector, so Northumberland sought to re-establish the traditional structure of the court. Membership of the Privy Chamber expanded dramatically to include senior figures of the Household and Council and many of Northumberland's military clients, and a number of Edward's companions. Among them were Sir Henry Sidney (whose father, Sir William, had been the first chamberlain of Edward's princely household), and the Irish boy Barnaby Fitzpatrick, later Lord Upper Ossory. Fitzpatrick entered the Privy Chamber on 15 August 1551, the same day as Northumberland's son Robert, who may also have been among Edward's earlier companions.

Northumberland probably had two motives for using the Privy Chamber in this manner. On the one hand he was able to create the illusion of Edward's independence. On the other, he could rely on a Privy Chamber dominated by his friends, family and followers, while the Privy Council contained a more balanced representation of the nobility. The key figures were those who combined membership of the Council with that of the Privy Chamber, and it was on their personal allegiance that his power rested.

Seymour was, however, sincere in one thing. His with Catherine Parr was a love affair: 'He spared no cost his lady to delight, or to maintain her princely royalty.' It culminated in Catherine's pregnancy. Coming after three infertile marriages and in Catherine's late thirties, the pregnancy delighted the parents-to-be, but it was naturally fraught.

As mindless of the gynaecolocical problems as he was of the political repercussions, Seymour anticipated a boy. In the event a girl christened Mary was born in August 1548, and Catherine died early in the following month, a fatality of the birth. The rumours about Seymour's indifference that then circulated were groundless.

Lord Seymour to Queen Catherine Parr   9 June 1548
Westminster

... I hear my little man doth shake his poll, trusting, if God should give him life to live as long as his father, he will revenge such wrongs as neither you nor I can, at this present, the (turmoil) is such. - God amend it!

 ... I bid your Highness most heartily well to fare, and thank you for your news, which were right heartily welcome to me. And so I pray you to show him, with God's blessing and mine; and of all good wills and friendship I do desire your Highness to keep the little knave so lean and gaunt with your good diet and walking, that he may be so small that he may creep out of a mouse hole. And so I bid my most dear and well-beloved wife most heartily well to fare.

 From Westminster, this Saturday, the 9th of June.

 Your Highness's most faithful, loving husband,

 T. Seymour

Seymour's personal tragedy coincided with a complete breakdown in his relations with his elder brother, the Protector Somerset. Although raised to the peerage and made Lord Admiral and a Privy Councillor in February 1547, Seymour had resented not being appointed Governor of Edward VI when Somerset had been named Lord Protector, and Seymour's clandestine marriage to Catherine Parr and his general conduct did little to improve the situation. By February 1548 the two brothers had quarrelled publicly, and in the following months Somerset had ample grounds to criticize the behaviour of Seymour. The Protector's fraternal feelings and patience were sorely tried.

Duke of Somerset to Lord Seymour   1 September 1548
Syon

After our right hearty commendations to your good Lordship. We have received your long letters to the date of the 27th of August, to the particularities whereof at this present we are not minded to answer, because it requireth more leisure than at this time we have.

But in the mean while, we cannot but marvel that you note the way to be so open for complaints to enter in against you, and that they be so well received. If you do so behave yourself amongst your poor neighbours, and others the King's subjects, that they may have easily just cause to complain upon you, and so you do make them a way and cause to lament unto us and pray redress, we are most sorry therefore, and would wish very heartily it were otherwise; which were both more honour for you, and quiet and joy and comfort to us. But if you mean it, that for our part we are ready to receive poor men's complaints, that findeth or thinketh themselves injured or grieved, it is our duty and office so to do. And though you be our brother, yet we may not refuse it upon you. How well we do receive them, it may appear in our letters; where we lament the case unto you, and exhort, pray, and admonish you so earnestly as we can, that you yourself would redress the same, that there should no occasion be given to any man to make such complaints of you to us ...

And this we do, not condemning you in every thing we write; for, before we have heard the answer, our letters be not so. But if the complaints be true, we require, as reason would, redress; and that you should the more earnestly look upon them, seeing you do perceive that the complaints do come to us. The which thing, coming as well of love towards you as of our office, can minister no occasion to you of any such doubt as you would make in the latter end of your letters.

We would wish rather to hear that all the King's subjects were of you gently and liberally entreated with honour, than that any one should be said to be of you either injured or extremely handled ...

Catherine Parr

KATHARINE PARRE

Catherine Parr, Henry VIII's sixth Queen. Despite her too clearly-voiced Protestant opinions, Catherine was an able manager of the King and his children. After his death, however, she rather kicked over the traces with her marriage to the dashing and dangerous Thomas, Lord Seymour of Sudeley.

By birth and kinship Catherine Parr was well connected with the leading families in the Western marches against Scotland and in the central Midlands. Both her grandfather Sir William and her father Sir Thomas had been Comptrollers of the Royal Household, and in addition Sir Thomas had held the lucrative post of Master of the Wards.

Few women's matrimonial advancement surpassed Catherine Parr's in Tudor England. Maternal scruples brought to an end the earliest overtures from members of the nobility, but she was still an adolescent when she married Sir Edward Burgh, a Midlands gentleman with a claim on the Grey of Codnor barony. Widowed before reaching the age of twenty-one, Catherine took as her second husband the third Lord Latimer in 1533. Within four months of Latimer's death in 1543 Catherine had been courted by Sir Thomas Seymour, and had rejected him in favour of Henry VIII. With two childless marriages behind her, Catherine presumably saw little probability in enlarging the royal family. Instead she saw in the King's proposal a call from God to work

for Protestantism. Her willingness to argue religion with her equally opinionated husband brought their marriage perilously close to an end when, irritated with her views, the King listened to allegations of heresy; but a timely submission saved her. Through her genuine concern and affection for Prince Edward and the two Princesses, she brought the King's family together again. After Henry VIII's death she married Seymour. She added to the fraternal divisions in the Seymour family by quarrelling over precedence with the Duchess of Somerset. Catherine died on 7 September 1547 after giving birth to a daughter, who did not survive infancy.

Although the extent of her own education remains open to doubt, Catherine was sympathetic towards whatever scholarship supported Protestantism. She encouraged Princess Mary to translate Erasmus's *Paraphrases* into English, and to undertake two devotional works of her own. Her penmanship using an up-to-date italic hand is further evidence of Catherine's own education and adaptability to changes in intellectual fashions.

By Christmas 1548 it was rumoured that Seymour, barely widowed three months, was to marry Princess Elizabeth, and that she was already expecting his child. The possiblity of a second clandestine marriage by Seymour disturbed the Protector Somerset and the Council, whom he further upset by a series of wild statements. On 17 January 1549 Seymour was arrested and, after being examined twice by the Council, he was accused of treason on 23 February. Attainted in Parliament, he was executed on 20 March. This sudden turn of events was reported to the Emperor Charles V by his ambassador.

Van der Delft to Charles V   8 February 1549
London

'He [Seymour] has been a great rascal.' [*ce a este grand meschant*]. I then asked them if it was really a criminal case as I had been told at Calais. Paget answered that as he hoped to reach his own house safely it was plain in every respect that the Admiral had intended to kill the King and the Lady Mary, and marry the Lady Elizabeth; that he had more greed than wit or judgement ... I have heard, however, from a well-informed source, the origin of the quarrel between the Admiral and the Protector. When the Admiral saw that his first proposal was set aside, and that his brother was made Protector of the Kingdom and the King's person, he went to him and asked him to countenance his plan to marry the Lady Mary. The Protector was displeased and reproved him, saying that neither of them was born to be king, nor to marry kings' daughters; and though God had given them grace that their sister should have married a king, whence so much honour and benefit had redounded to them, they must thank God and be satisfied; besides which he knew the Lady Mary would never consent. The other replied that he merely asked for his brother's countenance, and he would look after the rest. The Protector chid him again more sharply, and the Admiral went off and married the widow of the late King, showing his resentment against his brother openly, so that the quarrel between them and their competence to govern the King and kingdom were common topics of conversation ... Then he turned to other means of satisfying his great cupidity. He won over to his side several Gentlemen of the King's Chamber, and by kindness and gifts succeeded in gaining preference over his brother in the King's affections. He planned that the King should make a declaration to Parliament that he would rather have the Admiral than the Protector as his Governor ... The Council was informed of all this, and when the Admiral was finally discovered within the palace late at night, with a large suite of his own people, and the dog that keeps watch before the King's door was found dead, they determined to summon him to taken appear before them ... He was sent to the Tower at eight o'clock in the evening ...

The downfall of Lord Seymour was followed by a summer of discontent, with rebellions occuring in East Anglia and in the South-West. Failure by the Protector Somerset to act decisively to maintain law and order brought to a head long pent-up resentment against his autocratic manner of government. In the absence of Somerset from London, the Earl of Warwick, who had successfully defeated Ket's rebellion, engineered with other members of the Council the Duke's overthrow. Somerset tried to enlist the support of Lord Russell and Sir William Herbert, returning from Devon with their troops, in maintaining his authority.

Lord Russell and Sir William Herbert to   8 October 1549
the Duke of Somerset
Andover

Your Grace, we have received your letters, not without our great lamentation and sorrow to perceive the civil dissension which has happened between your Grace and the nobility. A greater plague could not be sent unto this realm from God; being the next way to make us, of conquerors, slaves, and to induce upon us an universal calamity and thraldom, which we pray God so to hold His holy hand over us as we may never see it.

And for answer, this is to signify, that so long as we thought that the nobility presently assembled had conspired against the King's Majesty's person, so long we came forward with such company as we have for the surety of his Highness, as appertaineth.

And now, having this day received advertisement from the Lords, whereby it is given us to understand that no hurt nor displeasure is meant towards the King's Majesty, and that it doth plainly appear unto us that they are his Highness' most true and loving subjects, meaning no otherwise than as to their duties of allegiance may appertain; so, as in conclusion, it doth also appear unto us, that this great extremity proceedeth only upon private causes between your Grace and them; we have, therefore, thought most convenient in the heat of this broil to levy as great a power as we may, as well for the surety of the King's Majesty's person, as also for the preservation of the State of the Realm, which whilst this contention endureth, by factions between your Grace and them may be in much peril and danger ...

From Andover, the 8th of October 1549
Your Grace's loving friends,
John Russell
Wm. Herbert

Russell and Herbert's refusal was the last straw: Protector Somerset had become an isolated figure politically. He exhorted the kingdom to rally to his defence and that of Edward VI, who accompanied him from Hampton Court to Windsor Castle during the crisis. His wife, whose pride and whose quarrel over precedence with Catherine Parr were commonly blamed for the estrangement of the two Seymour brothers and for many of Somerset's misfortunes and mistakes, did not understand the sudden downward turn of events. She approached the Comptroller Paget, who had long warned Somerset about the consequence of his actions. Paget disregarded the duchess, and on 12 October Somerset was arrested.

Anne, Duchess of Somerset   8 October 1549
to Comptroller Paget

Ah, good lord, what a miserable unnatural time is this? What hath my lord done to any of these noble men? or others? that they should thus rage and seek the extremity to him and his that never had thought in the like towards any of them. Ha, Master Comptroller, I have ever loved and trusted you, for that I have seen in you a perfect honest friend to my lord who hath always made the same account and assuredly bare you his good will and friendship as you yourself hath had best trial. God have given you a great wisdom and a friendly nature. I know you may do much good in these matters being a wise man. How can God be content with this disorder to danger the King and all the realm in seeking extremities? Oh, that I could bear this as I ought to do with patience and quietness, but it passeth all frail flesh to do. For knowing so well my lord's innocency in all these matters that they charge him with all, they be so untrue and most unfriendly credit that surely it hath been some wicked person or persons that first sought this great uproar. I say again if I could bear the time, I know well and assure myself that God will keep and defend him from all his enemies, as he hath always done hitherto. Good Master Comptroller, comfort my lord as I trust you do, both with counsel and otherwise, for I much fear he is sore grieved at the heart, first for the king and the realm, and as greatly to see these lords' friendships so slender to him as it doth appear and specially of some, albeit he hath pleasured them all. Alas, that ever any Christian realm should be so slandered. Thus to end with all I cry to you eftsoons show you, show your self like a worthy councillor and a servant to God and the King that these tumults might cease.
   Anne Somerset

Somerset's fall was not absolute. Although deprived of the Protectorate by Act of Parliament, he was released from the Tower in February 1550, and resumed his place on the Council not long after. The reason for this turn of events was the unstable balance of power in the Council between Warwick and the conservatives led by Thomas Wriothesley, Earl of Southampton. Warwick had resurrected Somerset as an ally *against* the conservatives; however, Somerset soon saw an alliance *with* the conservatives as a means of undermining Warwick. His intrigues proved his undoing. The duke's second arrest, trial and execution are recorded tersely in the journal kept by Edward VI.

Edward VI, journal   7 October 1551

... How, at St. George's day last, my lord of Somerset ... went to raise the people, and the Lord Grey before, to know who were his friends. Afterward a devise was made to call the Earl of Warwick to a banquet, with the Marquess of Northampton and divers other, and to cut of their heads ...

16 October 1551

This morning none was at Westminster of the conspirators. The first was the duke, who came, latter then he was wont, of himself. After dinner he was apprehended ...

24 October 1551

The lords sat in the Star Chamber and they declared the matters and accusations laid against the duke, meaning to stay the minds of the people.

1 December 1551

The Duke of Somerset came to his trial at Westminster Hall. The lords acquitted him of high treason, and condemned him of treason felonous, and so he was adjudged to be hanged. He gave thanks to the lords for their open trial, and cried mercy of the Duke of Northumberland, the Marquess of Northampton and the Earl of Pembroke for his ill meaning against them, and made suit for his life, wife and children ...

22 January 1552

The Duke of Somerset had his head cut off upon Tower Hill between eight and nine o'clock in the morning.

Somerset House

The Strand façade of Somerset House, the first large-scale classical building in England.

The nobility were expected to live in houses befitting their rank, and, where they lacked such houses, to build appropriately. Thus the Protector Somerset embarked on a spectacular series of building works at Bedwyn to replace the ancestral Seymour home at Wolf Hall - also at Reading, at Syon and at Chester Place on the Strand; while Lord Seymour undertook similar improvements at Sudeley Castle. Of these, Chester Place, renamed Somerset House, was the most ambitious scheme, being the London residence of the Lord Protector of the Realm. In its design and construction Somerset House was meant to outshine the string of palaces built by Henry VIII, and to outmode them.

Whoever prepared its plan was versed in the classical taste increasingly preferred for buildings as the Renaissance advanced, and was familiar with houses, such as Ecouen, that were then being built for the French aristocracy. Such classical features as were incorporated were sensitively and correctly applied to the long-established layout of an English house built around a courtyard. Its fundamental symmetry was revolutionary. The façade overlooing the Strand consisted of a centrally placed gateway of three storeys height with a triumphal arch at ground-level, and of projecting pavilions, also of the same height at each end. Aesthetically Somerset House was to have long-term consequences for English architecture, but in the late 1540s it must have appeared as no more than another quirky fad built by a nobleman and courtier. Few Englishmen outside a small circle of courtiers and intellectuals had the erudition to understand the significance of the 'triumphal arch' motif taken from Antiquity;

however, for the informed few the design doubtless confirmed their suspicions about the barely disguised ambition of the Protector.

Somerset House was more or less hewn out of a densely built area near Temple Bar. Three houses once belonging to bishops were demolished, and the church of St Mary le Strand was moved to a new site. Stone for the building was taken from the dissolved priory of St John of Jerusalem in Clerkenwell and from the cloisters and charnel house of Old St Paul's. Fittings and furnishings, particularly tapestries, came from further afield, notably from the third Duke of Norfolk's house at Kenninghall after his downfall in 1546-7, and from Lord Seymour's castle at Sudeley in 1549.

Notwithstanding the unscrupulous looting in which Somerset indulged, Somerset House cost him the phenomenal sum of £10,000 over three years, and was incomplete on his execution in 1552 when the property passed to the Crown and interior fittings such as the screen from the great hall were sold to meet Somerset's debts. The furnishings were ostensibly reserved for the use of Edward VI, but in fact they were shared out between Northumberland and his partisans. Northumberland also coerced Princess Elizabeth into exchanging Durham Place for Somerset House but, unfinished and stripped of its contents, it was beyond her means. The disadvantages of owning such a remarkable house perhaps confirmed Elizabeth as Queen in her natural disinclination to undertake any building works herself. Somerset House remained unfinished until it was assigned by King James to Anne of Denmark in 1603.

'The Alcibiades of England'

JOHN DUDLEY, DUKE OF NORTHUMBERLAND

'Now as to the Dudleys', objected Sir Philip Sidney in his 'Defence of the Earl of Leicester' of 1585, their enemies: 'saith they are no gentlemen, affirming the then Duke of Northumberland was not born so; in truth ... yet it would never have come into my head, of all other things, that any man would have objected want of gentry unto him ... '

The Sutton *alias* Dudley family originated in the North Midlands, where it can be traced back into the thirteenth century. Edmund Dudley of Atherington in Sussex, the father of the future Duke of Northumberland, made his career as an adviser, particularly on matters of finance, to Henry VII. Within two days of coming to the throne, however, Henry VIII ordered his arrest, and he was indicted for treason and executed.

On his mother's side, his nobility was both ancient and unblemished. The Lisle family were Norman stock, who had been ennobled as Baron Lisle in the fourteenth century.

The wardship of Edmund's son John was acquired by Sir Edward Guildford, who obtained the reversal of Edmund Dudley's attainder and the restoration in the blood of his ward. John Dudley grew up at Court, married Guildford's daughter and succeeded him as Master of the Royal Armoury.

John Dudley was a courtier by upbringing and inclination, rising in the personal service of Henry VIII and of Edward VI from Master of the

The Dudleys: traitors in two generations and dying out in the male line in three.

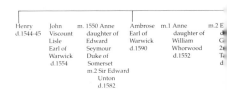

| Henry d.1544–45 | John Viscount Lisle Earl of Warwick d.1554 | m. 1550 Anne daughter of Edward Seymour Duke of Somerset m.2 Sir Edward Unton d.1582 | Ambrose Earl of Warwick d.1590 | m.1 Anne daughter of William Whorwood d.1552 | m.2 E |

Armoury to Chief Trencher to Chamberlain, and finally Great Master, of the Household. The embodiment of a Tudor courtier, Dudley relished intrigue. He combined an unfaltering desire for success with a capacity for leadership, which impressed his associates and subordinates, but which was marred by occasional indecision or reluctance to accept responsibility. Knighted by the Duke of Suffolk for valour in crossing the Somme in 1523, Dudley was ennobled as Viscount Lisle in 1542. For acquiescing in the Duke of Somerset's assumption of the Protectorate in 1547 and for surrendering the Admiralty to Somerset's brother Thomas, Lisle was elevated to the earldom of Warwick and got the Great Chamberlainship of the Household which he had been hankering after.

These rewards did nothing to enamour him of the Seymour family. In the autumn of 1549 he engineered the *coup d'état* which ended the Protectorate of the Duke of Somerset and which made Warwick regent in all but name. Somerset's eventual trial and execution, and Warwick's elevation to the dukedom of Northumberland in 1551 left the new duke as undisputed chief minister.

The King's sudden fatal illness precipitated the crisis. By the Succession Act of 1544 and Henry VIII's will the Catholic Mary was heir. To prevent the accession of Princess Mary and the restoration of Roman Catholicism, and to preserve his own political ascendancy, Northumberland encouraged the King to exercise his prerogative to designate a successor, and this Edward VI did with the 'Device for the Succession' in May 1553. According to the Device, the crown was to pass on the King's death and in default of sons of his own 'to Lady Jane Grey and her heirs male'. About the same time Northumberland married his son Guilford to Lady Jane Grey, thus making himself father-in-law to the heir-apparent, and arranged a series of other marriages linking the fortunes of Northumberland and his partisans, the Suffolks, the Pembrokes and the Sidneys.

These well-laid arrangements to provide for the succession, to maintain his dominion and preserve Protestantism collapsed when the King died suddenly on 6 July 1553.

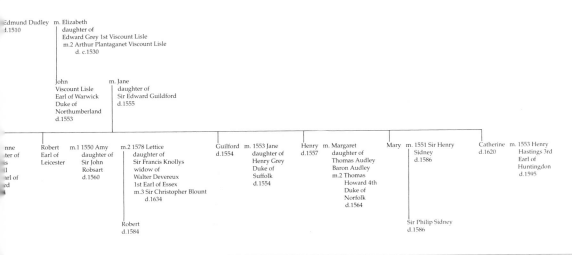

In the draft list of peerage creations which Henry VIII had drawn up alongside his will, John Dudley was to have been made Earl of Coventry. In the event, he got the earldom of Warwick, which had been held by the Beauchamps, from whom he was descended in the female line. The importance of female descent was also the key to the tragedy of Lady Jane Grey. Her mother was Frances, daughter of the Duke of Suffolk's marriage to Mary Tudor. This, under the terms of Henry VIII's will, made her heir to the throne immediately after his own children. The result was to turn her into a pawn in the family ambitions of the Seymours, the Dudleys - and her own dreadful parents. In 1546 her father, the third Marquess of Dorset, had placed her in the household of Queen Catherine Parr. At the death of Henry VIII, Lord Seymour tried to persuade Dorset to transfer Jane to his custody, but his marriage to Catherine Parr made this transfer unnecessary. Catherine's death in September 1548 reopened the matter, and Seymour successfully persuaded Dorset to let him have charge of Jane. Throughout, the bait was Seymour's proposal to marry Jane to her cousin Edward VI. For his part in the overthrow of the Seymour brothers Dorset was made Duke of Suffolk in October 1551.

Deposition of the Marquess of Dorset   February 1549
to the Council

First, immediately after the King our late master's death, one John Harrington, servant to the said Admiral, came to my house at Westminster, and amongst other things showed me that the said Admiral [Seymour] was like to come to great authority; and that being the King's majesty's uncle, and placed as he was, he might do me much pleasure; advising me ... to enter a more friendship and familiarity with him.

At the same time and place, the said Harrington advised me to be contented that my daughter Jane might be with the said Admiral; whereunto if I would agree, he said he durst assure me that the Admiral would find the means she should be placed in marriage much to my comfort. 'With whom', said I, 'will he match her?' 'Marry', quoth Harrington, 'I doubt not but you shall see him marry her to the King; and fear you not but he will bring it to pass, and then shall you be able to help all the friends you have.'

Upon these persuasions of Harrington, I repaired, within seven-night after, to the said Admiral's house at Seymour Place; and there, talking with him in his garden, he used unto me at more length the like persuasions as had been made by Harrington for the having of my daughter, wherein he showed himself so desirous and earnest, and made me such fair promises, that I sent for my daughter, who remained in his house from that time continually unto the death of the Queen.

The Palace of Westminster

The dais of Westminster Hall with the Courts of King's Bench and Chancery in session.

The great sprawling, medieval palace of Westminster was badly damaged by a series of fires under Henry VII. In 1512 'a great part' was 'once again burnt ... since which time it hath not been re-edified: only the great hall with the offices near adjoining are kept in good reparations, and serveth as afore for feasts at coronations, arraignments of great persons charged with treasons, keeping of the courts of justice etc.' The acquisition of the palace of York Place from Cardinal Wolsey in 1529 provided Henry VIII with a new and more convenient residence only a short distance away. From 1536 the ancient name of Westminster was transferred to the new palace and the old palace was declared only a 'member and parcel' of the new one. In all but official usage, however, the two remained quite distinct. The old palace continued to be called Westminster; the new one was nicknamed Whitehall. The latter was the royal residence; the former was used by the monarch only for certain great ceremonies, like the coronation banquet. Otherwise it was given over to administrative purposes.

Westminster Palace accommodated all the legal and administrative courts of Tudor England. Westminster Hall had long housed the Courts of Chancery, King's Bench and Common Pleas, separated only by light, easily removable partitions, and adjoining it were the Exchequer and offices for the Duchy of Lancaster. The Court of Requests occupied the Great Chamber of the palace, and the more recent Court of Star Chamber took its name from a chamber, 'the roof thereof is decked with the likeness of stars gilt'. The new financial courts established by Henry VIII between 1536 and 1542, Augmentations, First Fruits and Tenths, Wards and Liveries, and the Court of Surveyors,were also housed within the precinct.

This extraordinary density of 'courts' (that is, administrative departments as well as courts of justice) was further consolidated at the Reformation when in 1548-9 the chapel of the dissolved royal college of St Stephen's was made available as a permanent home for the House of Commons, the House of Lords making similar use of the Painted Chamber. The adaptation of the chapter house of Westminster Abbey as a muniment room with purpose-built coffers and shelving completed the process of converting the palace into the permanent administrative seat of government.

By the 1590s Westminster and government were synonyms in the popular imagination. John Norden observed: Westminster Palace 'is known to many, a terror to the multitude, and a golden mine to some ...'

Following Catherine Parr's funeral at Sudeley on 8 September 1548, Lady Jane Grey was removed to her parents' house at Bradgate. Lord Seymour immediately approached the Dorsets about Jane being placed in his care, to which they readily agreed. On the downfall of Lord Seymour, Lady Jane Grey returned a second time to her parental home. At the age of twelve and after three years' absence she was a stranger to the Dorsets. The return was something of a shock to the girl. Writing twenty years later, her tutor Roger Ascham remembered finding her at Bradgate reading Plato and asking why she did not take exercise in the park. Jane answered:

Roger Ascham, *The Schoolmaster*   1570

I will tell you and tell you a truth, which perchance you will marvel at ... One of the greatest benefits that ever God gave me is that He sent me, with sharp, severe parents, so gentle a schoolmaster. When I am in presence of either father or mother, whether I speak, keep silence, sit, stand, or go, eat, drink, be merry or sad, be sewing, playing, dancing, or doing anything else, I must do it, as it were, in such weight, measure and number, even as perfectly as God made the world, or else I am so sharply taunted, so cruelly threatened, yea, presented sometimes with pinches, nips, and bobs, and other ways (which I will not name for the honour I bear them), so without measure misordered, that I think myself in hell, till the time comes when I must go to Mr. Aylmer, who teacheth me so gently, so pleasantly, with such fair allurements to learning, that I think all the time nothing while I am with him. And when I am called from him I fall on weeping, because whatever I do else but learning is full of great trouble, fear, and whole misliking unto me ...

But, outside the schoolroom, the deadly game of high politics went on. With the ending of the Protectorate, the Earl of Warwick started to exercise power. Unfortunately this assumption of authority by the Earl coincided with a prolonged bout of sickness. Coming so soon after the *coup d'état* of October 1549 with the fate of Somerset and his supporters undecided and with the intentions of Warwick largely unknown, this sickness prolonged the period of confusion and political uncertainty. Richard Scudamore, secretary and court agent of Sir Philip Hoby, the English ambassador to the Emperor Charles V and the most vivid reporter on Edwardian politics, found the Council meeting round the earl's sickbed.

Richard Scudamore to Sir Philip Hoby   6 December 1549
Blackfriars, London

... I waited there Saturday, Sunday and Monday, but by occasion that my
lord [Warwick] was troubled with his disease kept his bed 2 days. And on
the Monday all the Council came thither except the Earl of Arundel,
the cause of whose absence I cannot learn, and the Earl of Southampton
who abideth still sick in his house. And that night I (fearing lest my said
Lord of Warwick should judge slackness in me for not getting good
attendance upon him) found the means to come to his speech putting him
in remembrance of his former pleasure, who said that he had not as yet
written but he would shortly. Seeing further that the King's highness with
all his most honourable Council had seen your whole discourse and your
doing therein they much commended allowing both your diligent service
and also your good intelligence. And my Lord of Warwick did grieve unto
you a very good report promising unto you such favour or pleasure as
shall lay in him either for your affairs about the Court ... or elsewhere.

Warwick's convalescence proved long drawn-out, and it was not until the summer of
1550 that the earl's health was fully restored. The replacement of figures suspected of
sympathising with the Duke of Somerset by partisans of Warwick's continued apace
throughout the period of convalescence. The simultaneous imprisonment of Sir Thomas
Arundell, thought to have been the Earl's 'chief counsellor' in Somerset's overthrow, and
the prorogation of Parliament were followed by a series of appointments which were to
set the tone of Warwick's regime for the next three years. This done, Warwick released
Somerset from the Tower. There was some confusion as to the correct sequence of events.

Richard Scudamore to Sir Philip Hoby   6 February 1550
Blackfriars, London

You shall understand that on Candlemas day the Marquess of Northampton
received his staff for the office of the Lord Great Chamberlainship,
the Lord of Wiltshire his staff for High Treasurership. And the same day
the Lord Wentworth was sent with a staff into London to my Lord of
Warwick's for the Great Mastership ... This be all that lately hath altered
their offices and received higher dignities, saving the Lord Marquess [of]
Dorset is Chief Justice of all the King's forests, parks and chases on this
side [of the river] Trent.

The Education of Women

A notable blue-stocking, Lady Jane Grey preferred her gentle tutor to her harsh go-getting parents.

Sir Thomas More observed: 'I do not see why learning in like manner may not equally agree with both sexes; for by it, reason is cultivated ... sowed with the wholesome seed of good precepts, it bringeth forth excellent fruit. But if the soil of woman's brain be of its own nature bad, and apter to bear fern than corn (by which saying many do terrify women from learning) I am of opinion ... that a woman's wit is the more diligently by good instructions and learning to be manured, to the end, the defect of nature may be redressed by industry.'

However, it was not the enlightened attitude of More in the education of his daughters which revolutionized the upbringing of women in the sixteenth century, but the example of Catherine of Aragon. An accomplished linguist and scholar in her own right, she saw to it that her one surviving child, Princess Mary, enjoyed an equally advantageous education. The example was followed for Princess Elizabeth and Prince Edward, and these precedents were copied by the nobility, courtiers and administrators. Aesthetic and intellectual standards played little part in this growing interest by parents

in their daughters' welfare, but an obsession with material advantage and a desire to be in fashion did: the Mores, the Cookes and the Cecils were exceptions in valuing things of the mind for their own sake.

Lady Jane Grey's daily routine as a child, from the age of seven, was not atypical. After prayers and breakfast she studied Greek and Latin. After dinner (that is, in the afternoon) she went on to music and to Spanish, Italian and French, with regular readings from classical authors and the Bible until supper. Instruction in dancing and needlework before going to bed completed the day. Then, as now, inattention and slow progress were causes for rebuke and discipline, and although girls were not subject to the floggings inflicted on boys, they were not spared verbal chastisement or mild physical punishment.

To complete their education, girls from noble and gentle families were often boarded out in other households, often for two or three years: Lady Jane Grey's boarded with Queen Catherine Parr. The more practical skills necessary for married life were acquired either from the example of other women or by personal experiment.

Sir Thomas More's daughters Cecily, Elizabeth and Margaret. Their tutors included Nicolaus Kratzer, the Astronomer Royal.

The Justiceship of Forests was Dorset's first reward for his support of the Duke of Northumberland. In 1551, after his part in destroying Somerset, he was given the Brandon dukedom of Suffolk. Two years later the alliance was cemented when, on 21 May 1553, Lady Jane Grey married Northumberland's eldest son Guilford Dudley at Durham House. Six weeks later on 6 July Edward VI died, somewhat unexpectedly. For two days there was no public announcement of the King's death. On 8 July Jane was taken from Chelsea to Syon, where she was told of the contents of the late King's will and was proclaimed Queen. Jane had protested vehemently at her accession to the throne, but brow-beaten by Northumberland, her parents, her husband and her kin the Sidneys, she reluctantly agreed. With the news of a concerted rising in favour of Princess Mary, Jane took the opportunity to resign the crown.

Queen Jane to Duke of Suffolk   July 1553

Sir, I better brook this message than my advancement to royalty. Out of obedience to you and my mother, I have grievously sinned and offered violence to myself. Now do I willingly, and obeying the motions of my own soul, relinquish the crown, and endeavour to solve those faults committed by others, if, at least, so great faults can be solved, by a willing and ingenuous acknowledgement of them.

Northumberland acted too late to stop the groundswell in favour of Mary, and at Cambridge he, too, proclaimed Mary Queen. Taken prisoner and lodged in the Tower, Northumberland was tried for treason, and on 18 August 1553 he was found guilty. Two days later he wrote a pleading letter to the twelfth Earl of Arundel, who proved to be Northumberland's match in political in-fighting. He had been one of the signatories to the Device settling the succession on Lady Jane Grey and one of the four peers doing homage to Queen Jane on 9 July. But on 19 July he had denounced him as a man of 'very small or no conscience at all', and then led the posse to arrest him at Cambridge. He was given Northumberland's office of Great Master of the Household by Queen Mary.

Duke of Northumberland to the Earl of Arundel   20 August 1553
Tower of London

Honorable Lord and in this my distress my especial refuge, most woeful was the news I received this evening by Mr. Lieutenant that I must prepare myself against tomorrow to receive my deadly stroke. Alas, my good Lord, is my cause so heinous as no redemption but my blood can wash away the spots thereof? An old proverb there is and that most true that a living dog is better than a dead lion. Oh that it would please her good Grace to give me life, yes the life of a dog that I might but live and kiss her feet and spend both life and all in her honourable service, as I have the most glorious father. Oh that her mercy were such as she would consider how little profit my dead and dismembered body can bring her, but how great and glorious an honour it will be in all posterity when the report shall be that so gracious and mighty a Queen had granted life to so miserable and penitent an abject. Your honourable usage and promises to me since these my troubles have made me bold to challenge this kindness at your hand. Pardon me if I have done amiss therein and spare not I pray your bended knee for me in this distress, the God of Heaven it may be will requite it one day on you or yours. And if my life be lengthened by your mediation and my good Lord Chancellor's [Stephen Gardiner, Bishop of Winchester] (to whom I have also sent my blurred letter) I will ever vow it to be spent at your honourable feet. Oh good my Lord remember how sweet life is and how bitter the contrary. Spare not your speech and pains ... But if no remedy can be found, either by imprisonment, confiscation, banishment and the like, I can say no more but God grant me patience to endure and a heart to forgive the whole world.

    Once your fellow and loving companion but now worthy of no name but wretchedness and misery.

    John Dudley

Northumberland's pleas were in vain and he was executed at Tower Hill on 22 August 1553, with the sons of his former rival, the Duke of Somerset, standing by. On mounting the scaffold Northumberland removed his gown of ash-grey damask and 'boldly' addressed the assembled crowd. The confession that he made so pleased the Marian regime that it circulated the text in full - perhaps with embellishments. But it did not win him a reprieve. Northumberland said his prayers and was beheaded.

Confession of Duke of Northumberland   22 August 1553

Good people, hither I am come this day to die, as you know. Indeed, I confess to you all that I have been an evil liver, and have done wickedly all the days of my life; and, of all, most against the Queen's highness, [of] whom I here openly ask forgiveness [and bowed his knees]: but not I alone the original doer thereof, I assure you, for there were some other which procured the same: but I will not name them, for I will hurt now no man. And the chiefest occasion hath been through false and seditious preachers, that I have erred from the Catholic faith and true doctrine of Christ. The doctrine, I mean, which hath continued through all Christendom since Christ. For, good people, there is, and hath been ever since Christ, one Catholic Church, which Church hath continued from him to his disciples in one unity and concord, and so hath alway continued from time to time until this day, and yet doth throughout all Christendom, only us excepted; for we are quite gone out of that Church ...

   For I pray you, see, since the death of King Henry the Eighth, into what misery we have been brought; what open rebellion, what sedition, what great division hath been throughout the whole realm; for God hath delivered [us] up to [our] own sensualities, and every day [we] wax worse and worse ...

   I have no more to say, good people; but all those which I have offended I ask forgiveness, and they which have offended me I forgive them, as I would God forgive me. And I trust the Queen's highness hath forgiven me: where as I was with force and arms against her in the field, I might have been rent in pieces without law, her Grace hath give me time and respect to have judgement ...

Scaffold Speeches

Sir Thomas Wyatt the Younger, executed for rebellion against Mary on 11 April 1554. In his speech he exonerated Princess Elizabeth from involvement in his rebellion and protested that he had never meant 'worse to the Queen's person than to mine own'.

Convicted felons and traitors enjoyed the traditional privilege of a last speech before execution. It was an opportunity to make their peace with man and God, to complete their confession in a public manner, and to testify to the correctness of their punishment. The purpose of public executions was to deter crime, and such speeches were to serve as warnings to the populace. They were not occasions for last-minute protestations of innocence.

The execution of noblemen for treason raised particular difficulties. Given that by rank they were to provide examples of political loyalty, their crime was the more heinous, yet rank also - and royal clemency - enabled them to escape the full horrors of drawing and quartering. However, many Tudor political trials were deeply suspect (those of the third Duke of Buckingham in 1521 and the Duke of Somerset in 1551 being obvious examples) and the spectacle of an innocent man being done to death by the machinations of his enemies was the epitome of tyranny. Thus when the fourth Duke of Norfolk began to plead his innocence in 1572 a very nervous sheriff prevented him from proceeding further.

The Duke of Northumberland's scaffold speech was perhaps the most dramatic of the century. It was certainly the most widely circulated; not only was it printed in English, but translations in Latin and all the major continental languages were also published. The reasons for such official interest are clear: it was a first-rate propaganda success for Mary's government. The duke's statement that he had been led into heresy by the 'new preachers'; that heresy in turn had

inspired his treason, and that only a return to the Church would restore civil peace and harmony, was precisely the case the government wished to see made. The 'apostasy' of the duke was so deeply embarrassing to those Protestants who had seen him as their champion that they too disowned him. Northumberland's recantation destroyed both his own reputation and whatever justification his advancing of Queen Jane may have had.

If Northumberland came up trumps in providing the example and speech expected of him by both the Marian regime and the vast throng at his execution, there was no precedent for queens to follow until the death of Anne Boleyn in 1536. As it was, Anne conducted herself with dignity: after a wry remark about the littleness of her neck she went to the scaffold where she cried mercy to God and King while asserting her fidelity to her husband, and ended by desiring everyone present to pray for Henry VIII as he was a good, gentle, gracious and amiable prince. In 1452 Catherine Howard broke down before her execution, but she managed to acknowledge publicly her adultery against Henry who had so graciously treated her. Jane Grey in 1554 acknowledged her assumption of the crown had been 'unlawful, and the consenting thereunto by me.' But Jane went on to say that she died 'a true Christian Woman', that is a Protestant. Equally embarrassing to Elizabeth I was Mary, Queen of Scots' assertion of Roman Catholicism: she hoped to be saved 'by and in the blood of Christ, at the foot of whose crucifix she would shed her blood.'

Northumberland's craven renunciation of Protestantism might have gratified Queen Mary's government. But it outraged his daughter-in-law Jane Grey, whose passionate religious convictions made her vehemently opinionated and very outspoken. When she was a prisoner in the Tower with her husband she commended the mercy of Queen Mary, but when at dinner on 29 August 1553 a companion mentioned her father-in-law's confession on the scaffold and his hopes for a pardon, Jane exclaimed:

> ... Pardon? Woe worth him! he hath brought me and our stock in most miserable calamity and misery by his exceeding ambition. But for the answering that he hoped for life by his turning, though other men be of that opinion, I utterly am not; for what man is there living, I pray you, although he had been innocent, that would hope of life in that case; being in the field against the Queen in person as general, and after his taking so hated and evil spoken of by the commons? and at his coming into prison so wondered at [reviled] as the like was never heard by any man's time. Who was judge that he should hope for pardon, whose life was odious to all men? But what will you more? Like as his life was wicked and full of dissimulation, so was his end thereafter.

But Jane had to face another turncoat - and one that touched her more personally. For in the autumn of 1553 her father's chaplain, Thomas Harding, reconverted to Roman Catholicism. In addition to his lapse from 'the truth of God's most holy word', what hurt Jane was that Harding had been her first tutor and had given the girl the grounding for her own convinced Protestantism.

> Lady Jane Grey to Thomas Harding   Autumn 1553
> Tower of London
>
> ... I cannot but marvel at thee and lament thy case, who seemed sometime to be the lively member of Christ, but now the deformed imp of the devil; sometime the beautiful temple of God, but now the stinking and filthy kennel of Satan; sometime the unspotted spouse of Christ, but now the unshamefaced paramour of Antichrist; sometime my faithful brother, but now a stranger and apostate; sometime a stout Christian soldier, but now a cowardly runaway. Yea, when I consider these things, I cannot but speak to thee, and cry out upon thee, thou seed of Satan ...

All this time Jane had been imprisoned in the Tower. But the implication of the Duke of Suffolk in Wyatt's rebellion and Wyatt's proclamation of Lady Jane Grey as Queen numbered Jane's days. Queen Mary tried to persuade Jane to convert to Roman Catholicism, and so avert death, but to no avail. Suffolk, a prisoner, expressed remorse for his past conduct towards Jane, and on the eve of their executions father and daughter were reconciled. Jane and her husband died on 11 February 1554, and Suffolk died two weeks later.

Lady Jane Grey to Duke of Suffolk   11 February 1554
Tower of London

Father, although it pleaseth God to hasten my death by one by whom my
life should rather have been lengthened, yet can I so patiently take it.
As I yield far more hearty thanks for shortening my woeful days, than if
the world had been given into my possession with life lengthened to my
will. And albeit I am well assured of your impatient dolours, redoubled
many ways, both in bewailing your own woe, and also, as I hear, especially
my unfortunate estate. Yet, my dear father, if I may, without offence, rejoice
in my mishaps, methinks in this I may account myself blessed, that,
washing my hands with the innocency of my part, my guiltless blood may
cry before the Lord, 'Mercy to the innocent'. And yet, though I must needs
acknowledge that, being constrained, and, as you well know, continually
essayed in taking the crown upon me, I seemed to consent, and therein
grievously offended the Queen and her laws; and yet do I assuredly trust
that this my offence, towards God, is so much the less, in that being in so
royal an estate as I was, my enforced hour never mixed with my innocent
heart. And thus, good father, I have opened my state to you, whose death
at hand, although to you perhaps it may seem right woeful, to me there is
nothing that can be more welcome ... if it be lawful for the daughter to
write so to her father, the Lord that hitherto hath strengthened you,
so continue you, that at last we may meet in Heaven with the Father,
Son, and Holy Ghost. Amen.

Queen Elizabeth's Eyes At Court

THE EARL OF LEICESTER

Whatever else may be said of them, the Duke and Duchess of Northumberland produced a large and happy family. Of their thirteen children, seven were alive at the time of the duke's execution. The five boys - John, Earl of Warwick, Lord Ambrose, Lord Guilford, Lord Robert (born on 24 June 1532) and Lord Henry - were also tried and found guilty of participating in their father's treason. The elder of the two girls, Mary, married to Sir Henry Sidney, escaped with her husband from the full effects of the disaster. The eight-year-old Catherine, though already betrothed to Henry, Lord Hastings, was still living with her mother.

Tudor opinion was divided on whether the sins of the father should be visited on the children. On the one hand it was the very principle upon which acts of attainder, whereby the descendants of traitors were barred from inheritance of land or title, were based. Yet one of Henry VIII's Councillors recalled from an earlier case 'the difference between the king's

Robert Dudley, Earl of Leicester. His flamboyant pose, rich dress, sword and coroneted and gartered coat-of-arms present him as the model of an aristocratic favourite.

The Armada portait of Queen Elizabeth I, with scenes of the Armada in the top corners.

laws and an instinct or law that is in nature' that permitted children to be spared. At his trial, John Dudley appealed for mercy for his sons, and some speculated that it was the hope of saving his children that lay behind his forswearing of his religion.

Only Lord Guilford followed his father to the block. He was executed with his wife Lady Jane Grey in February 1554. The other Dudleys received the Queen's clemency. The Duchess was able to retain most of her dower lands and a substantial estate of inheritance. Sir Henry Sidney went to Spain in 1554 to plead with Philip 'for the liberty of John, Earl of Warwick, and his brethren'. Thanks partly to his efforts, the four remaining brothers were released from the Tower and then pardoned in January 1555. But liberty came too late for Warwick, who died in October from the effects of imprisonment.

He was followed three months later by his mother. Her will, written in the weeks before her death, is a poignant document. Long and rambling, it is a testimony to her efforts to save what was left of her family.

Will of Jane, Duchess of Northumberland   December 1554-January 1555

Here followeth my last will and testament written with mine own hand.
First I bequeath my soul unto Almighty God and my body unto the earth
and to be buried without any solemnity, for my will is rather to have my
debts paid and my children and servants considered than my body that is
but meat for worms. I do commit unto the hands of my executors ... all the
whole lands of mine inheritance as my house of Halesowen for the behalf
of my children for to inherit my lands, the Queen's highness showing her
mercy and the King's majesty to my sons their pardons that they may
enjoy my lands ... I give my lord Don Diego de Acevedo the new bed of
green velvet with all the furniture to it, beseeching him even as he hath in
my lifetime showed himself like a father and a brother to my sons, so I
shall require him no less to do now their mother is gone ... I give to the
duchess of Alba my green parrot; I have nothing worthy for her else ...

King Philip's clemency was not entirely disinterested; he now possessed a direct claim
to the personal loyalty of the Dudley brothers. The debt was repaid in 1557 when the
three surviving brothers took part in the siege of St Quentin. There, before his own eyes,
Lord Robert later declared, Lord Henry was killed. Thanks possibly to his death, the four
remaining Dudley children were restored in blood by the Parliament of 1558.

In Lord Robert's case restoration did not stop there. The origins of his personal
relationship with Queen Elizabeth have been the subject of much curiosity, but reliable
evidence is very sparse. For all the speculation about a romance in the Tower in 1554,
the only statement by either Elizabeth or Dudley on the subject describes a childhood
friendship beginning in 1540-1. Other than that, all that can be established is that Lord
Robert was included among Elizabeth's friends in the report made by Philip's Councillor,
the Count of Feria, of an interview with her a week before she came to the throne.

Count of Feria to Philip II   14 November 1558
London

I have also been told (although not directly by her) of certain others with
whom she is on very good terms. They are the Earl of Bedford, Lord
Robert, Throckmorton, Peter Carew and Harrington. I have also been told
for certain that Cecil, who was King Edward's Secretary will also be
Secretary to Madam Elizabeth. He is said to be an able and virtuous man ...

It is quite likely that Dudley was with Elizabeth at Hatfield House when she received the news of her sister's death in the morning of 17 November 1558. One of her earliest acts was to appoint him Master of the Horse. His brother, Lord Ambrose, was appointed Master of the Ordnance shortly afterwards, while his sister, Mary Sidney, had become one of the Gentlewomen of the Privy Chamber by the time of the coronation. The Dudleys were thus at the centre of Elizabeth's Court from the first days of the reign.

By the summer of 1559 the closeness between Elizabeth and Dudley was the subject of widespread gossip and innuendo. What increased the potential for scandal was the fact that he was already married. When his wife died in mysterious circumstances on 8 September 1560, the rumours appeared confirmed. The reasons for his marriage in 1550 to Amy Robsart, the only child of the middling Norfolk gentleman-farmer Sir John Robsart, remain unclear. Nor is much known of their married life. For still unexplained reasons Amy Dudley spent most of 1558-60 near Abingdon in Berkshire - latterly at the former religious house at Cumnor where she died, thus giving rise to speculation that Dudley was deliberately keeping his wife in seclusion. She has left only two letters. One, probably written in 1558, deals with the management of the estates in Norfolk that she had inherited from her father. The other was written to her London dressmaker a fortnight before her death, and he attached it to the bill that he later sent to Dudley for payment. When it was discovered a century ago among Dudley's financial documents at Longleat House, its ordinariness destroyed the legend of the 'prisoner of Cumnor'.

Amy Dudley to [John] Flowerdew   7 August [?1558]
Mr. Hyde's [Denchworth, Berks]

Mr. Flowerdew, I understand by Grice that you put him in remembrance of that you spoke to me of concerning the going of certain sheep at Syderstone. Although I forgot to move my lord thereof before his departing, he being sore troubled with weighty affairs and I not being altogether quiet for his sudden departing, yet notwithstanding ... I neither may nor can deny you that request in my lord's absence ...

Amy Dudley to William Edney   24 August [1560]
Cumnor

... desire you to take the pains for me to make this gown of velvet which I send you with such a collar as you made my russet taffeta gown ...

The Court of Philip and Mary

King Philip and Queen Mary, shown as joint monarchs with their thrones, coats of arms and titles so lengthy that they have to be abbreviated to initial letters.

Mary Tudor was the first Queen regnant since Matilda; Philip the first king-consort. Their court was thus a novelty for which there was no real precedent. Its structure was further complicated by the circumstances of Mary's accession. She owed her success in 1553 to two distinct bodies of supporters: those who had rallied to her in East Anglia (the core of whom had been members of her household as princess, and in some cases that of her mother), and those members of the Council of Queen Jane who had defected to her after the Duke of Northumberland had left London. Both groups had a claim to her favour and her Council was unusually large.

The marriage to Philip was the work of three people: Mary herself, Lord Paget and the Emperor Charles V. Philip, already bethrothed to a Portuguese princess and advised that the chances of Mary bearing children were slim, agreed to it only out of deference to his father's wishes. The English Privy Council insisted on major restrictions to his powers as King. Wyatt's rebellion in January and February 1554, specifically intended to prevent the marriage, revealed its unpopularity. Philip therefore made major efforts to win friends in England. He created an English household duplicating his Spanish one and bestowed pensions from his own revenues on Privy Councillors and others who were important. He also encouraged the pardoning of the Dudley brothers and the surviving rebels of 1553 and 1554.

Philip arrived in England in July 1554, accompanied by a large section of the Spanish court, but he went to the Netherlands in August 1555 and returned only for a brief period between March and July 1557. In his absence the court was in fact that of a queen regnant. The most striking feature was the new role of the Privy Chamber, now staffed almost entirely by women drawn from Mary's former household. Where previously it had been at the centre of the politics of the court, under Mary it became a feminine inner sanctum. It was to serve the same function throughout the forty-five years of Elizabeth's reign.

The Master of the Horse

The Lord Robert Dudley master of the horses leading the palfrey of honour

The Lord Ambrose Dudley leading the second litter horse

The Queens Majesty in her litter under the canopy borne by

The Lord Giles Paulet leading the first litter horse

Elizabeth I's entrée into London, 14 January 1559. Lord Robert Dudley exercises his office as Master of the Horse by riding immediately behind the Queen's litter. He had also overseen arrangements for the coronation the following day.

By the later sixteenth century the Master of the Horse was the third of the major Household officers after the Lord Steward and the Lord Chamberlain. His position was less clearly defined, however, as the post had only recently emerged as one of consequence. Originally the Master of the Horse had been a deputy to the Constable and the Marshal and the office only became a distinct one in the fourteenth century. Until the middle of the sixteenth century it was usually held by a man of knightly rank, and came only fifth in the hierarchy of household officers, after the Treasurer and Comptroller but before the Vice-Chamberlain. Leicester's tenure, however, transferred the status of the office. Thereafter it was monopolized by the nobility, and became a great office of state - though on rather dubious grounds as it did not figure in the Act of Precedence of 1539.

The Master's functions are also obscured by the loss of most of the archives of his office prior to the Civil War. His major responsibility lay in the supervision of the stables. The main stables were located in the Royal Mews at Charing Cross, but there were also smaller stables in various royal houses and in a number of towns near London, together with several studs (called 'races') of which the largest was at Tutbury Castle in Staffordshire.

The office had military origins (one of its duties was to provide warhorses for the Royal Household), as well as some association with hunting, and it was not unusual for the Master to combine his office with another related one. Henry VIII usually appointed trusted companions of the chase or the tilt - Sir Thomas Knyvet, Sir Henry Guildford, Sir Nicholas Carew and Sir Anthony Browne. The longest-serving Tudor Master, however, was the Earl of Leicester (1558-87), and he probably displayed the greatest interest in equestrian matters.

Henry VIII had been concerned to improve the breeding of his horses and to introduce the new Italian arts of riding; Leicester shared his interests. It was he, for example, who persuaded Elizabeth to provide the wages for four apprentices to the Riding Masters. But it was also Leicester who established the office as one for a royal favourite. The Master was expected to attend the monarch whenever he or she appeared on horseback. Elizabeth's preference for Leicester's company and the personal contact involved (helping her to mount and dismount, for example) appeared to confirm the rumours that their relations had indeed extended to the physical.

Little is known of the circumstances of Amy Robsart's death. Lord Robert himself was then at Windsor with the Court, which had just completed a summer progress in Hampshire. The day before, he had written to the third Earl of Sussex in Ireland to order horses for the Queen. This letter helps to explain Sir William Cecil's complaint at the time that Dudley was encouraging Elizabeth to take up dangerous sports.

Lord Robert Dudley to the Earl of Sussex   7 September 1560
Windsor

My good Lord, the Queen's majesty thanks be to God is in very good health and is now become a great huntress and doth follow it daily from morning till night. She doth mean out of hand to send into that country [Ireland] for some hobbies [everyday riding horses] for her own saddle, specially for strong good gallopers, which are much better than her geldings, whom she spareth not to tire as fast as they can go ...

For the events at Cumnor we are dependent upon a series of letters between Dudley and his chief household officer, Thomas Blount of Kidderminster. They survive only as copies made in 1567 when Amy Dudley's half-brother, John Appleyard, claimed that Dudley had failed to investigate her death fully. The letters reveal the efforts that Dudley made to establish the truth - accident, foul play or suicide being suspected - though there is always the possibility that they were doctored. The first of the series gives Dudley's reaction to the news; the wandering grammar may reflect his shock.

Lord Robert Dudley to Thomas Blount   9 September [1560]
Windsor

Cousin Blount, immediately upon your departure from me there came to me Bowes, by whom I do understand that my wife is dead and as he sayeth by a fall from a pair of stairs. Little other understanding can I have of him. The greatness and the suddenness of the misfortune doth so perplex me until I do hear from you how the matter standeth, or how this evil should light upon me, considering what the malicious world will bruit, as I can take no rest. And because I have no way to purge myself of the malicious talk that I know the wicked world will use, but one, which is the very plain truth to be known ...

Particularly cryptic is a hastily scrawled (and undated) note from Dudley to Cecil, probably in the week after his wife's death, when he had retired from the Court to his house at Kew. Whether this was at his own volition or under orders from the Queen is still debated, as is the nature of his request to Cecil in the letter. Nevertheless, Cecil's visit, and the implied moral support he offered, helps to explain why Dudley's career at Court was not destroyed at this point.

Lord Robert Dudley to Sir William Cecil [?13 or 14 September] 1560

Sir, I thank you much for your being here, and the great friendship you have showed towards me I shall not forget. I am very loath to wish you here again, but I would be glad to be with you there. I pray you let me hear from you what you think best for me to do. If you doubt, I pray you ask the question, for the sooner you advise me thither, the more I shall thank you.

 I am sorry so sudden a chance should breed me so great a change, for methinks I am here all the while as it were in a dream, and too far, too far from the place I am bound to be, where methinks also this long idle time cannot excuse me for the duty I have to discharge elsewhere. I pray you help him that seems to be at liberty out of so great bondage. Forget me not though you see me not, and I will remember you and fail ye not ...

Amy Dudley's death by misadventure may have freed Dudley to marry Elizabeth, but it also overshadowed their relations with scandal. During the winter of 1560-1 Elizabeth's intentions were the subject of much speculation; by the end of 1561 this had died down. Nor was Dudley's ambition to marry the Queen his only iron in the fire. Equally important was the final restoration of his house, as his pleasure when the Queen granted his father's old titles to his brother Ambrose in December 1561 reveals.

Lord Robert Dudley to George, Earl of Shrewsbury 27 December 1561
The Court

... I thought good ... to participate unto your lordship these comfortable news which are that it hath pleased the queen's majesty of her great bounty and goodness to restore our house tothe name of Warwick, and as yesterday hath created my said brother earl hereof ...

Soon afterwards both brothers readopted the bear and ragged staff device made famous by the Beauchamp Earls of Warwick in the fifteenth century and revived by their father when he became Earl of Warwick in 1547. They also received many of his former estates. However, Robert Dudley's own promotion to the peerage did not occur until Michaelmas Day 1564, when Elizabeth, after considerable debate about his title, created him Earl of Leicester and Baron of Denbigh.

In October 1562, shortly after recovering from her near-fatal attack of smallpox, Elizabeth appointed both Dudley and the fourth Duke of Norfolk to her Privy Council. Dudley was already deeply involved in the making of foreign policy, and in particular with the maintaining of good relations with Mary, Queen of Scots. A letter he wrote then to the Scottish Secretary of State, William Maitland of Lethington, alludes to the great debate over the succession provoked by the Queen's illness.

Lord Robert Dudley to William Maitland of Lethington   27 October [1562]

My Lord, either I wrote in a piece of my last letter unto you that I wished you here for sundry causes to have spoken with you, or I meant to have written so to you. But to say truth, the extremity of our case was such that as I wot not well what I wrote of that woeful case. Thanks be to Almighty God, He has well delivered us for this present, for the Queen's majesty is now perfectly well out of all danger and the disease so well worn away as I never saw any in so short [time]. Doubtless, my Lord, the dispair of her recovery was once marvelous great, and being so sudden the more perplexed the whole state, considering all things, for this little storm shook the whole tree so far as it proved the strong and weak branches. And some rotten boughs were so shaken as they appeared plainly how soon they had fallen. Well this sharp sickness hath been a good lesson, and as it hath not been anything hurtful to her body, so I doubt not but it shall work much good otherwise. For ye know seldom princes be touched in this sort, and such remembrances are necessary in His sight that governeth all.
As further occasions and respects moveth me, I intend to write further by the next to you, for that my leisure is presently such as this bearer can tell. And shall pray you to use my writings when they come as I required you, for that I will be more frank with you than any other there, and do wish her Majesty [Mary, Queen of Scots] had two Lethingtons that she might spare one here. Fare you well and wish you humbly kiss her Majesty's hand on my behalf. In haste this 27 of October.
    Your assured,
    R. Dudley

As important as any formal position as a councillor was Dudley's intimacy with Elizabeth. She was extremely possessive of his company and refused for many years to allow him to take up embassies or military commands abroad. Even his temporary absences from the Court were begrudged, and his 'often sending' to her when away was expected. Elizabeth saved many of these private letters, and about twenty of them survive. Those that she wrote to him, on the other hand, appear (with the exception of the letter on p.170) to have been destroyed.

The earliest of Dudley's involved an awkward explanation. He had left the Court in August 1563 to greet his wounded brother on his return from commanding the expedition to Le Havre (a post that Dudley himself had wanted), despite the fact that many of the survivors were infected with the plague. After 1562 Elizabeth was very frightened by disease.

Lord Robert Dudley to Queen Elizabeth   7 August 1563
Bagshot

My most humble thanks, my most dear Lady, I must render as most bound for all, but in particular for this your gracious advertisement which I have received by your own handwriting ... And yet ten hundred deaths would I more suffer rather than by my evil chance the fear of any such sickness should happen to that dear person. And albeit to my judgement all doubt had been past, for the later and more perilous passengers hath been lightlier by others accounted of repairing to your presence, notwithstanding the natural care and love toward my brother might well much sooner have provoked me to desire the sight of him, yet surely both care of your person for fear of such danger and the occasion thereby to be absent from it, which thereby must force me, had been enough the least of both to have made me fast from the dearest and best sight that this world could show me. Wherefore my own Lady pardon me, though otherwise it will be painful enough to be so long from you, that I should do anything that might seem to any others careless of so great care as I am bound to have more than any other in this case ... So remaining your farther pleasure always, I humbly take leave. From Bagshot this Saturday.
 Most bounden for ever and ever,
 R.D.

In 1564 the relationship between Dudley (now Earl of Leicester) and the Queen came to the fore again, when a marriage to the Archduke Charles of Styria, son of Ferdinand I, the Holy Roman Emperor, was proposed. This was the most serious of Elizabeth's 'courtships', and it dominated court politics between 1564 and 1568.

The long debates over marriage to the archduke involved two distinct issues. At the beginning of the reign Elizabeth had made public her desire to remain single. What was not clear was whether her decision was an absolute one, or whether new circumstances might influence it. Should she change her mind, then the question of whether she should choose a foreign or a native husband arose. Against the established preference for a husband of royal blood was the memory of the widespread anxiety that her sister's marriage to Philip II of Spain had caused. This and Elizabeth's obvious affection for him were the strongest arguments in Leicester's favour.

During the progress of 1566 he gave his own views to a French diplomatic agent. This statement may, of course, have been made for foreign consumption, but it remains the most explicit surviving description of his relationship with the Queen.

Jacob de Vulcob, sieur de Sassy to   6 August 1566
Jacques Bochetel de La Foret
Stamford

I told him [Leicester] that their Majesties [Charles IX and Catherine de Medici] did not believe that she [Elizabeth] wished to choose a foreign prince for her husband. That point he would not concede to me at all, but showed nevertheless that he believed it to be so. Then speaking less guardedly he told me that his true opinion was that she would never marry. To convince me he added that he considered that he knew her Majesty as well as or better than anyone else of her close acquaintance, for they had first become friends before she was eight years old. Both then and later (when she was old enough to marry) she said she never wished to do so. Thereafter he had not seen her waver in that decision. However, if by chance she should change her mind and also look within the kingdom, he was practically assured that she would choose no one else but him, as she had done him the honour of telling him so quite openly on more than one occasion, and furthermore he enjoyed as much of her favour now as he had ever done.

The case against Leicester as Elizabeth's consort was outlined by Cecil in a memorandum he drafted in either 1566 or 1567 (excerpts of which are printed below). His own prejudice is evident. He constructs a damning indictment of Dudley, but he also displays a considerable amount of wishful thinking about the archduke, and says nothing about the crucial issue of religion.

Sir William Cecil, memorandum   1566 or 1567

Reasons against the Earl of Leicester
1. Nothing is increased by marriage to him either in { riches
                                                     { estimation
                                                     { power
2. It will be thought that the slanderous speeches of the Queen with the Earl have been true.
3. He shall study nothing but to enhance his own particular friends: to wealth, to offices, to lands and to offend others.
4. He is infamed by the death of his wife.
5. He is far in debt.
6. He is like to prove unkind or jealous of the Queen's majesty.

To be considered in the Marriage

Carolus	Earl of Leicester
in birth	
nevew	born a son of a knight
brother of Emperor	his grandfather but a solicitor
in degree	
an archduke born	an earl made
in wealth	
by report 3,000,000 ducats by year	all of the Queen and in debt
in education	
amongst princes	always in England
in reputation	
honoured of all	hated of many
named to the empire	his wife's death

The Nobility and Parliament

The opening of parliament, 1523. The King is enthroned in the centre; on the steps of the throne on Henry's right sit the two archbishops, Wolsey (taking precedence as Cardinal Legate) and Warham; below them are the bishops (in red) and the abbots (in black). On the left are the nobles with Norfolk, holding his baton as Earl Marshal, at the head. The Commons, and their speaker Sir Thomas More, are the gaggle top right.

The role of the nobility in sixteenth-century Parliaments remains a much-debated subject. The older near-exclusive concern with the House of Commons has been convincingly challenged, but the place of the House of Lords is still not entirely clear. After the death of Henry VII, Great Councils (of the Lords without the Commons) were no longer held, and this could be seen as a weakening of the independent power of the nobility. On the other hand, certain developments of Henry VIII's reign also strengthened it. The Act of Precedence of 1539 finally defined membership of the peerage and the House of Lords as co-terminous. The elimination of the abbots and priors from the House of Lords during the Reformation reduced the number of lords spiritual to the twenty-odd bishops and archbishops. This was of no small importance, for in the Parliament of 1529, for example, the lords spiritual had outnumbered the lords temporal.

The lords were summoned by personal writ, and the Crown would only license absences on provision of a valid reason (usually its own service or ill-health). They could initiate important legislation.

In 1593, for example, they increased the size of the proposed subsidy, despite the existence of the tradition that money bills were strictly a matter for the Commons.

The peers also retained extensive powers of patronage. Between a quarter and a third of members of the Commons regularly owed their seats to the influence of one peer or another, although often the rights of patronage came from an office granted by the Crown.

It has been claimed that in Mary's reign the Crown was prevented from introducing legislation strengthening Philip's rights in England owing to fears of opposition by the Lords. Certain other key episodes - the third Duke of Norfolk's introduction of the Six Articles bill in the Lords in 1539, or the attempt to pressure Elizabeth into marriage in 1566 - have been seen as reflecting their influence. Less clear, however, is the evidence for Parliament as the scene for factional struggles among the nobility, though there are signs of it in 1539, for example. Although here, the Court may have provided a more convenient location.

But though Leicester never became Elizabeth's husband, he always remained one of her intimates. This gave him an influence that most of her other councillors lacked. 'You know the Queen and her nature best of any man,' a member of the Court wrote in 1586. Much of his later reputation as a 'politician' came from his careful manoeuvring of her.

A revealing insight into the way this was done is provided by his advice to the French Protestant envoy, the cardinal of Chatillon, who arrived in England with a number of French exiles after the outbreak of the third 'War of Religion' in France in the autumn of 1568. The problem was Elizabeth's well-known reluctance to countenance rebels, ' those who have to do with princes' - even when those princes were hostile to her.

Earl of Leicester to Sir Nicholas Throckmorton   3 October 1568

Sir Nicholas, My Lord Steward [the first Earl of Pembroke], Mr. Secretary [Cecil] and I have written to you for an advice to be given to the cardinal upon the great resort and repair we hear from all parts that are come lately into the realm out of France, praying you to use our advice in such sort to him as he perceive no evil in our meaning either toward himself or his nation, for that in very deed there is no cause at all but only our chief respect is toward him that we may continue and show our good affections toward him the more largely. And without all doubt I know assuredly her Majesty hath a marvellous liking of him and one thing more than I looked for, which is her liking to hear of his wife, and is very desirous to see her and hath sent one expressly to visit her. But what her general opinion is to show public receiving of those that have to do with their princes you know as well as I, which causeth us to foresee lest too much open show may cause her in time to grow more weary of the cardinal, for that all the repair will now come to him. Wherefore it is reason they repair and deal with him, so we wish that he deal warily and wisely that he may do good in the cause. And when he will treat with her Majesty, that he come but in his former sort to her, that the open company appear not, that the [French] ambassador take not just cause to challenge the Queen's majesty for the maintenance of the King's adversaries and so to cause a stay, where we wish by little and little to have it so increase as it may break forth as it should indeed and must do if we look to her own safety and the realm's surety. Now you know my mind and ours, I doubt not of your wise handling thereof, our chief respect being to have the cardinal to keep his credit and recourse hither, who I trust shall do most good. In haste, 3 October.

   Your assured,
   R. Leycester

Leicester's support for the 'Protestant Cause' became more pronounced as Protestant rebellions spread in both France and the Netherlands in the 1570s. His reaction to the notorious assassination of the Admiral Coligny (brother of the Cardinal of Châtillon) and the massacre of the French Huguenot leadership in Paris on St Bartholomew's Day 1572 reflects the growing trend toward religious politics. More particularly, Leicester is also using the Massacre to support the Protestants (and English) party in Scotland, as opposed to the Catholic (and French).

Earl of Leicester to the Earl of Morton   7 September 1572
Woodstock

My lord, I think your lordship is not ignorant of the late most shameful and most cruel fait [deed] used in France against the Admiral and all others, the chief of the religion, being many hundred worthy and noble gentlemen murdered and slain in one day and night besides many thousands of zealous and good people likewise guiltlessly at the same time put to the sword. And as the act is most horrible to all true Christians so is it more to be lamented that it should hap to be done by the consent of such a prince [Charles IX] as hath so openly professed sincerity and with good and gracious dealings so entrapped the hearts of all good men to trust or rather to believe in his princely and upright meaning ...

These my lord be good warnings to all those that be professors of the true religion to take heed in time, for how great hope there was of this prince's indifference that way or rather good affection, I refer to your lordship that hath heard I am sure no less than we have done, which now seeing it to fall out as we do, we are to look more narrowly to our present estate. We cannot but stand in no small danger except there be a full concurrence together of all such as mean faithfully to continue such as they profess. And having always for my own part made no less reckoning of your lordship's good devotion toward the advancement of God's true religion than of my own which I know best, I think it my part upon these considerations to impart with your lordship so frankly thereof as the necessity of the case doth require ...

Your lordship's assured loving friend,

R. Leycester

By the 1570s Leicester had also become a leading domestic patron - artistic, literary and economic as well as political. In his journal the town clerk of Warwick, John Fisher, recorded an interview with him in 1571. It reveals both the pressure of lobbying on Privy Councillors as well as Leicester's benevolent response. Warwick and Coventry, which bordered his own estate at Kenilworth, had a particularly close association with him.

Journal of John Fisher   27 November 1571

At Greenwich on Wednesday being the 27th of the same month the Queen's majesty riding abroad and the said earl among other lords attending her highness the said Fisher had good opportunity and took such time as the said earl heard him at length ... and asked what good trade there was in the said town and how the poor were relieved. To which the said Fisher answered that the number of the poor was great ... 'I marvel [said the earl] you do not devise some ways among you to have some special trade to keep your poor on work as such as Sheldon of Beoley [Worcestershire] devised, which methinketh should not be only very profitable but also a means to keep your poor from idleness, or the making of cloth or capping or some such like. But I do perceive that every man is only careful for himself ... I could wish there were some special trade devised wherewith having a good stock both reasonable profit might arise and your poor set on work. Whereunto I would be glad to help, and in mine opinion nothing would be more necessary than clothing or capping to both which occupations is required many workmen and women and such may be employed as in no faculty else, for though they be children they may spin and card, though they be lame they may pick and free wool and do such things as shall keep them from idleness and whereof some commodity may grow. And therefore many such poor as I perceive you have, I would to God you would some ways devise that they might in sort be relieved and your commonwealth profited. And because I am of that country and mind to plant myself there I would be glad to further any good device with all my heart.'

The St Bartholomew's Massacre

The massacre of St Bartholomew's Day, Paris, 1572. Some three or four thousand were killed and of the Huguenot leaders only Henry of Navarre (the future Henry IV) and the Prince de Condé escaped.

The 'Wars of Religion' of the later sixteenth century were notorious for atrocities, the inevitable consequence of conflicts in which neither side regard its opponents as worthy of mercy. But no other had the impact of the massacre of the French Protestant leadership in Paris on St Bartholomew's Day (24 August) 1572. This arose from the belief, widespread throughout the Protestant world, that it had been planned long in advance and that Protestants had been deliberately lured to their fate. Moreover, Charles IX of France had also been negotiating an alliance with England to aid William of Orange and the Dutch rebels against Spain. This too was afterwards seen as part of the 'plot' by both Leicester and many in England, as well as those Englishmen, like Francis Walsingham (then Elizabeth's ambassador in Paris) and Philip Sidney, who witnessed it at first hand.

It is now known that the 'plot' was a myth. The Queen Mother of France, Catherine de Medici, had been panicked into allowing the massacre because she feared that France was about to be sucked into a war with Spain, which she desperately wished to avoid. But the plot appeared to confirm the growing belief in the existence of a 'Catholic League' intended to extirpate Protestantism from Europe. This had a major influence on later Elizabethan foreign policy. To those who believed it, it would be impossible in future to trust the word of a king of France or any other Catholic; the only allies who could be relied upon were fellow-Protestants. As Leicester's letter shows, the massacre led to renewed calls for a grand Protestant alliance. It also inspired the opposition of Leicester, Walsingham and Sidney to the proposed marriage between Queen Elizabeth and the Duke of Anjou at the end of the decade. The main argument for the marriage was as a means of creating a new alliance between England and France. In their view, the St Bartholomew's massacre had made such an alliance impossible.

Preaching the Gospel

If there was a single central concern of Tudor Protestantism, it was the preaching of the Gospel. Preaching was now to be the primary function of the clergyman; administration of the sacraments or pastoral work among his parishioners were of lesser importance.

The pre-Reformation Church had not neglected preaching. But sermons in the late Middle Ages had largely been the responsibility of the friars who almost unsupported had created and continued to stimulate a demand for preaching. The enthusiasm for sermons was virtually universal and seemingly insatiable. Many newly built churches were designed as preaching-houses with well-placed pulpits for the delivery of sermons and with pews for the comfort of the congregations. Until the Reformation the demand at Court was met by the Franciscans Observant at Greenwich and at Richmond, and later by the construction of the Preaching Place at the new palace of Whitehall. Outdoor sermons were particularly popular; Paul's Cross, the celebrated open-air pulpit beside Old St Paul's, was the chief place for sermon-mongers throughout the sixteenth century, and consequently a spot kept under close watch by Church and State alike. What was new at the Reformation was first: the elimination of physical expressions of sacramental worship, like altars and rood-screens; and second, an altered attitude to a clergyman's personal qualifications. A cleric who could not preach was regarded as unworthy of his calling. This new view of the duties of the clergy was embodied in the Injunctions issued by Edward VI in 1547 and revived by Elizabeth I in 1559. It was shared equally by both supporters of the Church as established by law and those (dubbed Puritans by the early 1570s) who pressed for further reform.

The demand for preachers led to the conversion of the clergy into a profession recruited from university graduates. The process of producing sufficient graduates to staff the 9000-odd parishes was a slow one and it was not fully complete by the eve of the Civil War. In order to supply them, the universities, especially in Elizabeth's reign, both expanded in size and gave a much greater prominence to the teaching of divinity. In view of the shortage of sufficient preachers a blind eye was generally turned towards minor expressions of non-conformity. Under the Injunctions of 1559 the bishops issued licences to those clergymen who were considered able to preach; this gave them some measure of control, but they found it difficult to prevent the more zealous from straying into controversial matters and politics in their sermons.

The gap between the demand for preachers and the supply gave Leicester and the other great Protestant noblemen considerable influence within the new Church. Their personal and official patronage enabled them to protect many preachers from the consequences of non-conformity. This benign tolerance towards dissent in the interests of expanding the preaching clergy was one reason why 'Puritanism' became so deeply embedded in the Elizabethan Church.

Two styles of preaching: Protestant left and Catholic right, from the title page of John Foxe's Book of Martyrs, *itself one of the key works of the English Reformation.*

The 'commonwealth' rhetoric Leicester used to Fisher commanded universal consent; a far more controversial aspect of the earl's patronage was his encouragement of Puritan preachers. Both as a Councillor and as Chancellor of Oxford University (to which he was elected in 1564) he had a major influence on the Church. During the 1570s growing attacks on the bishops by the Puritans ('uncharitable preaching') and the bishops' aggressive response frequently placed him in a difficult position, as an official letter to the University in 1580 shows.

Earl of Leicester to theVice-Chancellor   13 October 1580
and Convocation of Oxford University
The Court

After my right hearty commendations. Complaints have been made unto me by the space of these two or three years from time to time almost continually, touching disorderly and uncharitable preachings among you by some of the younger sort, which though I have much misliked, yet I have not much dealt in reprehension or reformation thereof for two causes: the one that I thought the men to be young that were named so to overshoot themselves [and] would in time see their own faults and amend them, the other that I would not seem to discourage any from preaching, knowing the great want of preachers everywhere. But now the fault, as it is informed, increasing daily and by example of sufferance to be more general and the complaint thereof not reaching to myself alone but to many others of the best sort, I was as well by further authority enforced as bound in respect of mine office there among [you] to look into it. And therefore to be as well informed more fully of the disorders as advised for the remedies, I sent for two or three of the preachers which had offended that way and for some five or six of the wiser and graver sort of the University whose advice I might use for redress.

   In conference with all whom I do find indeed disorders so great as it grieved me to hear and think the preachers that were here were themselves sorry. But for redress I have by advice of those doctors I sent for and other men of authority and wisdom here devised the enclosed orders, which I send and commend unto you as those that being well observed will, I hope, in time work some good reformation in this point, requiring you Mr. Vice-Chancellor and you the whole house to confirm them with your consents and authority ...

   Your loving friend and Chancellor,
   R. Leycester

By the end of the 1570s the long-standing relationships between the Queen and the leading figures of the Court found expression in numerous private jokes and allusions which are not always easy to understand now. The best-known of them were Elizabeth's nicknames for her intimates - her 'eyes' in Leicester's case (see p.170). In 1577 Leicester and his brother Warwick initiated what would become an extensive court patronage of the medicinal baths at Buxton in Derbyshire. This provoked a bantering exchange with the Queen, a great believer in her own herbal remedies, but sceptical of the benefits of the baths. Early in June she dictated to Sir Francis Walsingham a letter of thanks to the Earl and Countess of Shrewsbury for Leicester's entertainment. Much of the humour is derived from the implicit allusion to her disputes with Shrewsbury over the household expenses ('diets') of Mary, Queen of Scots. This letter may not have been sent, for a more formal version dated the 25th is now among Shrewsbury's papers. Even that pleased him so much that he endorsed it 'to be kept as the dearest jewel'.

Elizabeth I   4 June 1577
to the Earl and Countess of Shrewsbury

Right trusty etc., being given to understand from our cousin of Leicester how honourably he was lately received and used by you our cousin the Countess of Shrewsbury at Chatsworth and how his diet is discharged by you both at Buxton ... we think it meet ... to prescribe unto you a proportion of diet, which we mean in no case you shall exceed, and that is to allow him by the day two ounces of flesh, referring the quality to themselves, and for his drink the twentieth part of a pint of wine to comfort his stomach, and as much of St. Anne's sacred water as he listeth. On festival days, as is fit for a man of his quality, we can be content you shall enlarge his diet by allowing unto him for his dinner the shoulder of a wren, and for his supper a leg of the same, besides his ordinary ounces. The like proportion we mean you to allow our brother of Warwick, saving that we think it meet that in respect that his body is more replete than his brother's, that the wren's leg allowance on festival days be abated, for that light suppers agree best with rules of physic.

But however entrancing these courtly games, Leicester was growing increasingly unhappy about the absence of a Dudley heir. Both Warwick (as Cecil had unkindly pointed out in 1566) and the Earl and Countess of Huntingdon were similarly childless, which left the Sidney children as the nearest heirs. He also became emotionally involved with two widows. The first, Douglas, Lady Sheffield, bore him a son, Robert Dudley, in 1574. The circumstances of this affair are as mysterious as any episode in Leicester's life. In 1605 during a Star Chamber case over the inheritance to his estates between her son and Sir Robert Sidney, Lady Sheffield claimed that she and Leicester had made a secret marriage. This she was unable to prove; but among the papers of the case is an undated letter from him, possibly the most personal to survive.

Earl of Leicester to [Douglas, Lady Sheffield]   [undated]

My good friend, hardly was I brought to write in this sort unto you lest you might conceive otherwise thereof than I mean it, but more loath am I to conceal anything from you that both honesty and true good will doth bind me to impart unto you.

   I have, as you well know, long loved and liked you, and found always that faithful and earnest affection at your hand again that bound me greatly to you. This good will of mine, whatsoever you have thought, hath not changed from that it was at the beginning toward you. And I trust, after your widowhood began upon the first occasion of my coming to you, I did plainly and truly open unto you in what sort my good will should and might always remain to you, and showing you such reasons as then I had for the performance of mine intent as well as ever since ... And so without difference or question ever since it passed between us, till as you can remember this last year at one time upon a casual doubt you pressed me in a further degree than was our condition, wherein I did plainly and truly deal with you. Some unkindness began and after, a greater strangeness fell out, though, as I have told you since, for other respects, for notwithstanding that first unkindness we did often meet in friendly sort and you resolved not to press me more with that matter ... If I should marry I am sure never to have favour of them that I had rather yet never have wife than lose them, yet is there nothing in the world next that favour that I would not give to be in hope of leaving some children behind me, being now the last of our house ... To carry you away for my pleasure to your more great and further grief hereafter were too great a shame for me, when being too late known, the lack could not so easily be supplied as now it may, having both time and occasion offered you, neither should my repentance be excusable when no recompence could be made on my part sufficient to make satisfaction...

Several years later, Leicester's desperation for an heir led him to take the step he had refused Douglas Sheffield. In a discreet ceremony in September 1578, attended only by a small group of family and friends, Leicester married Lettice, Countess of Essex, mother of the second Earl. In the winter of 1580-1 a son was born; and when the little Robert, Lord of Denbigh, died in 1584 Leicester was shattered.

His marriage also coincided with a major debate over foreign policy. Elizabeth had recently rejected a proposal of military intervention in support of the Dutch rebels (which Leicester himself had offered to command), but instead sought to aid them in alliance with the French king's brother, the Duke of Anjou - an alliance that might be sealed by her marriage to Anjou. As he wrote to the English agent in the Netherlands, Leicester was himself at a loss to understand whether Elizabeth was serious.

Earl of Leicester to William Davison   26 February [1578]

Cousin Davison, I perceive the matters there [the Netherlands] goeth not well, which I am right sorry for and I am not deceived in my expectation, for I neither looked for better since her Majesty's forces joined not with them ... Now touching the other matter at home here for Monsieur [Anjou], which you desire to understand of, for that many speeches are of it, I think none but God can let you know yet. Only this I must say. Outwardly there is some appearance of good liking, for the messengers are very well used and her Majesty's self doth seem to us all that she will marry if she may like the person and if the person adventure without condition or assurance to come. If she then like him, it is like she will have him. His ministers say he will adventure his coming and stand upon that matter of liking &c. And this is all I assure you that can yet be said to you. For my own opinion, if I should speak according to former disposition, I should hardly believe it will take place. And yet if I should say conjecturally, by that I newly hear or find in her deep consideration of her estate and that she is persuaded nothing can more assure it than marriage, I may be of mind she will marry if the party like her. But till the issue come for that point, I can say little nor any more else I believe; yet thus much shortly shall we know certainly, whether he will come or no ... In some haste this 26 of February.

   Your loving cousin and friend,
   R. Leycester

Leicester was, however, widely regarded as the leading opponent of the match, and Anjou's agents were believed to have informed Elizabeth of his own secret marriage in the autumn of 1579 in an effort to destroy his influence. Her notorious sexual jealousy exploded. Leicester stood his ground, but his resentment at what he considered unfair treatment emerges clearly in a letter he wrote to Lord Burghley at the time.

Earl of Leicester to Lord Burghley [12 November 1579]

My lord, I have desired my Lord of Pembroke to excuse me to you and to pray your lordship to help to excuse my not coming this day. I perceive by my brother of Warwick your lordship hath found the like bitterness in her majesty towards me that others (too many) have acquainted me lately withal. I must confess it grieveth me not a little, having so faithfully, carefully and chargefully served her Majesty these twenty years as I have done. Your lordship is a witness I trust that in all her services I have been a direct servant unto her, her state and crown, that I have not more sought my own particular profit than her honour.

Her Majesty I see is grown into a very strange humour all things considered towards me, howsoever it were true or false as she is informed, the state whereof I will not dispute. Albeit I cannot confess a greater bondage in these cases than my duty of allegiance oweth, your lordship hath been best acquainted next myself to all my proceedings with her Majesty and I have ere now broken my very heart with you ... I ever had a very honourable mind in all my actions as near as my capacity might direct me (and with modesty be it spoken) toward her service in my poor calling. Even so was it never abased in any slavish manner to be tied in more than unequal and unreasonable bonds. And as I carried myself almost more than a bondman many a year together, so long as one drop of comfort was left of any hope, as yourself my lord doth well know, so being acquitted and delivered of that hope and by both open and private protestations and declarations discharged, methinks it is more than hard to take such an occasion to bear so great displeasure for. But the old proverb sayeth, they that will beat a dog will want no weapon ... God Almighty direct her Majesty and grant her many happy and prosperous years and your lordship as well to do as myself. In haste this Tuesday afternoon.

Your lordship's faithful friend,

R. Leycester

In time Elizabeth relented and, probably out of sympathy for the death of his son, appointed Leicester Lord Steward of the Household in the autumn of 1584. But her bitterness towards his wife remained. This cast a major shadow over the crowning and most controversial episode in his career: his command of the English expeditionary force in the Netherlands in 1585-7. By the summer of 1585 Elizabeth was left with no alternative but to aid the Dutch directly. Leicester's willingness to lead an army there was long established, but for a mixture of personal and political reasons she hesitated about sending him, and only gave way after learning of the surrender of Antwerp to the Spaniards in August. Leicester was laid up by a riding accident near Kenilworth when he received the news.

Earl of Leicester to Sir Francis Walsingham   28 August 1585
Stoneleigh

Good Mr. Secretary, I have this day received two letters from you, both much to one effect, and the substance being of her Majesty's good resolution now to proceed effectually in the causes of the Low Countries ... and that her Majesty did promise to send some nobleman to be their chief as heretofore was treated of, whom you thought should be myself, but first her Highness willed you to understand my own disposition now, whether I do remain in the same mind Antwerp being lost which I did before to be employed in that service. Truly Mr. Secretary that which moved me heretofore to be willing and ready to do her Majesty service in those parts was wholly and chiefly in respect of the cause offered which concerned God and her Majesty: God, touching religion which in my opinion is a sufficient cause for all true Christians to adventure their lives for; her Majesty, touching her safety as hath been to my seeming flatly and resolutely set down by all her Councillors, that there was never cause that happened in any prince's days whose estate both for their person and kingdom that was more nearly to be touched than her Majesty's, which for my part I have so assuredly conceived to be true, as if I be either a good Christian toward God or a faithful subject to her Majesty, I cannot but rest still of that mind.

Leicester's trials in the Netherlands - his acceptance of the governor-generalship against Elizabeth's opposition, his attempt to combat the leading army of Europe with small and under-funded forces, the difficulties of trying to deal with both Elizabeth and the Dutch, and the sadness caused by the death of Sidney - revealed him at his best and worst. Despite Elizabeth's savage repudiation of his governor-generalship, the extensive correspondence from this campaign contains the draft - the only one to survive - of a personal letter from the Queen to her favourite. In it the royal plural is abandoned and the 'mask of royalty' dropped.

Elizabeth I to Earl of Leicester   19 July 1586

Rob: I am afraid you will suppose by my wandering writings that a midsummer moon hath taken large possession of my brains this month, but you must needs take things as they come in my head, though order be left behind me ... I have fraught this bearer full of my conceits of those country matters and imparted what way I mind to take and what is fit for you to use: I am sure you can credit him and so I will be short with these few notes ... If there be fault in using soldiers or making of profit by them, let them hear of it without open shame, and doubt not but I will well chasten them therefor. It frets me not a little that the poor soldier that hourly ventures life should want their due that well deserve rather reward ... And if the treasurer be found untrue or negligent, according to desert he shall be used, though you know my old wont that love not to discharge from office without desert, God forbid ... Now will I end that do imagine I talk still with you and therefore loathly say farewell ô ô [i.e. 'Eyes' - his nickname] though ever I pray God bless you from all harm and save you from all foes with my million and legion of thanks for all your pains and cares.

As you know, ever the same, [Elizabeths motto, *Semper Eadem*]
E.R.

The Spanish Armada

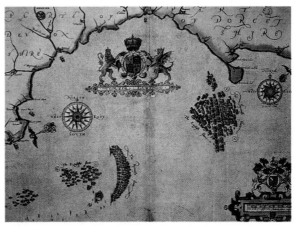

Above: the English, in loose formation, following the Spanish, in crescent formation, up the Channel and the engagement off Portland Bill (1-2 August, 1588).
Left: the decision to pursue the retreating Spaniards up the East coast, signed first by Howard (11 August 1588).

The voyage and defeat of the Grand Armada in 1588 was to be the best-remembered event of Elizabeth I's reign. Rumours and fears of a Spanish invasion had circulated since the beginning of the reign - not without justification, for Philip II's councillors had discussed a landing in England in 1559. They gained currency in the 1580s following the discovery of Spanish-inspired conspiracies in England and evidence of large-scale naval preparations in Spain after 1585. The English response was, if anything, over-confident - a cockiness about superiority at sea born of Sir Francis Drake's success in the Circumnavigation Voyage, and apparently confirmed by his raid on Cadiz in 1587. Although the Queen possessed only some twenty major warships, which could be supplemented by a similar number of large private vessels (out of the nearly two hundred mustered), these were considered equal to anything that the Spaniards could deploy.

Both the size and strength of the Armada and its sudden appearance in the Channel at the end of July 1588 took the English commanders by surprise. The inconclusive engagements off Plymouth and the Isle of Wight were a major disappointment. Only after the Armada's discipline was shattered by the fireship attack at Calais were any major Spanish ships lost, though not as many as Leicester reported.

The ensuing battle off Gravelines also prevented the Armada from picking up the Spanish army in the Netherlands ready for the invasion of England (thus defeating Philip of Spain's master-plan). But the heavy expenditure of shot and ammunition by the English in battle meant that Howard was unable to follow up his advantage. To the credit of the Spanish Captain-General, Medina Sidonia, the Armada regrouped and, despite stragglers, it proceeded into the North Sea until dispersed by storms. At the time Leicester wrote, the fate of the Armada on its long voyage home round Scotland and Ireland was unknown. It was at this stage that the great majority of the Spanish losses were suffered, and those mainly among the Armada's smaller and weaker ships.

But if a disappointment tactically, strategically it was a major English success; the Grand Armada, which had taken three years to prepare, had failed. The providential view of its defeat, which Leicester's letter also reflects, was no less important. God had intervened to protect England from her enemies. The belief in divine deliverance not only bolstered morale during the long war of attrition with Spain that followed, but inspired English Protestantism well into the seventeenth century.

Provoked beyond endurance by England's direct intervention in the Netherlands, Philip II decided to launch a direct attack on England. The Spanish Armada sailed in May 1588 and Leicester was given the command of the main army raised for the defence of London. Worn out by his exertions, he left the Court for Kenilworth and Bath at the end of August, having drafted a letter describing the victory (not altogether accurately) to an old friend in France, Henry, Duke of Montmorency.

Earl of Leicester to Henry, Duke of Montmorency   22 August 1588
St. James's Palace

Monsieur my brother, you already know that the king of Spain has been assembling a great fleet during the last few years, which recently he sent forth to conquer this kingdom, as the prisoners who have fallen into our hands have testified and admitted; but it pleased God, who governs the hearts of kings, to permit him no advantage over us and to favour the good and just cause, so that this fleet (whose smallest ship carried at least five hundred men) has been so met by ours and saluted by such cannon fire that few ships escaped damage and more than 5,000 soldiers were killed. Don Pedro de Valdes is a prisoner here, and in Holland Don Diego de Pimentel, *Maestre de Campo* [Field Marshal] of the *Tercio* [Army] of Sicily, which was composed of thirty companies of Spaniards and many members of the nobility; Don Pedro de Toledo escaped to Nieuport at night. We have certain news of seventeen great ships, some taken, some sunk; the others have been so scattered towards the north that we are sure that their force and fury has passed for this year. And because it was their intention that the Prince of Parma should embark at Dunkirk with another army to make a landing here while that from Spain was attacking our fleet, her majesty appointed me lieutenant-general of her forces to await the Duke of Parma with so good and able an army that the triumph for his *joyeuse entrée* [triumph] was already arranged; but now that the duke has seen the judgement God has delivered on the fleet, we believe that his plans, which were based on its arrival, will come to nothing, or even if the desire is still there, the means are lacking, so that in a short time God has revealed that it is He, the God of hosts, who disposes the plans and designs of men to His will. May this example serve as a solace and comfort to you in your daily trials and tribulations, for we need not doubt that God, for his glory, will give a happy outcome to the enterprises and just defence of Christian princes. To whom I pray, Monsieur, to grant you in good health a long and very happy life. From the Court at St. James the 22nd of August 1588.

Your very loving brother to do you humble service ...

On 29 August he wrote briefly to Elizabeth, who endorsed it 'his last letter'. Six days later he died from malaria at Cornbury in Oxfordshire.

Earl of Leicester to Elizabeth I   29 August 1588
Rycote

I most humbly beseech your Majesty to pardon your poor old servant to be this bold in sending to know how my gracious lady doth and what ease of her late pains she finds, being the chiefest thing in this world I do pray for and for her to have good health and long life. For my own poor case I continue still your medicine and it amended much better than with any other thing that hath been given me ... I humbly kiss your foot ...
    R. Leycester

Leicester's death was overshadowed by the celebration of the victory over the Armada, and he was buried quietly (as he had requested) in the Beauchamp Chapel of St Mary's, Warwick, where his son and 'sundry of my ancestors do lie'. By 1590 one of the greatest Tudor dynasties was extinct. In the finest of the literary tributes to him, Edmund Spenser saw in the suddenness of Leicester's demise a proof of the transitory nature of being.

Edmund Spenser, 'The Ruins of Time'

He now is dead, and all is with him dead,
Save what in Heaven's storehouse he uplaid:
His hope is failed, and come to pass his dread,
And evil men, now dead, his deeds upbraid:
Spite bites the dead, that living never baid [bit].
He now is gone, the whiles the fox is crept
Into the hole, the which the badger swept.
He now is dead, and all his glory gone,
And all his greatness vapoured to nought,
That as a glass upon the water shone,
Which vanished quite, so soon as it was sought.
His name is worn already out of thought,
Ne [nor] any Poet seeks him to revive;
Yet many Poets honoured him alive.

Running into the Sand

THE LAST OF THE SUFFOLK LINE

Charles Brandon, Duke of Suffolk's lengthy matrimonial adventures left two lines of descent. His marriage to Mary Tudor produced only girls, Frances and Eleanor, but his last wife, Catherine Willoughby, whom he had married in 1534, gave him two sons, Henry and Charles. They were roughly the same age as Edward VI, and were brought up in close contact with the King. Tragedy struck in July 1551, however, when both died suddenly of the sweating sickness - probably influenza. Their mother, Duchess Catherine, found some consolation in an increasingly intense commitment to Protestantism. Under the Catholic Queen Mary she chose exile, to return under Elizabeth I.

Meanwhile, Suffolk's granddaughters by the marriage of Frances to Henry Grey had been thrown into prominence by their claim to the crown. The oldest sister Jane had already paid the price under Mary; now it was the turn of the younger sisters, Catherine and Mary, to figure as front-runner candidates under Elizabeth.

England's stability hung by a thread in the first dozen years of Elizabeth's reign, for neither her sister nor her brother had survived more than seven years on the throne, and Elizabeth herself almost died of smallpox in 1562. England's neighbours were falling apart in religious civil wars, and England's own religious future seemed far from settled. In such an atmosphere the succession to Elizabeth became a highly charged issue. The Queen always refused to nominate a successor.

Elizabeth's own choice would probably have been Mary, Queen of Scots, but many of Elizabeth's subjects feared and hated Mary as a Scot and, even worse, a Catholic. A number of rival claimants were promoted, but the most promising was Lady Catherine Grey.

Mary's supporters answered by attacking Lady Catherine's claim on several grounds. None the less, the Grey partisans seemed to be having the best of the debate when Lady Catherine died unexpectedly in January 1568.

Wyngaerde's panorama shows the turreted house, Suffolk Place, which Suffolk built on Borough High Street, c.1515.

Henry, the second Brandon Duke of Suffolk and his brother Charles were apparently fine examples of the educated but still martial nobility valued at a Renaissance court - prototypes of the Elizabethan courtier - as Thomas Wilson, who had been their tutor at St John's College, Cambridge, claimed in his textbook on oratory two years later.

Thomas Wilson, The Art of Rhetoric   1553

... These two gentlemen were born in noble England, both by father and mother of an high parentage ... In their youth their father died, the eldest of them not being past nine years of age; after whose death their mother, knowing that wealth without wit is like a sword in a naked man's hand ... provided so for their bringing up in all virtue and learning, that two like were not to be had within this realm again.

When they began to wax [grow] somewhat in years, being in their primetide [early morning] and spring of their age, the elder, waiting of [on] the King's majesty that now is [Edward VI], was generally well esteemed, and such hope was conceived of his towardness [promise] both for learning and all other things, that few were like unto him in all the Court. The other, keeping his book among the Cambridge men, profited (as they all well know) both in virtue and learning, to their great admiration.

For the Greek, the Latin and the Italian, I know he could do more than would be thought true by my report. I leave to speak of his skill in pleasant instruments, neither will I utter his aptness in music, and his toward nature to all exercises of the body. But his elder brother in this time (besides his other gifts of the mind, which passed all other, and were almost incredible), following his father's nature, was so delighted with riding, and running in armour upon horseback, and was so comely for that feat, and could do so well in charging his staff [holding his lance], being but fourteen years of age, that men of war even at this hour moan much the want of such a worthy gentleman ...

The elder's nature was such that he thought himself best when he was amongst the wisest, and yet contemned [disdained] none, but thankfully used all, gentle in behaviour without childishness, stout of stomach without all pride, bold with all wariness, and friendly with good advisement [consideration]. The younger, being not so ripe in years, was not so grave in look, rather cheerful than sad, rather quick [lively] than ancient [venerable]; but yet if his brother were set aside, not one that went beyond him ...

The mother of these two paragons, the Duchess Catherine, was a formidable character herself - particularly where the Protestant religion was concerned. It was from northern Poland, her refuge in exile, that Duchess Catherine wrote to her old acquaintance, Sir William Cecil, fifteen weeks after Elizabeth's accession, to chide him in typically biblical language for the new regime's slow progress back to a purely Protestant Church. She had little time for the sort of political caution which had led Protector Somerset off the reformers' track and threatened to do the same to Cecil and Elizabeth.

Catherine, Duchess of Suffolk, to Sir William Cecil   4 March 1559
Crozan, Lithuania

... I would to God all our whole nation were ... one in Jesus Christ, as behoveth [it should be]. Nay, if there be but 11 about her majesty's person that savour [care for] one thing in Him, she is happy, and the whole realm. But alack, the report is otherwise, which is an untolerable heaviness [sadness] to such as love God and her; yea, and that such as should rather be spurs holdeth her Majesty of [back from] her own good inclination, running most back, among which you are specially named. Wherefor, for the love I bear you, I cannot forbear to write it.

And, if it shall please you to heed a simple woman's mind, undoubtedly the greatest wisdom is not to be too wise, which, of all others, you should by experience chiefliest know. For if there were anything whereby that good duke, your old master, deserved and felt the heavy stroke of God, what is there else whereof men may accuse him, but only that when God had placed him to set forth His glory (which yet of himself he was always ready to do) but being still plucked by the sleeve of [by] worldly friends, for this worldly respect or that, in fine [finally] gave over his hot zeal to set forth God's true religion as he had most nobly begun, and turning him to follow such worldlings' devices, you can as well as I tell what came of it: the duke lost all that he sought to keep, with his head to boot ... Wherefor I am forced to say with the prophet Elijah, how long halt [waver] ye between two opinions?... If the mass be good, tarry not to follow it, nor take from it no part of that honour which the last Queen, with her notable stoutness, brought it to and left in ... But if you be not so persuaded, alas, who should move the Queen's majesty to honour it with her presence, or any of her Councillors?...

With my hearty prayer that He will so assist you with His grace that you may chiefliest and only seek Him as his elect and chosen vessel ... So far yours as you are God's.

K. Suffolk

Catherine, Duchess of Suffolk

The tomb, at Spilsby, of Catherine Willoughby, Duchess of Suffolk, with her bust and that of her husband, Richard Bertie, a gentleman of her household.

Catherine Willoughby, born in 1519, was the only child of her father, the eleventh Lord Willoughby, and stood to inherit his title and lands worth £900 or more a year - perhaps half the value of the estates of Charles Brandon, Duke of Suffolk, in the 1520s. On her father's death in 1526, Suffolk bought her wardship from the King, intending to marry her to his son, Henry, Earl of Lincoln, then aged three. But Lincoln was sickly, and when the French queen died in 1533 Suffolk did not wish to gamble on his son's survival and risk losing Catherine's lands. So he married her himself. Six months later Lincoln died. She had two sons by the Duke, who survived him to become the second and third Dukes of Suffolk, but both died in 1551. In 1553 Catherine married Richard Bertie, an educated gentleman of her household, by whom she had a daughter and a son, Peregrine, who became the thirteenth Lord Willoughby on her death.

All this was far from extraordinary, and does not explain why Catherine enjoyed the accolade of the composition of a ballad and a play about her life within a few years of her death in 1580. She became a contemporary heroine by dint of her zeal for the more thoroughgoing forms of Protestantism. By the end of Brandon's life she was starting to move in the reformist circles at Henry VIII's court which would push on the Reformation under Edward; in the next few years she encouraged such preachers as the German exile Martin Bucer and the fiery social critic Hugh Latimer; and in Mary's reign her conscience drove her and Bertie out of Catholic England.

They began their exile in Wesel, in north-eastern Germany; moved on to Weinheim, in the Rhine Palatinate, often travelling incognito, enduring hardships and surviving swashbuckling adventures; and ended up in Lithuania by invitation of the king of Poland and one of his Calvinist noblemen. In summer 1559 they came home to Lincolnshire, and Catherine occupied the last two decades of a very full life with raising her son and daughter, such occasional duties as the keeping of Lady Mary Grey, and consistent support for those who urged further Church reform on Elizabeth's cautious government. In literature as in reality she was one of the best English examples of a classic European type, the noble patroness of the Reformation.

The marriage between Somerset's son, Edward, Earl of Hertford and Lady Catherine Grey had been clandestine: only the birth of a son in 1561 made it public knowledge. This match by a claimant to the throne was invalid without royal consent, and aroused the Queen's suspicions of plotting (the more so as the Seymours themselves were so closely connected to the Tudors). The earl and countess were confined to the Tower, and the bridegroom's mother was quick to disclaim responsibility.

Anne, Duchess of Somerset, to Sir William Cecil   [August 1561]

Good Master Secretary, hearing a great bruit [rumour] that my Lady Catherine Grey is in the Tower, and also that she should say she is married already to my son, I could not choose but trouble you with my cares and sorrows thereof. And although I might, upon my son's earnest and often protesting unto me the contrary, desire you to be an humble suitor on my behalf, [that] her tales might not be credited before my son did answer; yet, instead thereof, my first and chief suit is that the Queen's majesty will think and judge of me in this matter according to my desert and meaning. And if my son have so much forgotten her Highness' calling him to honour, and so much overshot his bounden duty, and so far abused her Majesty's benignity, yet never was his mother privy or consenting thereunto.

I will not fill my letter [with] how much I have schooled and persuaded him to the contrary, nor yet will desire that youth and fear may help excuse or lessen his fault, but only that her Highness will have that opinion of me as of one that, neither for child nor friend, shall willingly neglect the duty of a faithful subject. And to conserve my credit with her Majesty, good Master Secretary, stand now my friend, that the wildness of mine unruly child do not minish her Majesty's favour towards me. And thus, so perplexed with this discomfortable rumour, I end, not knowing how to proceed, nor what to do therein. And therefore, good Master Secretary, let me understand some comfort of my grief from the Queen's majesty, and some counsel from yourself, and so do leave you to God. Your assured friend to my power,

Anne Somerset

The couple were not very effectively separated in the Tower, and in February 1563 they produced a second son, though a royal commission had decided in 1561 that their marriage was invalid. This time Hertford was heavily fined, and in August, when plague in London threatened to spread into the Tower, he was sent to live with his mother in Middlesex, while Catherine was confined to the house of her uncle, John, Lord Grey, at Pirgo in Essex. Lord Grey tried to use his distant family connection with Sir William Cecil to help her, but to no avail. Cecil probably sympathised with the Grey cause, but dared not offend the Queen by doing so openly: his friend and colleague, Sir Nicholas Bacon, fell into temporary disgrace in 1564 for his slight involvement with a campaign to have Lady Catherine recognized as heir to the throne, an affair which brought brief imprisonment for Lord Grey.

John, Lord Grey of Pirgo, to Sir William Cecil   12 December 1563
Pirgo

The augmenting of my niece's grief, in the want of the queen's majesty's favour, enforceth me (besides my duty in nature) every way to declare and recommend unto you her miserable and woeful state. This three or four days she hath for the most part kept her bed, but altogether her chamber; in such wise as I thought once I should have been driven to have sent for some of the Queen's physicians. And I never came to her but I found her either weeping, or else saw by her face she had wept.

    Wherefor, good cousin Cecil, for the mutual love which ought to be betwixt Christian men, and for the love wherewith God hath loved us, being His, procure, by some way or means, the Queen's majesty's further favour towards her. For, assuredly, she never went to bed all this time of her sickness, but they that watched with her much doubted how to find her in the morning, for she is so fraughted with phlegm, by reason of thought, weeping, and sitting still, that many times she is like to be overcome therewith; so as, if she had not painful [careful] women about her, I tell you truly, cousin Cecil, I could not sleep in quiet. Thus with my hearty commendations to you, and to my good lady, my cousin, I wish you the same quiet of mind as to myself. From my house at Pirgo, the 12th of December, 1563, By your loving cousin and assured friend to his power,
    John Grey

Hertford was released after Lady Catherine's death in 1568. But in 1565 her sister Lady Mary had made an equally disastrous and more bizarre match, again without royal consent. She married Thomas Keys, the Queen's Serjeant Porter, a widower of fairly humble extraction; they provided considerable material for the unkinder wits of the Court, for he was noted for his large frame and she was almost a dwarf. They too were separated, and Mary's succession of keepers included the Duchess of Suffolk, who found it hard to provide for her impecunious charge.

Catherine, Duchess of Suffolk, to Sir William Cecil   9 August 1567
Greenwich

Good Master Secretary, according to the Queen's commandment, on Friday at night last, Master Hawtry brought my Lady Mary to the Minories to me, even as I was appointed to have gone to Greenwich ... All the stuff that I had left me when I came from the other side of the sea, and all that I have since scraped for and gotten together, will not sufficiently furnish our houses in Lincolnshire ... Wherefor I was fain to declare the same lack of stuff to Master Hawtry, praying him that my lady's stuff might come before [her] for the dressing up of her chamber. But would God you had seen what stuff it is ... She hath nothing but an old livery feather bed, all to-torn and full of patches, without either bolster or counterpaine, but two old pillows, the one longer than the other, an old quilt of silk, so torn as the cotton of it comes out ...

    Wherefor I pray you heartily, consider of this, and if you shall think it meet [proper], be a means for her to the Queen's majesty, that she might have the furniture of one chamber for herself and her maid; and she and I will play the good housewives, and make shift with her old bed for her man. Also I would, if I durst, beg further some old silver pots to fetch her drink in, and two little cups to drink in, one for beer, another for wine ... I cannot yet, since she came, get her to eat, in all [in so much as] that she hath eaten now these two days not so much as a chicken's leg. She makes me even afraid of her [life] ... And so I end my long begging letter ...

Serjeant Keys died in 1571, and Lady Mary was released in 1573, dying childless five years later. Catherine's descendants did succeed to the earldom of Hertford, but never stood much chance of gaining the throne. Neither did the line of Lady Margaret Strange, the only daughter of Lady Eleanor Brandon (the younger daughter of Charles Brandon and Mary, the French queen). The Suffolks had not died out, but the French queen's claim to her brother's kingdom had run into the sand.

Medicine and Welfare

All the great aristocratic households included a physician with a fee equivalent to a well-known lawyer's. Where a physician on the staff was beyond the means of gentle families, there were surgeons, physicians and apothecaries based in any town of importance, and a number of itinerant practitioners. These men provided electuaries and drugs, treatment and potions, on the understanding often that they were free of all claims, damages or blame, whether the patient recovered or not. The vast majority of the population had to rely upon commonsense and to draw upon a common fund of knowledge, using medicinal herbs growing wild or cultivated in physic gardens. The remedy most frequently employed was bleeding, blood being let at different points of the body according to the diagnosis much in the same way as the pin is inserted at different points by the practitioners of acupuncture today. The efficacy of some other traditional remedies, such as the seventh Earl of Shrewsbury's use of oil of stag's blood for the relief of gout, is more open to doubt.

Medicine in England underwent a transformation in the sixteenth century, not in its theory, but in its organization. This was partly on account of a growing professionalism among medical practitioners: the College of Physicians was set up in 1518 and the established guilds for barber-surgeons and for apothecaries regulated their membership more closely. Better provision for instruction was also made, particularly in anatomy (with dissections to illustrate the lecture), and in surgery through endowment of Lord Lumley's Lecture in 1582.

Of more immediate consequence was the disruption caused in running hospitals at the Dissolution of the Monasteries. Until then the religious foundations had provided and maintained a network of infirmaries, almshouses, orphanages and poorhouses. The responsibility for these philanthropic charities now devolved largely on the municipalities. The City of London set an example in saving St Bartholomew's Hospital in 1544 and St Thomas's in 1552. The nobility either supported these civic ventures indirectly or took the responsibility for re-endowment upon their own shoulders, as did the Earl of Leicester at Warwick in 1571.

Far left: the title page of John Gerard's herbal, which dealt with the medicinal properties of plants.

Left: Henry VIII's physician, Sir William Butts. His Knighthood and his foundation of a county family mark the moment at which medicine became a lay profession.

Household Stuff

A late Tudor chest made for the Hobsonne family. Chests were used for storage; they could also double as tables or benches.

'Household-stuff' was the contemporary expression for goods belonging to a person, to a house or to a household. It fell into five distinct categories: beds and bedding, other pieces of furniture, wall hangings, plate, and utensils. All these items, being movable, were treated legally as separate from the buildings where they were kept, and as the possessions of particular individuals. In some noble or gentle families, however, particular pieces were regarded as heirlooms inseparable from a title or an office or a property, thus to be transmitted from holder to holder. Whatever their rank, women were expected to bring household-stuff as part of their marriage-portion, and further items were settled on them at marriage by their husbands as part of their dower. Ideally each child of a marriage was provided with his or her own stuff. Thus, household-stuff figures prominently in marriage settlements, general family provisions, testaments and wills.

The quality of these domestic possessions reflected, and was expected to reflect, the status of the owner. Where appropriate domestic furnishings were withheld as they were by the third Duke of Norfolk from his estranged wife, this was considered a justifiable cause for complaint. Where a person of quality lacked suitable stuff, it was a subject for concern; the Duchess of Suffolk was both overcome by the wants in this respect of Lady Mary Keys (herself a duke's daughter) and non-plussed by her kinswoman's improvidence.

One significant change occurred with domestic furnishings during the sixteenth century. Although movable, they ceased to be transferred regularly from one house or set of lodgings to another. Forty-six wagons conveyed the third Duke of Buckingham's possessions to Penshurst in 1519 in anticipation of Henry VIII's arrival. Later in the century Lord Burghley furnished Burghley House, Theobalds and his London residence permanently throughout. It became incumbent upon a host to provide everything necessary to accommodate a guest, and accordingly the Duchess of Suffolk was herself guilty of a social misdemeanour in not herself providing for Lady Mary Keys.

Furniture was often included with the accommodation which went with household office, and such furniture was customarily considered a perquisite of office either to be taken away on retirement or to be acquired on the death of the head of the household. The abuse of this right in noble households led to dissension as did any attempt to curtail the practice.

'Beware of High Degree'

THE HOWARDS UNDER ELIZABETH I

Thomas Howard, fourth Duke of Norfolk, and his second wife Margaret Audley. These fine portraits, by Hans Eworth, commemorate a happy marriage that ended tragically with the Duchess's death in childbirth the following year.

If the fortunes of the Howards under Henry VIII had represented a plunge from recovery to renewed disaster, their story from Mary's accession to Elizabeth I's death is a revolution in the old sense of the word: a full circle from prosperity through catastrophe to revival.

It began with the family lawyers engaged in the herculean task of rebuilding a ducal estate from the wreck into which it had been plunged by the regimes of Edward VI. In the middle of this busy reconstruction Thomas Howard, fourth Duke of Norfolk and elder son of the poet Earl of Surrey, reached manhood. As England's premier noble, he would have to negotiate the minefield created by the succession issue, yet he lacked the skill or the nerve to do so.

The duke was an attractive individual, the exact opposite of his unpopular grandfather; and in equal contrast his family was close, although not immune from personal tragedy - all his three wives died in childbirth. The death of his third wife proved too much, and the duke suffered a mental breakdown. Although apparently recovered by spring 1568 he was hardly in the best psychological state to face the political crisis which was unfolding.

The cause was Mary, Queen of Scots, now a fugitive in England. One solution was to marry her to England's only duke; but fatally, Norfolk did not take Queen Elizabeth into his confidence as he was drawn into the scheming. His own plans became mixed in with the plots of the Catholic northern Earls of Northumberland and Westmorland, and, after a highly uncomfortable interview with Elizabeth on 6 September 1569, the Duke's nerve broke; he fled the court for his East Anglian estates. His arrest followed as the earls sprang their rebellion.

The duke might well have recovered his position if he had not continued to dabble in the affairs of Mary, Queen of Scots. Ridolfi's plot to replace Elizabeth with Mary as queen sealed Norfolk's fate when the Council learned of it; once more he was arrested, and condemned by his peers. A miserably protracted five months after Elizabeth had signed his death warrant he was executed, on 2 June 1572, and once more the Howards were facing catastrophe.

'Last farewell' written in his New Testament by Thomas Howard, fourth Duke of Norfolk, to his steward, William Dyx, 10 February 1572. It begs him to counsel and advise his two older children, Philip and Anne.

Disaster was not universal; by now there were several cadet branches of the family who were not associated with the duke's fall, notably Lord Howard of Effingham. However, for the main line two decades of desperation followed. The problem was that, against the express wishes of the fourth Duke, many of his family reconverted to Catholicism; most notable among them was his son and heir, Philip Howard, thirteenth Earl of Arundel. It was only after Arundel's death in prison in 1595 that the Howard fortunes began to show signs of recovery.

To the duke's intense grief his second wife, Margaret Audley, died giving birth to his son William in 1564; they had enjoyed five years of happy marriage. The Bishop of Norwich, here writing to the duke's old Protestant tutor, John Foxe, the author of the Book of Martyrs, was determined that the funeral should not become an occasion for the Catholic-inclined Dean of Norwich and his East Anglian sympathisers to put on a display of traditional ritual. The bishop's delight at the success of his Protestant one-upmanship rather overbalances his pastoral concern for the duke, as can be seen from his repetition of similar material in both English and Latin to two different correspondents; it is also clear that he indulged in a little exaggeration to his more distant Swiss friend!

Bishop Parkhurst of Norwich to John Foxe   29 January 1564

... My Lord Dean of Christ's Church [Cathedral, Norwich] was appointed by the duke's council to preach at the burial of the duchess: the which thing he had done, if I had not sent my letters to them, offering my service in this behalf, for although the other could do much better than I, yet I thought it my bounden duty to do all things that I might ['to God's glory' inserted] to do honour to the duke's grace. Therefore the dean buried her, and I made the funeral sermon 24 January. All things were done honourably, *sine crux, sine lux, at non sine* tinkling [without cross or candle but not without bell-ringing]. There was neither torch, neither taper, candle, nor any light else, besides the light of the sun; singing there was enough ...

Bishop Parkhurst to the Swiss reformer Josiah Simler   17 February 1564

The wife of the Duke of Norfolk died in childbed on the 10th of January, and was buried at Norwich on the 24th of the same month. I preached her funeral sermon. There were no ceremonies at the funeral, wax candles or torches. Except the sun nothing shone, which sadly annoyed the papists. Nothing of the kind has been ever seen in England, especially at the funeral of a peer or peeress ...

Noble Funerals

Bishop Parkhurst of Norwich knew that he was playing for high stakes at the funeral of the Duchess of Norfolk in 1564. The Protestant Settlement was only five years old, and the rites of death were the area of Church ceremony where Catholicism and Protestantism were furthest apart. So the funeral would be a demonstration of whether the Howards - the most powerful family in the bishop's diocese - were accepting or rejecting the new dispensation.

However, all noble funerals were important occasions. Just as today, it was at rites of passage - births, marriages and deaths - that the family had its strongest sense of belonging and identity. In the case of the death of a nobleman, the scale of the funeral demonstrated his power and acquaintance beyond his own household and relatives; it must be made something for everyone to remember, not just by the magnificence of the ceremony but by the scale of hospitality to those attending. Because of these social and political needs the scale of aristocratic funerals was little affected by the Reformation, despite the radical changes of meaning and ritual gesture which were made in the actual liturgy. Indeed, in one respect Protestantism probably increased the sense of occasion through its emphasis on the sermon, with its possibilites for dramatic rhetoric to praise the deceased and over-awe the living.

The expense of noble funerals could be crippling. The costs included new mourning clothes not just for the household, but for relatives and friends as well;

Sir Philip Sidney's funeral in 1587: the coffin is caried, not drawn by horses, and there are only four heraldic banners.

the board, lodging and fees for a swarm of heralds and their staff, with all the attendant heraldry painting; the funeral feast and doles to the poor, the torches, the music, the bells, the embalming of the corpse and of course, the truly monumental expense of the tomb itself as funeral monuments swelled in size as Purgatory faded away from England. Sir Philip Sidney's funeral in 1587 was the most splendid and probably the most expensive that any commoner had received in England, for it was a political as well as a personal gesture. A year later his uncle the Earl of Leicester's funeral cost the truly staggering figure of £4,000. Death could be a financial disaster for the family as well as a personal tragedy.

A full-size image of Queen Elizabeth lies on her coffin; twelve banners of the coats of arms of her ancestors are carried.

It was the duke's grief at the death of his third wife which helps to explain the potential bunglings that led to his arrest in 1569. But there were worse fates than arrest in Tudor England, and still Norfolk hoped to regain the Queen's favour; so he sent her an elaborate New Year's gift to test the waters, putting the attempt into the hands of the person most likely to succeed: Leicester. Leicester broke the news of the outcome to him with what sounds like genuine regret.

Earl of Leicester to Duke of Norfolk   2 January 1571

I know not almost with what face I may in this sort write to you, my good Lord, having given such assurance of it beforehand, which is fallen out so far contrary, but as I warrant myself alway of the good opinion I know you have of my unfeigned good will, so do I most faithfully ascertain your Grace that this doing is both contrary to my knowledge and expectation. The matter is touching your New Year's gift to her Majesty ... I delivered your letter first; she took it and read it twice over and commended it to be both very wisely and dutifully written. Then I showed her your token, to the which she made some stay [hesitation] to receive, but said 'you shall thank him from me, and tell him that I have received his letter and do keep it, and like the manner of his writing very well. But I may not take any gift or token from him till we be better friends.' In this sort, somewhat pleasantly I told her Majesty there was no fault in you that you were no better friends, and what fault soever hath been, you had tasted of a long displeasure for it, and yet if she were not satisfied both as you had written to herself, so had you sent to me to say to her you were content to suffer whatsoever further she would lay upon you, so it might satisfy or redeem her favour again. 'Surely I cannot say', saith she, 'but his letter is very dutiful, but -' and so shaked her head. 'Well, Madam, I pray you, see yet the token of his good will'; and so opened the case, and she took the jewel in her hand, and, I perceive, did not think before it had been so rich or fair as it was indeed till she had seen it. Then did she commend it beyond measure, and thought there had not been such a one to be got in all London, and valued it with the pearl at least £500. Thus held she it, and perusing it almost a quarter of an hour and more: in the end, 'I am sorry', saith she, 'that the cause is such between us yet, that I may not take it; and yet say I do not refuse it in token of any new or worse conceit than the old cause which still grieves me, but because till the matter be at other point than yet it is, it is not convenient for me to receive such a gift from him.' Still I pressed her Majesty to it with all the persuasions I could, but by no means would she take it ... and perceiving no persuasions would serve, I have thought good to return it ...

There were many troubles for a duke's gaoler, as can be seen from a whole series of worried letters to high authority from Sir Owen Hopton, governor of the Tower of London. As the execution approached, the Duke grew more bitter, threatening to denounce from the scaffold those with whom he had collaborated in his plotting, particularly his own secretary William Barker and Mary's agent, Bishop Lesley of Ross: an alarming threat to the proprieties of executions. Later, Hopton did his best to spare the feelings of the dowager Countess of Surrey, his near neighbour at his Suffolk home, as her son prepared for execution: the poor lady had seen first her husband and now her eldest son go to the scaffold. The countess at least had the consolation of a second husband of her own choosing; she had married her steward, Thomas Steynings.

Sir Owen Hopton to Lord Burghley 19 January 1572
Tower of London

Right honourable, my singular good Lord: I think it my duty to advertise you that the duke as yet is determined to speak very evil of the Bishop of Ross and Barker, and as it were to attribute all his traitorous actions to the wrongful accusations of the bishop and Barker, which course swerveth from that charity and repentance which others of equal degree hath at such times used, wherefore, considering the rash disposition of the papists to interpret everything to the worst, I would (if it should not offend you) stay him from that uncharitable speech. What the ghostly counsel of the Dean of Paul's and Mr. Foxe may do, I know not, but if they cannot win him, I trust your Honour and the rest will foresee it; praying you to pardon my boldness in writing, considering I do it of dutiful zeal ...

Sir Owen Hopton to Earl of Leicester 3 February 1572
and Lord Burghley
Tower of London

Right honourable, whereas the Duke of Norfolk hath earnestly desired me to speak with Mr. Steynings that my lady his wife (the duke's mother) might make haste to repair homeward, and not to tarry here at London, for that it is to her great charges, and he unable to make up expenses; besides, he greatly feareth that if she should happen to be in town at the time of his execution, the sudden news thereof might happen to be the death of her, whose life he chiefly desireth. Now for me to do anything without your privities [knowledge] I will not ...

New Year's Gifts

As the Duke of Norfolk knew only too well when he engaged in his sad New Year's duel of emotions with the Queen, a great deal hung on the act of giving and receiving. The delicate diplomacy about the New Year's gift was much the same as that which can surround one's Christmas card list today; the difference was that, at the Tudor Court, the diplomacy could be a matter of life and death. A gift could turn into a weapon. Henry VIII was hideously embarrassed at New Year 1532 when Catherine of Aragon, still his legal wife despite the presence of Anne Boleyn in the consort's rooms at Court, ostentatiously sent him an elaborate and distinctive cup. He went to great lengths to make sure that he was not forced formally to receive it and so acknowledge his continuing marriage to Catherine.

New Year's gifts of the Tudor Court are sad phantoms today; by their nature, most of the Crown's presents of plate have long been melted down and put to other uses. On the other hand Holbein's designs preserve at least the appearance of some of the greatest; they also help us to visualize the long lists of elaborate jewels which are such a feature amid the records of the Tudor Court. But these lists are more than inventories of objects; they are also

A New Year's gift for Henry VIII. Holbein designed the universal timepiece (hour-glass, sundials and clock) as Sir Anthony Denny's present to the King in 1544. Henry, like many middle-aged males, was fascinated by mechanical toys.

precious witnesses to a set of unwritten rules that reveal much of the life which surrounded the monarch. Take, for instance, the surviving gift list for Queen Mary's Court in 1557. Here can be seen a picture of the court in its dual role: both an intimate domestic society around the Queen, and also an assemblage of all those most powerful in Marian England - 271 names, ranging from the Queen's cousin and Archbishop of Canterbury, Cardinal Reginald Pole, down to tradesmen who served the court. From gentlefolk, cash was quite an acceptable present for the Queen, ranging from £66 15s from the controller of Mary's household down to £4 from some of her ladies. But the gentry also came up with interesting presents, such as Sir John Mason with his map of England, or Sir Henry Neville's lute with Habsburg portraits painted on the case.

Cash did not come so appropriately from those further down the social scale, but often court tradesmen would give items suitable to their trade: so the Serjeant of the Pastry gave Mary a quince pie and the court hosier gave three pairs of hose, while Miles Huggarde, an energetic propagandist for the government, gave 'a book written' which was no doubt his own. In return, Mary sent gilt cups and covers or carefully graded smaller pieces of plate to all who had sent her New Year's gifts, just as her father had done. She also took good care to give to a rather larger number than had sent her gifts, setting an example of good lordship to her social inferiors. Little changed under Elizabeth.

New Year's gifts from the Crown were carefully standardized, and were a great mark of favour - as was being allowed to send one to the monarch in the first place. To join the list indicated that one had arrived as part of the court circle; with luck real power would follow. And the life of a royal favourite was measured out with more than the coffee-spoons of T. S. Eliot's Prufrock. The exact number of ounces of plate in the royal gift was a register of success: the meteoric rise of Sir Christopher Hatton in Queen Elizabeth's affections, for instance, can be gauged from the fact that, once on the royal gift list, he never received less than four hundred ounces of plate from the Queen, at a time when the highest in the land never got more than two hundred ounces, and most got fifty.

The Rebellion of the Northern Earls

St Cuthbert's Cathedral, Durham. Durham was the centre of the Northern Rebellion of 1569.

Rebellion was only one element in the political crisis of 1568-70 which centred on the arrival of Mary, Queen of Scots and the plans to marry her to the fourth Duke of Norfolk. The devoutly Catholic party in the North around the Earls of Northumberland and Westmorland opposed the scheme because of Norfolk's Protestant sympathies. But they had not formulated any coherent plans when news came in October 1569 of the crisis in which the Duke of Norfolk gave himself up to the Crown. Norfolk sent a message to Westmorland (his brother-in-law) begging him not to rise, but the earls felt that if they did not act now, the Catholic cause would be lost for ever.

Throughout October the atmosphere grew more tense. The Council in the North, presided over by the third Earl of Sussex, cross-questioned the earls about the unrest. Finally, on 9 November, Northumberland raised his followers in defiance of the Protestant regime. An emotional demonstration, with celebrations of Mass, took place in Durham Cathedral on 14 November. An improvised force moved south to confront Sussex in the York area; Sussex, even less well equipped, was helpless. Yet the rebels failed to press home their advantage. Worried by reports of a royal army moving north, and discouraged by their lack of support, they retreated without even taking York. Although the rebels captured Hartlepool and successfully besieged the loyalist garrison at Barnard Castle, the royal army had linked up with the loyalist forces from Newcastle by the week before Christmas.

The earls fled. Westmorland went into lifelong exile with a number of rebel leaders, but Northumberland was betrayed in Scotland and eventually beheaded in York in 1572.

Norfolk spent much of his last days in the Tower of London constructively, writing long letters of advice to his children. Repeatedly in his letters he emphasized that his family should avoid Roman Catholicism. This was not in fact his last letter, but he can hardly be blamed for thinking that it would be.

Duke of Norfolk to his children   20 January 1572
Tower of London

Dear Children,
This is the last letter that ever I think to write to you, and therefore if you loved me, or that you will seem grateful to me for the special love that I have ever borne unto you, then remember and follow these my last lessons. O Philip, serve and fear God above all things; I find the fault in myself that I have, God forgive me, been too negligent in this point. Love and make much of your wife, and therein, considering the great adversity you are now in by reason of my fall, is your greatest present comfort and relief, besides your happiness in having a wife which is endued with so great towardness in virtue and good qualities and in person comparable with the best sort ...

Show yourself loving and natural to your brothers and sisters and sisters-in-law. Though you be very young in years, yet you must strive with consideration to become a man, for it is your own presence and good government of yourself that must get friends. And if you take that course, then have I been so careful a father unto you, as I have taken such order as you, by God's grace, shall be well able, beside your wife's lands, to maintain yourself like a gentleman ...

I would wish for you the present to make your chief abode at Cambridge, which is the place fittest for you to prosecute your learning in, and besides is not very far hence [from Audley End, near Saffron Walden], whereby you may within a day's warning be here to follow your own causes, as occasion serveth. If after a year or two you spend your time in some house of the law, there is nothing that will prove more to your commodity, considering how for the time you shall have continual business about your own law affairs; and thereby also, if you spend your time well, you shall be ever after better able to judge in your own causes. I too late repent that I followed not this course that now I wish to you, for if I had, then my case perchance had not been in so ill state as now it is ... Beware of high degrees! To a vainglorious proud stomach it seemeth at the first sweet: look into all chronicles and you shall find that in the end it brings heaps of cares, toils in the state, and most commonly in the end utter overthrow ...

and into their state now, and then judge whether my lessons be true or not ... Beware of the Court, except it be to do your prince service, and that as near as you can in the meanest degree; for place hath no certainty, either a man by following thereof hath too much to worldly pomp, which in the end throws him down headlong, or else he lieth there unsatisfied, either that he cannot attain to himself that he would, or else that he cannot do for his friends as his heart desireth.

... If your brothers may be suffered to remain in your company, still I would be most glad thereof, because continuing still together should still increase love between you. But the world is so catching of everything that falls, as I believe Tom being after my death the Queen's majesty's ward, shall be begged by one or another. But yet you are sure to have your brother William left still with you, because (poor boy) he hath nothing to feed cormorants withal, to whom you will as well be a father as a brother; for, upon my blessing, I commit him to your charge, to provide for ...

Lastly, delight to spend some time in reading of the Scriptures, for therein is the whole comfort of man's life; all other things are vain and transitory. And if you be diligent of reading of them they will remain with you continually to your profit and commodity in this world ... And upon my blessing beware of blind papistry, which brings nothing but bondage to men's consciences. Mix your prayers with fasting, not thinking thereby to merit, for there is nothing that we of ourselves can do that is good; we are but unprofitable servants. But fast, I say, thereby to tame the wicked affections of the mind, and trust only to be saved by Christ's precious blood, for without your perfect faith therein there is no salvation ... I write somewhat the more herein, because perchance you may heretofore heard, or perchance may hereafter hear, false bruits that I was a papist. But trust unto it, I never since I knew what religion meant, I thank God, was of other mind than now you shall hear that I die in, although I cry God mercy I have not given fruits and testimony of my faith as I have ought to have done, the which is the thing that I do now chiefliest repent.

... And now, dear and loving children, farewell. God I hope will be your comfort and guide, and I hope ere it be long to be rid out of this wretched world, to follow my dear wives and your mother in the heavenly joys, whither I pray God send me, and you afterwards, when it shall be his will and pleasure to take you out of this vale of misery. Amen ... Written by the hand of your loving father, and father-in-law, now being ready and willing to part out of this world, I hope unto life everlasting,

TN

Law and Landed Estates

Survey of Moulsham, Essex by John Walker (1591). Surveyors, along with lawyers, provided the key techniques for the efficient management of great landed estates. Surveying improved rapidly in the sixteenth century; the law only got more complicated.

Land was the bedrock of aristocratic wealth, and a nobleman must have some acquaintance with the intricacies of Tudor land law if he was to have any grip on his own affairs. After at least four centuries of gradual development away from feudal practice, land law had become so complex that it resembled nothing so much as an abstruse branch of mathematics. The upheaval in the land market caused by the dispersal of Church property was a stimulus to further complication: this was a great age of legal innovation. In order that Tudor landed gentry should not run into disaster through ignorance of these complexities, the Inns of Court in London, took on an extra role as finishing schools for the rich. It was a slightly uncomfortable situation for the Inns, which found themselves with two different sorts of clients: serious students of the law and young gentlemen who had come to gain a smattering of law.

Gentlemen needed to be able to recognize the reality behind the elaborate legal fictions which made possible the conveyancing of land. These had two goals: to circumvent the slowness and inflexibility of early medieval legal procedure, and to safeguard the holding of it from one generation to the next. The feudal system of land tenure had long been in decay, but all its forms remained within the law. And increasingly the benefits of those forms were in the hands of the ultimate feudal lord, the Crown, which was determined to exploit them. The law, therefore, became a war between royal lawyers trying to preserve the Crown's legal rights and family lawyers trying to erect fictional forms of ownership and conveyance which would defeat the Crown's claims.

The law had an ambiguous attitude to the whole battle-ground: lawyers might, after all, be beholden either to their private clients or to their royal masters. Moreover, each court acted as if it was a private corporation responding to market forces, trying by new forms of legal action to attract business from other courts. Even among private clients there would be conflicting interests in developing the law: fathers might want to see forms of conveyance which would tie up their estates away from a spendthrift son or a confiscation caused by political disaster; sons might be seeking ways of raising some quick cash by selling off land apparently in the grip of a trust.

Norfolk's hopes that his family would remain Protestant and apolitical were doomed to disappointment: faith (in the case of his son and heir, Philip, Earl of Arundel) and ambition (in the case of his brother Lord Henry Howard) were too strong. Their resultant difficulties with the Council are chronicled in Sir Henry Neville's breezy letter to his Puritan brother-in-law, Nathaniel Bacon. Some of the gossip is enjoyably and inaccurately scandalous.

Sir Henry Neville to Nathaniel Bacon   19 December 1583
Greenlands

Good brother, after my hearty commendations... For my going to the Scots Queen, it is put off till the spring for that my Lord of Shrewsbury doth request to come up and somewhat sickly; also my lady [the Countess of Shrewsbury, 'Bess of Hardwick'] shows to come up before him for that she would maintain her first complaint against my lord, which is in some part that her husband hath gotten a child by the Scots queen, some say two ... You hear how the Earl of Arundel is commanded to attend and [the Earl of] Northumberland committed to Mr. Leighton [Sir Thomas Leighton], but they will do well enough. I fear their friends will weigh them with gold. My Lady of Arundel very much detected of papistry. My Lord Harry [Henry Howard, later Earl of Northampton] is at Mr. Sadler's, whom I hope will after a while kiss the Tower [of London]. He deserves it well. He prays daily as loud as he can cry, '*Ave Maria, Ave Maria*'. I think to the Scots queen [a play of words for the name Mary] he means there will some more matter fall out - I hope shortly! Thus must I end for this time.
At Greenlands, 19 December,
   Your loving brother Henry Neville

After his formal conversion to Roman Catholicism in 1584 Arundel found it more and more difficult to continue his life at Court, and he determined to flee to France. He gave this letter to his sister, Lady Sackville, to explain his actions to the Queen, but it was never delivered; soon after setting sail for France he was arrested and thrown into prison.

Earl of Arundel to Elizabeth I   11-14 April 1585

As the displeasure of a prince is a heavier burden to bear than the hard conceit [opinion] of a meaner and inferior person, so it is not lawful for any and less convenient for them to settle an opinion of mislike before either there appear either some cause sufficient to procure it, or there be fault committed worthy to deserve it. [There follows a long rehearsal of his career] ... I began to call to remembrance the heavy sentence which had lighted upon those three of my ancestors who immediately went before me. The first being my great-grandfather [third Duke of Norfolk], who was so free from all suspicion of any fault, as because they had no colour of matter to bring him to his answer, they attainted him by Act of Parliament, without ever challenging him to his answer. The second being my grand-father [Henry, Earl of Surrey] was brought to his trial, and condemned for such trifles as amazed the standers by at that time, and it is ridiculous at this time to all that hear the same ... The last being my father, was arraigned according to the law and condemned by his peers. God forbid that I should think that but that his triers did that whereunto their consciences did lead them ... yet all his actions did plainly declare and his greatest enemies must needs confess that he never carried any disloyal mind to your Majesty nor intended any undutiful act to his country ...

The first day of this Parliament when your Majesty with all your nobility was hearing of a sermon in the Collegiate Church of Westminster above in the chancel, I was driven to walk by myself below in one of the aisles. And one day this last Lent when your Majesty was hearing another sermon in the chapel at Greenwich, I was forced to stay all the while in the Presence Chamber ... Wherefore since I saw that it would of necessity be shortly discovered, and withal what a watchful and jealous eye was carried over all those that were known to be recusants [those who refuse (from Latin *recusare* to attend services of the Established Church]; nay, calling to mind how all their lodgings were continually searched, and to how great danger they were subject, if any Jesuit or seminary priest [priests trained abroad in Roman Catholic seminaries] were found within their houses ... I did think it my safest way to depart the realm, and abide in some other place, where I might live without danger to my conscience, without offence to your Majesty, without the servile subjection to mine enemies ...

The result of Arundel's trial in Star Chamber was a £10,000 fine and imprisonment 'during the Queen's pleasure', which would in his case turn out to be for life. Once more Sir Owen Hopton as governor of the Tower of London found himself gaoler to the head of the Howard family; and the Council's worries about Arundel soon forced Hopton to make the earl's imprisonment as rigorous as it could be. Yet Arundel still vigorously protested his loyalty to the Queen. He wrote to his old guardian, Lord Burghley, hoping that he could obtain the toleration offered to certain favoured Catholics, and be freed to serve her as the crisis with Spain reached new heights. However, the Elizabethan regime could ill afford to show weakness when England's premier nobleman refused to renounce Catholicism; two months later, with no result from his pleas, Arundel was setting his sights lower - he simply wanted a less strict imprisonment in the Tower and access to his wife and children.

Earl of Arundel to Lord Burghley   21 July 1587
Tower of London

My special good Lord, I have just cause to think myself very unhappy that after all these miseries which I have endured two years and now almost a half, I can by no means obtain her Majesty's favour to be released of this miserable imprisonment. But as in all my distresses next unto God, your lordship's most fatherly dealing and honourable favour is my greatest comfort, so can I not tell whither to fly for refuge but unto your Lordship, without whose goodness from time to time I know my great miseries would be far greater, and my most wretched estate more wretched (if it may be) than it is at this present. Wherefore I am humbly to beseech your lordship to move her Majesty that I may have the liberty of the Tower and access of my wife and children unto me. Of this suit, my good Lord, I can have no doubt; and therefore am the bolder to trouble your lordship therewith; for I cannot think that her Majesty will deny this unto me, having been long since punished for my fault, and ever a most true and loyal subject unto her, which was never yet denied to those that have been convicted of high treason, after that it pleased her Majesty to extend her favour for the saving of their lives. The liberty of the Tower I desire for avoiding the present and imminent danger of my life. For the access of my wife and children unto me, as I am bound in duty unto God and by the law of nature to desire, so I do assure myself that I shall have this common and ordinary favour allowed, which even by the bond of Christianity I may look to obtain, and which her Majesty or her predecessors have seldom or never denied to any of their poor Christian subjects.

Sermons at Court

The Preaching Place, Whitehall. Bishop Hugh Latimer preaches to the Court; King Edward VI listens from the window of the Council Chamber. Latimer's court sermons did not spare the feelings of his auditors.

From the late Middle Ages divine service had been a feature of many great occasions, and these services invariably had a sermon relating the particular event to the greater schemes of the Almighty. With the Reformation, such sermons naturally took on a more controversial quality. This partisanship helps to explain the fourteenth Earl of Arundel's reluctance to attend the sermons preached before Queen Elizabeth: their content was likely to be heavily political, particularly in the highly charged atmosphere of the 1550s and 1580s.

The Queen herself was not above intervening in sermons if she thought that the message was going in an unpalatable direction. It was folly indeed for Dean Nowell of St Paul's to launch a veiled but unmistakeable attack on the furnishings of her private chapel in a Lenten sermon of 1563: Elizabeth had had enough of clergy lecturing her on these popish survivals, and he had only himself to blame when she noisily interrupted. Similarly, Bishop Rudd of St David's went dreadfully astray in a Lenten sermon of 1596 with some over-elaborate sacred mathematics which seemed to imply that the Queen's death was imminent; he got a humiliating dressing-down from the royal pew as the service ended.

A sign of the increased importance of preaching at Court from the time of Henry VIII's religious revolution was his considerable expenditure on an open-air Preaching-Place within his own Palace of Whitehall. It was a timber construction with a classical loggia surmounted by a balustrade around the open space and a covered pulpit like a tabernacle in the middle; the royal family would watch from the Privy Council Chamber, which opened off the main gallery of the royal apartments directly off the King's Bedchamber. Although designed in imitation of the famous medieval open-air pulpit in the middle of the cloisters of Old St Paul's, it was built in the fashionable Italianate Renaissance style by Robert Trunckey. Situated in the former Privy Garden, the new amenity emphasized how much preaching was to become part of court ceremonial. It was demolished, ironically enough, by Oliver Cromwell's Puritan regime in 1649-50.

Writing to a friend appointed to preach at Court, probably the brilliant preacher Hugh Latimer, Archbishop Cranmer gave some good advice on how to secure the maximum 'laud and praise', which gives us some idea about Henry VIII's preferences. The preacher should stick to expounding Scripture according to its literal sense, without the traditional medieval elaborations of method. He should not get involved in discussing current theological disputes, particularly ones in which he himself had been involved. Even so, the preacher should not be afraid to rebuke moral offence or superstition. In other words, Latimer's evangelical views would be acceptable to the King if expressed with tact. Last, but not least, the sermon should be no longer than 'an hour, or an hour and an half at the most'; otherwise the King and Queen 'shall have small delight to continue throughout with you to the end'.

Arundel's second trial in 1589 was a shambles from the Council's point of view, as they had hoped that it would convincingly discredit him. The result was that, although a guilty verdict was brought in, and the earl condemned to death, the Queen decided not to sign the warrant. Arundel was not told of this; and facing death, feeling that he had nothing more to lose, he made a bold statement of his faith:

Earl of Arundel, declaration   1589

... I here protest before his divine Majesty and all the holy court of Heaven that I have committed no treason and that the Catholic and Roman faith which I hold is the only cause (as far as I can any way imagine) why either I have been thus long imprisoned, or for which I am now ready to be executed. And I do most firmly, resolutely and unmoveably hold and believe this one, Holy, Catholic and Apostolic faith. And as I will die in the same, so am I most ready at all times, if need be, to yield my life for defence thereof. And whatsoever the most sacred Council of Trent hath established touching faith and manners, I believe and hold. And whatsoever it hath condemned, I condemn in my soul, and renounce here under my hand, and abjure from the bottom of my heart ... And thus I will conclude with beseeching almighty God the father of mercies and God of all consolation to grant peace unto his Church, charity and grace to mine enemies, salvation and felicity to the Queen, and realm, and to me as an untimely fruit (being born before my time) and the meanest of all his servants a constant perseverance in his holy faith and the love of his divine Majesty. Amen. By me a most humble and obedient child of the Catholic Roman Church,
    Philip Howard

Arundel's long imprisonment and troubles finally destroyed his health in 1595, and even before the last sudden illness which killed him, he knew that the end could not be far off. He wrote to his wife, seeking forgiveness for his callous neglect of her in his youthful days at Court.

Earl of Arundel to Anne, Countess of Arundel   1595

Mine own good wife, I must now in this world take my last farewell of you, and as I know no person living whom I have so much offended as yourself, so do I account this opportunity of asking you forgiveness, as a singular benefit of Almighty God, and I most humbly and heartily beseech you even for his sake, and of your charity to forgive me all whereinsoever I have offended you, and the assurance thereof is a great contentment to my soul at this present, and will be a greater I doubt not when it is ready to depart out my body; and I call God to witness it is no small grief to me that I cannot make you recompense in this world for the wrongs I have done you; for if it had pleased God to have granted me longer life, I doubt not but you should have found me as good a husband to my poor ability by his grace, as you have found me bad heretofore ...

Despite Arundel's tragedy, the 1590s saw the beginnings of recovery for the Howards: a new presence at Court, and a return to positions of influence for themselves and their dependants, signalled by appearances in various county commissions of the peace. The first straw in the wind came in 1590 when Edward Coke (then a family lawyer and also an ambitious schemer whose energies would gain him high office and legal fame) won them a signal victory against the Crown: he successfully argued that the core of Howard East Anglian estates were exempt from royal forfeiture. However, it was the accession of James I which completed the revolution in the Howards' fortunes.

Lord Henry Howard, with his impeccable nose for political atmospheres, had already sensed that James was the man to follow, and he had spent much time in Elizabeth's last years secretly corresponding with him about the succession to the throne. Now, to his delight, the good times had come; for Howard, they would bring the earldom of Northampton and some years of supreme power in James's counsels. Excitedly he wrote to Sir Thomas Egerton, the Lord Keeper of the Great Seal, after meeting James in his triumphant progress south to claim a new kingdom.

Lord Henry Howard to Sir Thomas Egerton   April 1603

... Your lordship's letter was so judiciously and sweetly written as, although on two sundry times before in private discourse I had performed the part of an honest man, yet I could not forbear to present it to the sacred hand of his Majesty, who not only read it over twice with exceeding delight, witnessed by his own mouth to all in his chambers, but beside commanded me to give you very great thanks for the strong conceit you hold of him, and to let you know that he did hope that longer acquaintance would not make you like him worse, for he was pleased with persons of your parts [talents] and quality ...

This fortnight's experience, to one that converseth so near to the person whom he would most carefully and watchfully observe, may give some light of the person's inclination with whom he doth converse; and therefore I dare confidently assure your lordship upon my soul and without all flattery, that in the days of my life I never met with so sweet a disposition in subject nor sovereign, nor a person that deserved better to be chosen king, though right and nature had not raised him.

I have at this time somewhat in hand, by his Majesty's direction, that concerns his service; wherefore, referring other matters and more large discourse till my fortune shall be to attend your lordship at more leisure, where your eye and observation shall fortify this dutiful conceit, I humbly take my leave, and will ever rest, as I am deeply bound,

Most affectionately and faithfully devoted to do you some service ...

The Man who was the 'Flower of the Age'

SIR PHILIP SIDNEY

When Philip Sidney visited Paris in 1572 King Charles IX made him, as 'Baron of Sidney', a Gentleman of the Chamber, 'considering how great the house of Sidney is in England.' In England, Sidney was a plain esquire and his father a mere knight; so he is a prime example of a man more honoured abroad than at home and more respected by succeeding ages than by his own.

The Sidneys were an old gentle family (going back to the reign of Edward I). But they were brought near to greatness by their connection with two of the great Tudor dynasties: the Brandons and the Dudleys. Yet time after time inopportune deaths - either their own or of monarchs - robbed them of their destiny. They ended the Tudor century, as they had begun it, as gentlemen and knights (though ennoblement came swiftly under the Stuarts).

The foundations of the family fortunes were laid in the fifteenth century when Nicholas Sidney married the aunt of Charles Brandon, the future Duke of Suffolk. The Brandon connection launched the career of Sidney's eldest son, William (d. 1554). On the pretext of studying the language, William Sidney resided, as Suffolk's unofficial agent, at the court of Margaret, Regent of the Netherlands, as her dalliance with Suffolk unravelled; he accompanied Suffolk on his mission to escort the widowed Queen Mary back from France, and rode home with Suffolk's letter submitting himself to Henry VIII's will after the couple's illicit marriage. Once Suffolk and Mary had been publicly married in England, it was again Sidney who was sent to Francis I to beg him to save Mary's honour by continuing to keep her earlier marriage secret. He also fought gallantly in Henry VIII's early wars; was knighted (not by Brandon, but by the future third Duke of Norfolk) in 1512, and about this time became an Esquire of the Body 'with the fee'. As such he was closer to the King than any but the intimate servants of the Privy Chamber. Sir William

Sidney's eldest son, named Henry after his godfather, the King, was born in 1529, and ten years later became one of the royal Henchmen. The Henchmen were boys of good birth who were entrusted to the King to be brought up at Court. As such, they formed the natural companions for Prince Edward. Sir William Sidney's position as the Prince's chamberlain cemented the tie and Henry became one of Edward's intimate friends, notwithstanding a difference of eight years in their ages. With Edward's accession there may have come a period of estrangement under Somerset's regime. But after Somerset's fall, Henry was made one of the Gentlemen of the Privy Chamber in 1550, and promoted to one of the four Chief Gentlemen in 1551. Shortly before, in March 1551, Sidney had married Lady Mary Dudley, oldest daughter of the Duke of Northumberland.

This marriage determined the family's future. Henceforward, they were central to the Dudley affinity, and eventually the Dudley heirs. Two years later, in 1553, Sidney was deeply involved in the attempt to put his sister-in-law Lady Jane Grey on the throne. Queen Mary bore no grudges, however; Sidney became chief intermediary between the Court and his erstwhile patrons, the Dudleys, while King Philip stood as godfather to his oldest son. With Elizabeth I's accession, fortune changed once more. Sidney's brother-in-law, Lord Robert Dudley became the Queen's favourite; and his wife Lady Mary became one of Elizabeth's favourite attendants as a Gentlewoman of the Privy Chamber.

But the expected greatness did not come. Sidney was a natural courtier: polished, well-educated and something of an aesthete. But under Elizabeth all his appointments were on the periphery, in the Welsh marches or in Ireland. As a shrewd administrator, and also as a skilled military commander, he was well suited to these jobs. But it was a question of out of sight, out of mind (if not out of favour). At the end of his first period as Lord Deputy of Ireland he was offered a barony. He was not, however, offered a land grant to support the title. As he felt his own estates insufficient he refused the offer.

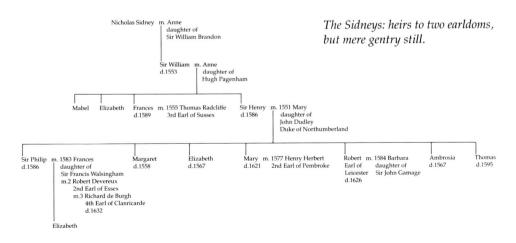

The Sidneys: heirs to two earldoms, but mere gentry still.

The following letter to Sir Francis Walsingham (whose daughter was to marry his son Philip) chronicles Sidney's cheated hopes. The tone is high-rhetorical and sometimes exaggerates. For instance, Lady Sidney certainly emerged from her 'owl's desert' to attend the Court, despite her disfigurement by smallpox.

Sir Henry Sidney to Sir Francis Walsingham   1 March 1583
Ludlow

...since by your letters of the third of January to my great discomfort I find there is no hope of relief of her Majesty for my decayed estate in her Highness's service (for since you gave it over I will never make more means, but say, *Spes et fortuna, valete* [Hope and fortune, farewell]). I am the more careful to keep myself able, by sale of part of that which is left, to ransom me out of the servitude I live in for my debts; for as I know, Sir, that it is the virtue which is, or that you suppose is, in my son that you made choice of him for your daughter, refusing haply far greater and far richer matches than he, so was my confidence great that by your good means I might have obtained some small reasonable suit of her Majesty; and therefore I nothing regard any present gain, for if I had, I might have received a great sum of money for my good will of my son's marriage, greatly to the relief of my private, biting necessity...

As that sweet prince [Edward VI] grew in years and discretion, so grew I in favour and liking of him, in such sort as by that time I was twenty-two years old he made me one of the four Principal Gentlemen of his Bedchamber. While I was present with him he would always be cheerful and pleasant with me, and in my absence gave me such words of praise as far exceeded my desert ... Lastly not only to my own still felt grief but also to the universal woe of England he died in my arms.

...When I went to Newhaven [i.e. Le Havre] I left her [Mary Sidney] a full fair lady, in mine eyes at least the fairest, and when I returned I found her as foul a lady as the smallpox could make her, which she did take by continual attendance of her Majesty's [Queen Elizabeth] most precious person (sick of the same disease), the scars of which (to her resolute discomfort) ever since hath done and doth remain in her face, so as she liveth solitarily *sicut nycticorax in domilicio suo* [like an owl that is in the desert, *Psalm 102: 6*].

...When I came to the Court [on his final return from Ireland] to know how I was entertained, I confess well, but not so well as I thought and in conscience felt I had deserved... Not-withstanding all these painful services I was accounted *servus inutilis* [an unserviceable servant] for that I had exceeded a supposed commission...

The accession of Queen Elizabeth in 1558, with his brother-in-law Sir Robert Dudley a favourite of the new queen, had seemed to augur great things for Sidney. After a three-year stint of service in Ireland he was recalled in 1559 and given the prestigious presidency of the Council in the marches of Wales, which he held until his death in 1586. Twice he combined his work in the marches with the thankless lord deputyship of Ireland. As an affectionate father he determined that his children should not suffer neglect on account of his workload. The solution adopted by him, and by many fathers in similar circumstances, was to send his sons away to boarding school. First to go was Philip, who in 1565, aged eleven, went to the recently established public school at Shrewsbury. His parents remembered their duty in writing to him while away from home, even if their letters were occasionally stuffy.

Sir Henry and Lady Mary Sidney to Philip Sidney   1566

Son Philip,

I have received two letters from you, one written in Latin, the other in French; which I take in good part, and will you to exercise that practice of learning often; for that will stand you in most stead in that profession of life that you are born to live in. And now, since this is my first letter that ever I did write to you, I will not that it be all empty of some advices which my natural care of you provoketh me to wish you to follow, as documents to you in this your tender age.

Let your first action be the lifting up of your mind to the Almighty God by hearty prayer; and feelingly digest the words you speak in prayer…

Apply your study to such hours as your discreet master doth assign you, earnestly; and the time I know he will so limit as shall be both sufficient for your learning and safe for your health. And mark the sense and matter of that you do read, as well as the words; so shall you both enrich your tongue with words and your wit with matter, and judgment will grow as years grow in you.

Be humble and obedient to your masters, for, unless you frame yourself to obey others – yea, and feel in yourself what obedience is, you shall never be able to teach others how to obey you.

Be courteous of gesture and affable to all men, with diversity of reverence according to the dignity of the person. There is nothing that winneth so much with so little cost.

Use moderate diet so as, after your meal, you may find your wit fresher and not duller, and your body more lively and not more heavy. Seldom drink wine, and yet sometimes do, lest, being enforced to drink upon the sudden, you should find yourself enflamed. Use exercise of body, yet such as is without peril to your bones or joints …

From Shrewsbury in 1568 Philip Sidney, aged only thirteen, went to Christ Church, Oxford. While at the University the intellectual promise shown at school came to fruition, and he gathered his first circle of admirers. A long-established friend of the Sidney family, Sir William Cecil, whose academic progress had foreshadowed Sidney's, took a keen interest in the boy. This encouraged Sidney, after consulting the Earl of Leicester, to propose a marriage between Philip and Cecil's daughter Anne, the earl undertaking to provide his nephew with an allowance of £266 13s. 4d. a year. But this matrimonial alliance uniting three of the families dominating the first part of Queen Elizabeth's reign, the Cecils, Dudleys and Sidneys, was not to be. Cecil, with his eye on great things, blew cool; and Sidney, overwhelmed by the affairs of Ireland where he had resumed his post, lost the vital papers.

Sir Henry Sidney to Sir William Cecil   24 February 1570
Dublin

I have such a familiar of penury as I think never none endured as a Prince Deputy. What should I in particular dilate it, when I am forced to borrow, yea almost to beg for my dinner? How then doth my servants, how then my soldiers, but most of all, how doth the poor country, which hath borne all, without receiving any thing, this ten years past? ... With this I am, I thank my good hap, hated of all here. Of the nobility, for deposing their tyranny; of the merchant, for that, by my persuasion, he hath so far trusted the soldiers, as not receiving his money is become bankrupt (and indeed so are some); of the gentleman, for that he cannot get his rent of his tenants, through their keeping of the soldiers. The husbandmen cry out of me, and will do no work, for that they are never paid so long for bearing the soldiers; the soldiers have twice refused to go to the field, for that the horseman is not able to shoe his horse, nor the footman to buy a pair of shoes to his feet; and when I punish one of them for any offence done to the husbandman the rest are ready to mutiny ...

   Now for our particulars, and for our children. I am sorry that you find coldness anywhere in proceedings, where such good liking appeared in the beginning. But, for my part, I never was more ready to perfect that matter, than presently I am: assuring you, for my part, that if I might have the greatest prince's daughter in Christendom for him, the match spoken of between us on my part should not be broken. Articles, I confess, I received, signed (as I remember) by my Lord of Leicester and you, and well allowed by me, but where they be God knoweth ... The paper I cannot find. But this for truth, Sir, I was never more joyous of the match than now I am ...I pray you commend me most heartily to my lady ...

Elizabeth I's Ladies

Monument to Blanche Parry, Chief Gentlewoman of Elizabeth's Privy Chamber, in St Faith's, Bacton, Hereford and Worcester Blanche Parry, who had served Elizabeth since the 1540s, is shown kneeling beside her mistress. There is a second monument to her by the west door of St Margaret's, Westminster, the Court church. On the other side of the doorway is a memorial to her colleague, Lady Dorothy Stafford, who 'served Queen Elizabeth forty years lying in her Bedchamber, esteemed of her'.

As an unmarried queen, Elizabeth I kept about her a body of women to attend on her person and to look after domestic matters, both at the royal palaces and on progresses. There was a central, feed staff attached to the Privy Chamber, including at any one time four Ladies of the Bedchamber, seven or eight Gentlewomen of the Privy Chamber and four Chamberers. The two principal offices were those of Chief Gentlewoman and Mistress of the Robes. There were also six Maids of Honour who, though not formally on the Privy Chamber staff, performed functions within that department. And numerous other ladies of high rank could be drafted in for service when needed, especially on ceremonial occasions.

Elizabeth treated her ladies as an extended family; she expected loyalty and discreet behaviour from them, and took a very close interest in their marital prospects. The most notable upheaval in this regard was when Lady Catherine Grey, a Maid of Honour and a possible successor to the throne, secretly married William Seymour, Earl of Hertford; Elizabeth feared a plot within her own Privy Chamber. Her ladies frequently engaged in liaisons with prominent courtiers which, when discovered, she greeted with fury as an affront to her own honour.

Elizabeth's ladies had little direct influence on political affairs, though their access to the Queen's ear often made them useful intermediaries, particularly on matters of patronage. Their concerns were straightforwardly financial: contemporaries complained bitterly about their greediness in extorting bribes and the resulting system has been described as a 'free market economy of favour'.

As Philip Sidney was destined for a career at Court and in politics, and not in the Church, he left Oxford in 1571 without taking a degree. In 1572 his uncle Leicester got him a licence to visit the Continent 'for his attaining the knowledge of foreign languages', and introduced him 'young and raw' to Francis Walsingham, then English ambassador in France. While in Paris Sidney witnessed the massacre of Huguenots on St Bartholomew's Eve. From France he travelled to Germany where he struck up a lifelong friendship with the Protestant scholar and controversialist, the homosexual Hubert Languet and to 'this harmony of an humble hearer to an excellent teacher' Sidney later attributed all his knowledge. The pair travelled together, and when apart they corresponded prolifically.

Philip Sidney to Hubert Languet   4 February 1574
Padua

For many reasons I was very much gratified by your last letter, which displayed nothing but the affection which so pleases me. I am delighted that you approve of my intention to stop studying astronomy ...

As for Greek, I should wish to absorb only enough to understand Aristotle well; for although several translations appear every day, I still suspect that they do not express the author's ideas distinctly and exactly enough, and besides, I am very much ashamed to "follow only the little brooks, and not to see the very fountainhead," as Cicero says. Of Aristotle's works, I think that one must read his *Politics* in particular. This I say because you advise me to turn my mind to moral philosophy.

Of the German language, my dear Hubert, I quite despair, for it has a certain harshness about it, as you well realize—so much so that at my age I have no hope of ever mastering it, not even to the point of simple understanding. Still, to obey you I shall sometimes practise it with our friend Delius, particularly while I am toasting him.

I readily confess that I am often more melancholy than either my age or my activities call for; but I have fully proved by experience that I am never less liable to moods of melancholy than while I am pitting my weak mental powers against some difficult challenge. But enough of this.

With regard to your ardent request for my portrait, I am happy because this is clear evidence of the affection for me which, to my delight, I have long noticed in you. At the same time I am sad because you hesitate to ask such slight favours of me. For even if our friendship were not true and perfect ... I still have received such favours from you that you can demand much more than this from me as a debt. As soon as I return to Venice I shall have it done either by Paolo Veronese or by Tintoretto, who easily occupy first rank in this art.

While Sidney was at the court of the Emperor Maximilian II at Vienna, tragedy struck his family at Ludlow when on 22 February 1575 his sister Ambrosia died. On hearing the news Philip returned home from the Continent; meanwhile Queen Elizabeth wrote personally to condole with Sir Henry Sidney on the bereavement.

Elizabeth I to Sir Henry Sidney   February 1575

Good Sidney,

   Although we were well assured that by your wisdom and great experience of worldly chances and necessities, nothing can happen with you so heavy, but you can and will bear them as they ought to be rightly taken, and namely such as happen by the special appointment and work of Almighty God, which he hath lately showed by taking unto Him from your company a daughter of yours, yet forasmuch as we conceiving the grief you yet feel thereby (as in such cases natural parents are accustomed) we would not have you ignorant (to ease your sorrow as much as we may) how we take part of your grief upon us; whereof these our letters unto you are witness; And will use no further persuasions to confirm you, respecting the good counsel yourself can take of yourself, but to consider that God doth nothing evil, to whose holy will all is subject and must yield at times to us uncertain. He hath yet left unto you the comfort of one daughter [Mary] of very good hope, whom if you shall think good to remove from these parts of unpleasant air (if it be so) into better in these parts, and will send her unto us before Easter, or when you shall think good, assure yourself that we will have a special care of her, not doubting but as you are well persuaded of our favour toward yourself. So will we make further demonstration thereof in her, if you will send her unto us. And so comforting you for the one, and leaving this our offer of our good will to your own consideration for the other, we commit you to Almighty God.

Sir Henry Sidney's lord deputyship in Ireland brought him into close contact with the first Earl of Essex, from early in 1575 Earl Marshal of Ireland. Another marriage for Philip was soon under discussion with Essex's daughter, Penelope. The difficulty was that both the Devereux and Sidney families were in severely straitened financial circumstances. However, Essex was still hopeful that the monetary impediments would be overcome when he died in September 1576. Essex's executor, Edward Waterhouse, tried to realize the late earl's pipedream. He failed. But later Sidney was to develop a literary romance with Penelope Rich, as she became, that finally acquired a touch of the real thing.

Edward Waterhouse to Sir Henry Sidney   14 November 1576
Chartley

The funerals of the Earl of Essex have been deferred till now that they be appointed to be honourably finished at Carmarthen the 24th of this month. I have forborne to write to your lordship, since my arrival in this realm, because I would give free scope to all men to utter their opinions concerning my behaviour hear in such causes as I had to deal in; and I doubt not, but you have heard enough of it; but, if any reports have come unto your lordship's ears, that in the causes of my Lord of Essex, I have dealt indirectly, I assure your lordship, they have done me wrong; for, as I have justified him and his doings against all the world, without respect of fear, or favour, for have I been free from malicious thoughts, and have quenched all sparks that might kindle any new fire, in these causes, which I hope be buried in oblivion, wherein I stand to the report of Philip Sidney, above any other.

The state of the Earl of Essex being best known to myself, doth require my travail for a time in his causes; but my burden cannot be great, when every man putteth to his helping hand. Her Majesty has bestowed upon the young earl's marriage, and all his father's rule in Wales, and promiseth the remission of his debt. The Lords [i.e. of the Council] do generally favour and further him; some for the trust reposed, some for love to the father, other for affinity with the child, and some for other causes. And all these Lords that wish well to the children, and, I suppose, all the best sort of the English Lords besides, do expect what will become of the treaty between Mr. Philip, and my Lady Penelope. Truly, my Lord, I must say to your lordship, as I have said to my Lord of Leicester, and Mr. Philip, the breaking of from this match, if the default be on your parts, will turn to more dishonour, then can be repair with any other mariage in England. And, I protest unto your lordship, I do not think that there is at this day so strong a man in England of friends, as the little Earl of Essex, nor any man more lamented than his father, since the death of Kind Edward.

The Irish Question

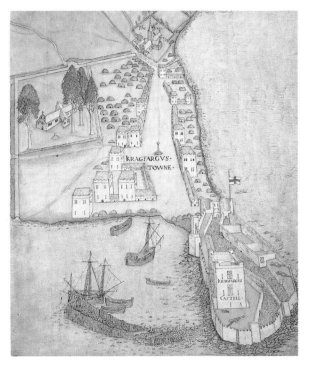

Carrickfergus, Ulster. The drawing, made about 1560, was designed to bring the ruinous state of the fortifications to the government's attention. Sidney restored the castle and planted a garrison there in 1567-8. At the same time he created the country of Carrickfergus by taking in territory from the 'wild Irish'. These territories were the site of the disastrous colonization schemes of the second Earl of Essex.

When Henry VII came to the English throne in 1485 he found that Ireland enjoyed virtual home rule under the great marcher lords. Only the 'obedient English' in the Pale around Dublin were consistently loyal to the Crown. Poyning's Law of 1494-5 notionally made the Irish Parliament subject to the will of the English Council. But this was almost impossible to enforce, and in 1534 Earl 'Silken Thomas' of Kildare and head of the Fitzgeralds renounced allegiance to Henry VIII on the grounds that the King had been excommunicated by the Pope.

An expedition under Sir Thomas Skeffington captured 'Silken Thomas' and five of his uncles, who were hanged at Tyburn in 1537 as an example. In 1541 Parliament declared Henry 'King of this land of Ireland, as united, annexed and knit forever to the imperial crown of the realm of England'. The long-term aim was for all Irish estates to be held or reconfirmed under English law, as was successfully carried through in Wales. To this end Philip and Mary began the policy of 'plantations', to increase the number of English landowners and tenants directly loyal to the Lord Deputy; but these early efforts largely failed.

There were constant uprisings and when they were not fighting the Crown, the lords were often fighting each other. Elizabeth I 'grew weary with reading the Irish despatches' of successive Lord Deputies attempting to impose order. Sir Henry Sidney believed this could only be done by the direct rule of presidencies, with governing councils, on the model of the North and Wales, though this was a costly option. But the settlers never received adequate military protection, and many were driven out.

Hugh O'Neill, Earl of Tyrone, led a well-planned campaign of resistance, with help from the Spanish. This led to open rebellion in 1598, when an English army under Sir Henry Bagnall was massacred. Essex's muddled and vacillating campaign the next year was almost as disastrous. But his sucessor Charles Blount, Lord Mountjoy, wore Tyrone down and finally routed his forces in 1601. James I inherited a pacified Ireland, though one whose basic problems were hardly resolved.

The failure of one matrimonial scheme with a marcher lord (Essex) did not prevent another - and a far greater catch - the second Earl of Pembroke from coming forward with a proposal of marriage to Philip's younger sister, Mary. Despite their disparity in age, the earl being a widower in his forties and Mary an adolescent, the alliance had the sanction of Leicester who was anxious to attach Pembroke more closely to his political circle. With Leicester's support at every turn of the negotiations a marriage settlement was swiftly concluded, and the marriage itself took place on 21 April 1577.

Sir Henry Sidney to Earl of Leicester   4 February 1577
Dundalk

Your lordship's later written letter I received, the same day I did the first, together with one from my Lord of Pembroke to your lordship, by both which I find, to my exceeding great comfort, the likelihood of a marriage between his lordship and my daughter, which great honour to me, my mean lineage and kin, I attribute to my match in your noble house; for which I acknowledge myself bound to honour and serve the same to the uttermost of my power; yea, so joyfully have I at heart that my dear child's so happy an advancement as this is as, in truth, I would lie a year in close prison rather than it should be broke … I am poor; my estate … wants much to make me able to equal that which I know my Lord of Pembroke may have. £2000 I confess I have bequeathed to her, which your lordship knows I might better spare her when I am dead than £1000 when living. And if your lordship will give me leave, that I may feed my eyes with the joyful sight of their coupling I will give her a cup worth £500. Good my Lord, bear with my poverty, for, if I had it, little would I regard any sum of money but willingly would give it, protesting before God Almighty that if he, and all the powers on earth, would give me my choice for a husband for her, I would choose the Earl of Pembroke. I write to my Lord Pembroke, which herewith I send your lordship; and thus I end, in answering your most welcome and honourable letter, with my hearty prayer to Almighty God to perfect your lordship's good work, and requite for you the same; for I am not able … Good my Lord, send Philip to me; there was never father had more need of his son than I have of him. Once again, good my Lord, let me have him.

'Astrophil and Stella'

Philip Sidney's most sustained achievement in verse, *Astrophil and Stella*, remains the greatest enigma of his life. The Petrarchan sequence of 108 sonnets, interspersed with eleven 'songs', explores the vicissitudes of unrequited love in the 'star-lover's' vain pursuit of his 'star', and was advertised by Thomas Nashe, who in 1591 issued an edition without the consent of Sidney's widow, as a moral fiction showing 'the tragicomedy of love ... the argument cruel chastity, the prologue hope, the epilogue despair'. But the work is not total fiction. Astrophil ('Astrophel' in many early texts, perhaps to minimize the identification) is in part Philip himself - he mentions his father's campaigns in Ulster (sonnet 30), his own prowess at jousting (sonnet 41) and the stars on his armour (sonnet 104). Equally clearly, continual punning on the word 'rich' (sonnets 24, 35 and 37) identifies 'Stella' as Penelope Devereux, sister of the Earl of Essex and, after November 1581, wife of Lord Rich. Sidney may have met Penelope at the Devereux castle of Chartley in 1575 when the Queen travelled there after the Earl of Leicester's lavsih entertainments at Kenilworth, but she would only have been thirteen to his twenty-one. The following year her father expressed a deathbed wish that the two of them should marry, but nothing came of it, perhaps because her father died so heavily in debt that her chances of receiving her marriage-portion were slight. Her mother, however, promptly married Leicester, and Sidney and Penelope may then have seen something of each other at Leicester House when in London.

But in the poems Astrophil bewails the fact that he had no interest in Stella before marriage made her unattainable. Yet, as Sidney lay dying, he allegedly said: 'There came to my remembrance a vanity wherein I had taken delight, whereof I had not rid myself. It was my Lady Rich. But I rid myself of it, and presently my joy and comfort returned.' The fact that this passage was omitted from many early manuscripts suggests that contemporaries found the idea of even a would-be adulterous Sidney as difficult to square with the saintly image as later generations have done.

More importantly, it should be remembered that the conventions of Petrarchan love poetry (frustrated male, unattainable but provocatively attractive female) had such currency throughout the Renaissance because they mirrored the relationship between a courtier seeking advancement and the patron/monarch who might or might not grant his wish - all the more so when that monarch was female. Sidney's frustrations were political as much as sexual. The real in-joke for the original readers of these poems, as they circulated in manuscript, may have been that they transposed his situation at Court to a fictionalized relationship with an attractive and intelligent member of the Leicester/Essex circle.

The actual quality of the verse is various. Its importance lies in its quantity - no one had written so many sonnets in English before - and in the allusions to the enigmatic Stella. For these, following from Surrey's equally enigmatic 'Geraldine' poems, created a fashion for the sonnet-sequence charting the uncertain course of love.

Come, Sleep; O Sleep! the certain knot of peace.
The baiting-place of wit, the balm of woe,
The poor man's wealth, the prisoner's release,
Th' indifferent judge between the high and low;
With shield of proof shield me from out the prease
Of those fierce darts Despair at me doth throw;
Omake in me those civil wars to cease;
I will good tribute pay, if thou do so.
Take thou of me smooth pillows, sweetest bed,
A Chamber deaf to noise and blind of light,
A rosy garland and a weary head;
And if these things, as being thine by right,
Move not thy heavy grace, thou shalt in me,
Livelier than elsewhere, Stella's image see.

Sonnet 39

Overleaf: Isaac Oliver's 'Allegory of Virtue Confronting Vice' belongs to the same world of courtly love as Sir Philip Sidney's 'Astrophil and Stella', although the mood is coarser. Oliver equates scenes of the chase in the background (hawking, the boar-hunt and duck-shooting) with the pursuit of sexual pleasure in the foreground. There is also the parallel commonplace of withdrawal from the city (left distance) to the country. But the commonplace is stood on its head as the country is the scene of Vice, where Virtue (left foreground) is embodied in a city lady.

Although his outstanding talent was universally recognised, and notwithstanding his many connections, Sidney's career in the service of the Queen was slow to take off - at least according to his own exalted opinion of his merits. Waiting in the wings, while his uncle Leicester and others hogged the limelight, did not appeal to Sidney. His lack of advancement frustrated and embittered him. There were good reasons for withholding promotion from him, for he had several decidedly unpleasant characteristics. One of these traits was a violent rage which he did little to try to curb. The following letter shows the tone of imperious bullying that he adopted with an inferior, his father's secretary, whom he accused of leaking Philip's letters.

Philip Sidney to Edward Molyneux   31 May 1578
The Court

Mr. Molyneux,
 Few words are best. My letters to my father have come to the eyes of some. Neither can I condemn any but you for it. If it be so, you have played the very knave with me; and so I will make you know, if I have good proof of it. But that for so much as is past. For that is to come, I assure you before God, that if ever I know you do so much as read any letter I write to my father, without his commandment or my consent, I will thrust my dagger into you.

Another was inordinate pride in his Dudley ancestry and the fact that he was a 'duke's daughter's son'.

Sir Philip Sidney's 'Defence of the Earl of Leicester'   1585

I am a Dudley in blood, that duke's daughter's son, and do acknowledge though in all truth I may justly affirm that I am by my father's side of ancient and always well esteemed and well-matched gentry, yet I do acknowledge I say that my chiefest honour is to be a Dudley and truly am glad to have cause to set forth the nobility of that blood whereof I am descended… [He sets out family connections with many of the great old noble houses]… Many other houses might herein be mentioned but I name these because England can boast of no nobler …

Sidney had already remonstrated with the Queen to her face about her determination to marry the Duke of Anjou. He drafted the following letter to Elizabeth to drive home his point in language which went to the very limit of what a subject could decently use to his sovereign. It may only have been an exercise in getting things off his chest; it is quite unclear whether it was actually sent.

Philip Sidney to Elizabeth I   c. 1580

Most feared and beloved, most sweet and gracious Sovereign; to seek out excuses of this my boldness, and to arm the acknowledging of a fault with reasons for it, might better show I knew I did amiss, than any whit diminish the attempt; especially in your judgement, who is able lively to discern into the nature of the thing done …because my words, I confess shallow, but coming from the deep wellspring of most loyal affection, have already delivered to your gracious ears what is the general sum of my travelling thoughts therein, I will now but only declare what be the reasons that make me think the marriage of Monsieur to be unprofitable for you. Then will I answer the objections of those fears which might procure so violent a refuge … As for this man, as long as he is but Monsieur [heir-presumptive to France] in might and a papist in profession, he neither can nor will greatly stead you. And if he grow king, his defence will be like Ajax's shield, which weighed down rather than defended those that bore it.

   Against any contempt at home, if there by any, which I will never believe, let your excellent virtues of piety, justice and liberality daily, if it be possible, more and more shine. Let some such particular actions be found out (which is easy, as I think to be done) by which you may gratify all the hearts of your people. Let those in whom you find trust, and to whom you have committed trust in your weighty affairs, be held up in the eyes of your subjects. Lastly, doing as you do, you shall be as you be: the example of princes, the ornament of this age, the comfort of the afflicted, the delight of your people, the most excellent fruit of all your progenitors, and the perfect mirror to your posterity.

Altogether, these were difficult years for Sidney. The Queen's displeasure on hearing of his uncle Leicester's marriage had been extended to him. Sidney had also had a violent altercation with the seventeenth Earl of Oxford when in September 1579 the earl, uninvited, had joined him in a game of tennis at Whitehall.

Sir Fulke Greville, *Life of Sir Philip Sidney*   Early 17th century

Being one day at tennis, a peer of this realm, born great, greater by alliance, and superlative in the prince's favour, abruptly came into the tennis-court, and speaking out of these three paramount authorities, he forgot to entreat that which he could not legally command … at last with rage (which is ever ill-disciplined) he commands them to depart the Court. To this Sir Philip temperately answers that if his lordship had been pleased to express desire in milder characters, perchance he might have led out those that he should now find would not be driven out with any scourge of fury. This answer (like a bellows) blowing up the sparks of excess already kindled, made my lord scornfully call Sir Philip by the name of puppy … The French commissioners unfortunately had that day audience in those private galleries whose windows looked into the tennis-court.
They instantly drew all to this tumult, every sort of quarrels sorting well with their humours especially this. Which Sir Philip perceiving, and rising with inward strength by the prospect of a mighty faction against him, asked my lord with a loud voice that which he heard clearly enough before. Who (like an echo that still multiplies by reflections) repeated this epithet of puppy the second time. Sir Philip … gave my lord a lie, impossible (as he averred to be retorted) in respect all the world knows puppies are gotten by dogs and children by men.

… They both stood silent a while like a dumb show in a tragedy, till Sir Philip, sensible of his own wrong, the foreign and factious spirits that attended, and yet even in this question between him and his superior, tender to his country's honour, with some words of sharp accent led the way abruptly out of the tennis-court, as if so unexpected an accident were not fit to be decided any farther in that place. Whereof the great lord making another sense continues his play without any advantage of reputation as by the standard of humours in those times it was conceived.

… This stirred a resolution in his lordship to send Sir Philip a challenge. Notwithstanding, these thoughts in the great lord wandered so long between glory, anger and inequality of state as the Lords of her Majesty's Council took notice of the differences, commanded peace, and laboured a reconciliation between them.

Honour: Quarrels and Duels

Zuccharo's sketch of the Earl of Leicester presents the traditional 'man of honour'.

Sir Thomas Elyot wrote that honour was subordinated to the crown.

Honour was initially the code of behaviour of a military caste established by blood and lineage. It centred on the public esteem given to the virtues of the warrior, listed in the popular *Boke of St Albans* (1486) as fortitude, prudence, wisdom, hope and steadfastness - qualities that a campaigner should cultivate - while in peacetime courtliness and justice were the only additional necessary attributes.

Such virtues might be acquired by someone not gently born, but normally they were expected to be proper marks of a sound lineage, and the code was always most strongly invoked in relation to the good name of the family or clan. Honour bound a man to his liege lord in a way that often took precedence over his loyalty to the monarch; its language underpinned most of the significant rebellions of the century, including the Pilgrimage of Grace, the Northern Rising and the Essex Rebellion.

Henry VIII and his successors tried to make the Crown the sole fount of honour and brought the heralds under royal commission. Their visitations of the shires to check for irregularities were clear indications of a state-centred system, the more so after 1555 when they were formally subordinated to

the Earl Marshal. The royal will was assisted by Sir Thomas Elyot's unsophisticated but influential *The Boke named The Governor* (1531), which recast the honour code in terms of the popular humanism of the day. It promoted the idea of an educated magistracy enforcing the law in local communities, recognizing that the only true allegiance was that of a subject to his sovereign, and through his sovereign to God. He proposed a virtue of wisdom and understanding, as much at war with vice and error as with the country's enemies - ideas which the new grammar school education and the Protestant ethic reinforced.

Sir Philip Sidney instinctively inclined to the old family-based code, but his education and the advice of men like Languet led him to a refined version of what Elyot proposed. *Arcadia* charts for its aristocratic heroes a course beyond military glory, through earthly to divine love, and so to patience and magnanimity, ideal qualities for a newly Protestant governing class. Falstaff's 'catechism' - 'What is honour? A word ... Who hath it? He that died o'Wednesday' (*Henry IV, Part I*, Act 5, Scene 1) - gives voice to a timeless cynicism, but it also sounds the death knell of the whole honour culture.

Sidney's sense of alienation from the Court was as much self-induced as the result of loss of favour. He sought silence in the approved fashion by withdrawing from the Court to the country. During early 1580 he lived in Wiltshire, either at or near his sister Mary, Countess of Pembroke's home at Wilton. He put his time to good use by completing the first version of the *Arcadia*, now known as the *Old Arcadia*. The long prose romance in five books is a stylized embodiment of courtly *mores*. Although originally meant only to entertain his sister and a circle of friends, his sister brought out a version completed with material from the *Old Arcadia* in 1593. This was for two hundred years the most popular work of fiction in the English language.

Philip Sidney, *Arcadia*, dedicatory epistle   c. 1580
to the Countess of Pembroke

To my dear lady and sister, the Countess of Pembroke.
   Here now have you (most dear, and most worthy to be most dear lady) this idle work of mine: which I fear (like the spider's web) will be thought fitter to be swept away, than worn to any other purpose. For my part, in very truth (as the cruel fathers among the Greeks were wont to do to the babes they would not foster) I could well find in my heart to cast out in some desert of forgetfulness this child, which I am loath to father. But you desired me to do it, and your desire to my heart is an absolute commandment. Now it is done, only for you, only to you: if you keep it to yourself, or to such friends who will weigh errors in the balance of good will, I hope, for the father's sake, it will be pardoned, perchance made much of, though in itself it have deformities. For indeed, for severer eyes it is not, being but a trifle, and that triflingly handled. Your dear self can best witness the manner, being done in loose sheets of paper, most of it in your presence, the rest, by sheets, sent unto you as fast as they were done. In sum, a young head, not so well stayed [governed] as I would it were (and shall be when God will), having many fancies begotten in it, if it had not been in some way delivered, would have grown a monster, and more sorry might I be that they came in, than that they got out. But his chief safety shall be the not walking abroad; and his chief protection, the bearing the livery of your name; which (if much good will do not deceive me) is worthy to be a sanctuary for a greater offender. This say I, because I know the virtue so; and this say I, because it may be ever so; or, to say better, because it will be ever so. Read it then at your idle times, and the follies your good judgement will find in it, blame not but laugh at. And so ... you will continue to love the writer, who doth exceedingly love you; and most heartily prays you may long live, to be a principal ornament to the family of the Sidneys.

Sidney was careful, however, not to alienate himself totally from the Court. The following letter to Leicester shows him deploying on his own behalf the sort of tactical strategy that he so deplored in the conduct of England's foreign policy.

Philip Sidney to Earl of Leicester   2 August 1580

Right honourable and singular good Lord. I have now brought home my sister, who is well amended both of her pain and disease. For myself, I assure your lordship upon my troth, so full of the cold as one cannot hear me speak: which is the cause keeps me yet from the Court, since my only service is speech and that is stopped. As soon as I have gotten any voice I will wait on your lordship, if so it please you, although it be contrary to that I have signified to her Majesty of my want. I doubt not her Majesty will vouchsafe to ask for me, but so long as she sees a silk doublet upon me, her Highness will think me in good case. At my departure I desired Mr. Vice-Chamberlain [Sir Christopher Hatton] he would tell her Majesty necessity did even banish me from the place. And, always submitting myself to your judgement and commandment, I think my best, either constantly to wait [i.e. be in attendance] or constantly to hold the course of my poverty, for coming and going neither breeds desert nor witnesseth necessity. Yet if it so please your lordship, I hope 3 or 4 days this cold will be past, for now truly I were a very unpleasant company keeper. My lord [Pembroke] and my sister do humbly salute you, and I remain to do your commandment as far as my life shall enable me. God preserve your Lordship in all happiness. At Clarendon this 2nd of August 1580.

Your lordship's most humble and most obedient
Philip Sidney

Wilton and 'Arcadia'

Sir Philip Sidney, with gorget (neck armour) and sword, as the soldier and man of action. But at Wilton, the country house of his sister Mary, Countess of Pembroke, Sidney became the author of Arcadia, a prose romance of retreat from worldly affairs. Where conventions stop and real feelings begin is hard to say.

Like Penshurst, Wilton has acquired an almost legendary status because of its link with the Sidneys. John Aubrey compared it to 'an Arcadian place and a paradise', noting that under the Countess of Pembroke it was 'like a college, there were so many learned and ingenious persons. She was the greatest patroness of wit and learning of any lady in her time'. When Philip Sidney retired there in the spring of 1580, however, it had no such associations.

Philip Sidney probably completed the *Old Arcadia* for Mary in the weeks before and after her confinement. But this brotherly gesture was in its way a reaction to family and political tensions, which Wilton symbolized as much as it offered refuge from them. Philisides in the book, a melancholy shepherd, is not a literal self-portrait, but his world-weariness certainly reflects Sidney's personal and political frustrations.

Sidney's death gave him the status of a Protestant martyr and his sister cultivated the role of keeper of the shrine, authorizing the reputable printer William Ponsonby to publish most of his writings during the 1590s to forestall inferior pirated versions. In this context both the Sidneys, brother and sister, gained reputations as generous and discerning patrons of the arts; which was somewhat out of proportion to the facts. The death of all the senior Dudleys and Sidneys between 1586 and 1590 ended, at least for a generation, Wilton's reputation as a court-away-from-court; later that golden reputation grew along with that of Sir Philip Sidney. But, for most discerning contemporary readers, *Arcadia* was a work of political disenchantment as much as the 'vain amatorious poem' that Milton judged it to be. Equally, we must be careful of taking its nostalgia too literally - either as a comment on past aristocratic glories or on present degradation. For nostalgia depends on exaggerating both.

The Education of Men

According to John Aubrey, the 'mad fighting young fellow' William Herbert who became first Earl of Pembroke could neither read nor write (though documents do exist with his name inscribed in capitals). But his namesake and grandson, the third Earl, was himself a poet and a reader able, said Ben Jonson, to 'countenance a legitimate poem'. William Shakespeare's father could not sign his own name. On the other hand, John Tiptoft, the fifteenth-century butcher Earl of Worcester, had studied at Padua as well as Oxford; while Sir John Fastolf's secretary, William Worcester, quoted Cicero in arguing for the resumption of the Hundred Years' War.

So talk of an 'educational revolution' in the sixteenth century goes too far. What happens instead is that a high-level education becomes the norm. Sir Philip Sidney's experience is typical (though his talent was not). He went to Shrewsbury School followed by Christ Church, Oxford. The curriculum at the former centred on Livy, Caesar, Sallust, Cicero, Socrates and Xenophon, all of whom had been politicians as well as authors. The statutes also provided for readings in Vives, Virgil, Ovid and Terence, but even here (as in the rule that first-form scholars 'declaim and play one act of a comedy' every Thursday) the emphasis was on acquiring the skills necessary for subtle or forceful self-expression, not on literary appreciation for its own sake. Sidney was also bought books on French grammar, Calvin's catechism (the Puritanism of the headmaster, Thomas Ashton, weighed in Sidney's father's choice of the school) and on the writing of secretary hand.

Oxford's medieval reputation as the home of the humanistic movement was eclipsed early in the century by Cambridge's pre-eminence as a centre of Greek scholarship, but both universities declined markedly during the Reformation, reaching a low ebb by mid-century, when Oxford had barely a thousand students. This rose to seventeen hundred by Sidney's time and exceeded two thousand in the 1590s, when Lord Herbert was there.

The curriculum was divided into the trivium of grammar, rhetoric and logic, and the quadrivium of mathematical sciences (arithmetic, geometry, astronomy and music). The emphasis was on the former, and students were prepared for their formal testing in university and college 'disputations' or public debates. Richard Carew recalled that in 1569: 'Being a scholar in Oxford of fourteen years age and three years standing ... I was there called to dispute extempore (*impar congressus Achilli* [an unequal encounter with Achilles]) with the matchless Sir Philip Sidney in presence of the Earls Leicester, Warwick and divers other great personages'.

So the Dudleys observed the chief fruits of the education of their potential heir: the skills of language (especially Latin, the international language), argument and self-presentation befitting a courtier, diplomat and administrator. Sidney himself stressed to his brother Robert that learning was a practical preparation for their station in life: 'So you can speak and write Latin, not barbarously, I never require great study in Ciceronianism, the chief abuse of Oxford' and he put the horsemanship and weapons training of a soldier on a par with intellectual attainments. Less grandly, Shakespeare's Justice Silence bears the cost of having a son at Oxford and expects him soon to go to one of the Inns of Court (*Henry IV, Part II*, Act 3, Scene 2), the law schools in London where many of the gentry rounded off their preparation for public affairs and the administration of their estates. By the end of the century this was an established pattern of education for members of the ruling class at all levels.

A woodcut of Christ Church, Oxford, where Sir Philip Sidney was a student from 1568 to 1571.

223

By the autumn of 1580 Sidney was back in London and once more at Court. He was living at Leicester House and clearly assisting his uncle in the conduct of business. He found time to write to his brother Robert, now embarked in turn on continental travel. His emphasis on horsemanship and sword-fighting (he despised mere fencing as effeminism) is a forceful corrective to the picture of Sidney as an aristocratic intellectual.

Philip Sidney to Robert Sidney   18 October 1580
Leicester House, Temple Bar

My dear brother: For the money you have received, assure yourself, for it is true, there is nothing I spend so pleaseth me as that which is not for you. If ever I have ability, you will find it; if not, yet shall not any brother living be better beloved than you of me… For your countenance, I would for no cause have it diminished in Germany; in Italy your greatest expense must be upon worthy men and not upon householding. Look to your diet (sweet Robin) and hold up your heart in courage and virtue; truly, great part of my comfort is in you ... take a delight to keep and increase your music; you will not believe what a want I find of it in my melancholy times. At horsemanship when you exercise it, read Crison Claudio and a book that is called *La Gloria de l'Cavallo* withal, that you may join the thorough contemplation of it with the exercise, and so shall you profit more in a month than others in a year, and mark the bitting, saddling and curing of horses. I would, by the way, your worship would learn a better hand: you write worse than I, and I write evil enough. Once again have a care of your diet and consequently of your complexion; remember *Gratior est veniens in pulchro corpore Virtus* [Virtue is more pleasing coming in a handsome body]. Now, sir, for news I refer myself to this bearer; he can tell you how idle we look on our neighbours' fires, and nothing is happened notable at home save only Drake's return, of which yet I know not the secret points, but about the world he hath been, and rich he is returned. Portugal, we say, is lost [annexed by Spain] and, to conclude, my eyes are almost closed up, overwatched with tedious business. God bless you, sweet boy … When you play at weapons, I would have you get thick caps and bracers, and play out your play lustily, for indeed ticks and dalliances are nothing in earnest, for the time of the other and the other greatly differs; and use as well the blow as the thrust: is good in itself, and besides exerciseth your breath and strength, and will make you a strong man at the tourney and barriers. First in any case practise the single sword, and then with the dagger; let no day pass without an hour or two such exercise; the rest study, or confer diligently, and so shall you come home my comfort and credit. Lord, how I have babbled!

Never, of course, had the Queen been anything like as ungrateful as Sidney claimed in his more posturing moments. He had been a Cupbearer since 1576; become a Member of Parliament in 1581; escorted the Duke of Anjou out of England in 1582 (a congenial task); he was knighted early in 1583, and made joint Master of the Ordnance with his uncle the Earl of Warwick in 1585. With these prospects opening up before him, in September 1583 he married Frances, daughter of Secretary Walsingham. However, this marriage did not at first have the Queen's blessing. Elizabeth did not much like marriages, particularly in her inner circle (the Walsinghams were Boleyn cousins). She might also have seen it as an alliance strengthening a group on the Privy Council anxious for England to intervene militarily on the Continent.

Sir Henry Sidney to Sir Francis Walsingham   1 March 1583
Ludlow

I have understood of late that coldness is thought in me in proceeding in the matter of marriage of our children. In truth, Sir, it is not so, nor so shall it ever be found; for compremitting the consideration of the articles to the earls named by you, and to the Earl of Huntingdon, I most willingly agree, and protest, and joy in the alliance with all my heart. But since, by your letters of the 3rd of January, to my great discomfort I find there is no hope of relief of her Majesty for my decayed estate in her Highness' service. I am the more careful to keep myself able, by sale of part of that which is left, to ransom me out of the servitude I live in for my debts; for as I know, sir, that it is the virtue which is, or that you suppose is, in my son, that you made choice of him for your daughter, refusing haply far greater and far richer matches than he, so was my confidence great that by your good means I might have obtained some small reasonable suit of her Majesty; and therefore I nothing regarded any present gain, for if I had, I might have received a great sum of money for my good will of my son's marriage, greatly to the relief of my private biting necessity …

Three times her Majesty hath sent me her Deputy into Ireland, and in every of the three times I sustained a great and a violent rebellion, every one of which I subdued … I returned from each of these three deputations £300 worse than I went …

Truly, Sir, by all these I neither won nor saved; but now, by your patience, once again to my great and high office - for great it is in that in some sort I govern the third part of this realm …

For, alas, Sir! how can I, not having one groat of pension belonging to the office? I have not so much ground as will feed a mutton. I sell no justice … I trust you do not hear of any order taken by me ever reversed, nor my name or doings in any court ever brought in question …

The Sidneys, the Herberts and the New World

Sir Philip Sidney's interest in the New World took several forms. As early as 1576 he invested in an expedition led by Martin Frobisher, and did so again in the following two years. In 1577 he was convinced that Frobisher had found gold, and his continental adviser, Hubert Languet, was concerned that he was being distracted from his central role in the religious politics of Europe. In fact, he saw the two as complementary, for he shared the view, widely held in Protestant England, that the way to defeat Spain was to attack the colonies in America, which were believed to be the source of Spain's enormous wealth.

In fact Frobisher's ore proved worthless, and Sidney became disillusioned about the economic prospects. But his close association with the occult magician, Dr John Dee, suggests another dimension; Dee mixed a practical interest in maps and navigation with mystical notions of England as mistress of a religiously inspired northern empire in the Americas, and wrote a vast Latin work on the conversion of its people to Christianity. These notions were not simply an extension of antagonisms between Protestant and Catholic, but looked to a time when such divisions might be transcended and Christendom reunited.

It was partly in this spirit that Sidney became involved, in 1582-3, in Sir Humphrey Gilbert's plans for an American colony. The project involved men with Catholic sympathies, who looked to the New World as a place to pursue their faith without being disloyal to England. Members of the Council, including Walsingham, apparently backed the scheme; Sidney was certainly engaged in negotiations and actually sold a patent of his own for New World colonization to a Catholic sympathiser, Sir George Peckham. Then, in 1585 Sidney nearly joined Sir Francis Drake's West Indies voyage. But this was largely out of frustration at the Queen's initial refusal of Leicester's request, following English intervention in the Netherlands, to appoint Sidney as the Governor of Flushing.

A generation later Sidney's brother Robert and his Herbert nephews, the Earls of Pembroke and of Montgomery, were conspicuously prominent in efforts to open up the New World to the advantage of England. Sir Robert Sidney subscribed to the second Virginia charter in 1606, and he and Pembroke became members of the council of the Virginia Company in 1609.

Montgomery joined them three years later, when all three of them became 'incorporators' in the North-West Passage Company. Pembroke was a member of the Bahamas Company, the Herberts were 'incorporators' in the Guiana Company of South America, and both acquired interests in the West Indies. Clearly the anti-Spanish motive was primary, but running through all these dealings was a sense of Protestant England and her increasingly prominent place in the world.

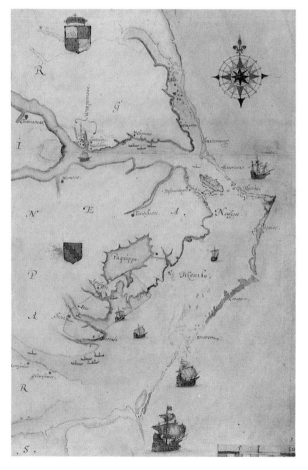

A map of Virginia showing the island colony of Roanoake. The map was drawn by a member of the expedition, John White, who later became governor of the colony.

Sidney's vision extended far beyond Europe, however. A contemporary of Sidney's at Christ Church had been Richard Hakluyt, who in 1582 dedicated to him the first edition of *Divers Voyages touching the Discovery of America*. Sidney epitomized the excitement caused by English explorers. As early as 1575 he had invested in Martin Frobisher's quest for the North-West Passage, and during 1584–5 he supported Sir Walter Ralegh's plan to colonize Virginia. Indeed he found himself torn between joining the expedition (commanded by Sir Francis Drake) and taking part in England's intervention in the Netherlands. But when Elizabeth (at Leicester's insistence) offered him the governorship of Flushing, he chose the Netherlands. Nevertheless, knowing of Sidney's interest and help in the Roanoke venture, the first Governor of Virginia wrote to him advocating further attacks upon the Spanish and describing the setting up of the colony.

Ralph Lane to Philip Sidney   [17] August 1585
[Roanoke, Virginia]

My most noble General; Albeit in the midst of infinite business, as having, amongst savages, the charge of wild me of mine own nation…
nevertheless I would not omit to write these few lines of duty and affection unto you … If her Majesty at any time find herself burthened with the King of Spain, we have by our dwelling upon the island of St John and Hispaniola for the space of five weeks so discovered the forces thereof, with the infinite riches of the same, as that I find it an attempt most honourable, feasible and profitable, and only fit for yourself to be chief commander in … To conclude: finding by mine own view his forces at land to be so mean, and his terror made too great amongst us in England, considering that the reputation thereof doth altogether grow from the mines of his treasure, and the same in places which we see here are so easy both to be taken and kept by any small force sent by her Majesty, I could not but write these ill-fashioned lines unto you, and to exhort you, my noble general, by occasion not to refuse the good opportunity of such service to the Church of Christ, of great relief from many calamities that this treasure in Spaniards' hands doth inflict unto the members thereof, very honourable and profitable for her Majesty and our country, and most commendable and fit for yourself to be the enterpriser of.

Sidney soon justified the Queen and Leicester's confidence in making him Governor of Flushing. He put heart back into the dispirited troops under his command, and soon he was taking a lead in the offensive against the Spanish. In September 1586 Leicester decided to follow up his recent military good fortune by intercepting a convoy supplying Zutphen. In the attack Sidney's horse was killed, and he was hit by a musketshot in the left thigh. Clearly shaken by the event, Leicester made his report back to England.

Earl of Leicester to Sir Thomas Heneage   [23] September 1586
Zutphen

Albeit I must say it was too much loss for me [referring to the small losses in the battle], for this young man he was my greatest comfort, next her Majesty, of all the world, and if I could buy his life with all I have to my shirt I would give it. How God will dispose of him I know not, but fear I must needs, greatly, the worse; the blow is in so dangerous a place and so great; yet did I never hear of any man that did abide the dressing and setting his bones better than he did. And he was carried afterwards in my barge to Arnhem, and I hear this day he is still of good heart and comforteth all about him as much as any may be. God of His mercy grant me his life, which I cannot but doubt of greatly. I was abroad that time in the field giving some order to supply that business which did endure almost two hours in continual fight, and meeting Philip coming upon his horseback not a little to my grief. But I would you had stood by to hear his most loyal speeches to her Majesty, his constant mind to the cause, his loving care over me, and his most resolute determination for death, not one jot appalled for his blow, which is the most grievous that ever I saw with such a bullet; riding so a long mile and a half upon his horse ere he came to the camp; not ceasing to speak still of her Majesty; being glad if his hurt and death might any way honour her Majesty. For hers he was whilst he lived and God's he was sure to be if he died; prayed all men to think that the cause was as well her Majesty's as the [Low] Countries' [Netherlands'], and not to be discouraged, for you have seen such success as may encourage us all, and this my hurt is the ordinance of God by the hap of the war. Well, I pray God, if it be His will, save me his life, even as well for her Majesty's service's sake as for mine own comfort.

After an unsuccessful operation to remove the shot and with the onset of gangrene Sidney died on the following 17 October. Sidney's embalmed body was transported back to London with full honours, and on 16 February 1587 he was buried in Old St Paul's in a funeral service of unprecedented splendour for a person of his rank. This funeral was as much a memorial service to a national hero as a political statement by Leicester, Walsingham and their adherents, and it was the ancestor to modern state funerals.

Funeral of Sir Philip Sidney   16 February 1587

His burial was ordered by Robert Cook, Clarencieux King of Arms:
first proceeded 32 poor men in black gowns, according to his age;
then Serjeants of the Band, fife and drum, ensigns trailed; Lieutenant of
Foot, Corporals, trumpets, guidon [i.e. standard] trailed; Lieutenant of his
Horse, conductors to his servants; the standard borne by a gentleman;
his gentlemen, and yeoman servants, 60; physicians and surgeons, steward
of his house, esquires, of his kindred and friends, 60; knights of his kindred
and friends, 12; preacher and chaplains; the pennon [i.e. flag] of his arms
borne; the horse for the field, led by a footman; a page riding with a
broken lance; a barbed horse led by a footman; a page on horseback
carrying a battle-axe, the head downward; yeomen-ushers to the Heralds;
the great banner borne by a gentleman; Portcullis bearing the gilt spurs;
Bluemantle the gauntlets; Rouge Dragon the helmet and crest; Richmond
the shield of arms; Somerset the coat of arms ... the corpse covered with a
velvet pall, carried by 14 yeomen; 2 bannerols [banners] following;
Sir Robert Sidney, chief mourner; mourners assistants; 4 knights;
two gentlemen-ushers to the noblemen ...
  So general was the lamentation for him, that, for many months after,
it was accounted indecent for any gentleman of quality, to appear at Court
or City, in any light or gaudy apparel.

The deaths of Sir Henry Sidney and Sir Philip in 1586 left Sir Philip's younger brother Robert heir of the Sidney family. The deaths of his uncles Leicester in 1588 and Warwick in 1589 effectively made him head of the Dudley interest as well. Although lacking the political acumen of his father and the intellect of his brother, Sidney won the respect of his contemporaries by his skill as a soldier and by settling the debts he had inherited. During the 1590s he supported the second Earl of Essex, who had married Sir Philip's widow Frances. At the accession of James I Sidney was himself ennobled, obtaining a barony in 1603, and then consecutively two titles, on which his Dudley kin had a lien, the viscountcy of Lisle (1605) and the earldom of Leicester (1618) before his death in 1626.

Guardians of Claimants to the Throne

THE TALBOTS

A tradition of service in local government, in the royal household and in war at home and abroad distinguished the Talbot family from the fourteenth century onwards, earning them the earldom of Shrewsbury in 1442. Successive earls acted as courtiers, councillors, and as defenders and promoters of the Crown's interests in the provinces, with occasional military commands. George, sixth Earl of Shrewsbury, was ten years older than Elizabeth I. His early upbringing had

The Talbots and their dynastic marriages with the Cavendish offspring of Bess of Hardwick. From Bess's children sprang four ducal titles: Kingston, Devonshire, Newcastle and Portland.

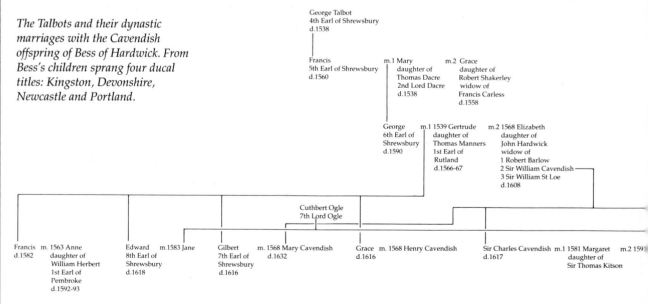

George Talbot
4th Earl of Shrewsbury
d.1538

Francis
5th Earl of Shrewsbury
d.1560

m.1 Mary
daughter of
Thomas Dacre
2nd Lord Dacre
d.1538

m.2 Grace
daughter of
Robert Shakerley
widow of
Francis Carless
d.1558

George
6th Earl of
Shrewsbury
d.1590

m.1 1539 Gertrude
daughter of
Thomas Manners
1st Earl of
Rutland
d.1566-67

m.2 1568 Elizabeth
daughter of
John Hardwick
widow of
1 Robert Barlow
2 Sir William Cavendish
3 Sir William St Loe
d.1608

Cuthbert Ogle
7th Lord Ogle

Francis   m. 1563 Anne
d.1582   daughter of
William Herbert
1st Earl of
Pembroke
d.1592-93

Edward   m.1583 Jane
8th Earl of
Shrewsbury
d.1618

Gilbert   m. 1568 Mary Cavendish
7th Earl of   d.1632
Shrewsbury
d.1616

Grace   m. 1568 Henry Cavendish
d.1616

Sir Charles Cavendish m.1 1581 Margaret   m.2 159
d.1617   daughter of
Sir Thomas Kitson

The standard of the Earl of Shrewsbury, in the Talbot colours and dominated by their badge of the dog or 'Talbot'.

been largely spent at Court, and it was there that he became acquainted with the future Queen. Styled Lord Talbot from 1538, he was present at the coronation of Edward VI in 1547 before embarking on a career of military service and management of local affairs. By 1549 he had been named a member of the Council in the North, a post which he continued to hold in virtue of his local standing until his death.

As Lord Talbot he was summoned to Parliament in March 1553, and signed the device settling the succession upon Lady Jane Grey. This was not held against him by Queen Mary, who pardoned him and gave him military commands.

The Talbots also weathered the political crisis of Queen Elizabeth's accession. Having succeeded to the earldom in 1560, Shrewsbury was invested with the Garter in 1561 and made Lord Lieutenant of Yorkshire, Nottinghamshire and Derbyshire four years later. As the leading aristocrat and landowner in the region, a supporter of the Elizabethan regime and of the Anglican Settlement, and a trusted friend of the Queen, the earl was an obvious choice as guardian of Mary, Queen of Scots after her flight from Scotland in May 1569. This thankless task, lasting for fifteen years, kept the earl away from Court, drained his finances and helped to sour his second marriage - to Elizabeth (Bess) of Hardwick. The letters reveal a bitter and somewhat crusty old figure fighting 'a woman of masculine understanding and conduct, proud, furious, selfish and unfeeling': a woman whose obsession was to provide for the children of her first marriage to Sir William Cavendish.

William Cavendish m. 1582 Anne
1st Earl of   daughter of
Devonshire   Henry Keighley
d.1626

Elizabeth Cavendish m. 1574 Charles Stuart
d.1582   Earl of Lennox
                                  d.1576

Arabella m. 1610 William Seymour
d.1612   Marquess of Hertford
                      later Duke of Somerset

On 9 February 1568 the sixth Earl of Shrewsbury married the thrice-widowed Elizabeth (Bess) Hardwick at Sheffield. The forty-six-year-old earl had six children living from his first marriage, and his slightly younger bride four by her previous marriage to William Cavendish. On the same day as this wedding two of the earl's children married two Cavendishes, thus interlinking the two families very closely. Although their marriage originated in a political and social alliance, at its outset the earl was enamoured of Bess.

Earl of Shrewsbury to Countess of Shrewsbury   April 1568

Of all the joys I have under God, the greatest is yourself. To think that I possess so faithful, and one that loves me so dear, is all and the greatest comfort that this earth can give. Therefore God give me grace to be thankful to him for his goodness shown unto me, a vile sinner ... I thank you, my sweetheart, that you are so, willing to come when I will. Therefore, dear heart, send me word how I might send for you, and till when I may have your company, and meantime I long daily for your coming. I your letters con very well, and I like them so well they could not be amended, and have sent them up to Gilbert. I have written to him how happy he is to have such a mother as you are.

   Farewell, only joy.

Only three months after the Shrewsburys' wedding, Mary, Queen of Scots fled to England in May 1568. Her flight was a cause of acute embarrassment to her cousin Queen Elizabeth. The unresolved question as to whether Mary was responsible for the murder of her husband Darnley meant that Elizabeth could not receive her at Court. Instead it was decided to lodge her (as a prisoner in all but name) at Tutbury Castle in Staffordshire and appoint the Earl of Shrewsbury as her guardian. With her memories of the luxurious French court and her extravagant tastes, Mary found Tutbury uncomfortable and disagreeable.

Mary, Queen of Scots to the French ambassador   31 January 1570
Tutbury

I am in a walled enclosure, on the top of a hill, exposed to all the winds and inclemencies of Heaven. Within the said enclosure, resembling that of a wood at Vincennes, there is a very old hunting lodge, built of timber and plaster cracked in all parts, the plaster adhering nowhere to the woodwork and broken in numberless places, the said lodge distant 3 fathoms or thereabouts from the walls and situated so low that the rampart of earth, which is behind the wall, is on a level with the highest part of the building, so that the sun can never shine upon it on that side nor any fresh air come to it, for which reason it is so damp that you can not put any furniture in that part without its being in 4 or 5 days completely covered with mould. I leave you to think how this must act upon the human body, and in short the greater part of it is rather a dungeon for base and abject criminals than the habitation fit for a person of my quality or even of much lower. The only apartments that I have for my own person consist - and for the truth of this I can appeal to all there that have been here - of 2 little miserable rooms, so exceedingly cold especially at night, that but for the ramparts and entrenchments of curtains and tapestry which I have made, it would not be possible for me to stay in them in the daytime, and out of those who have sat up with me at night during my illnesses, scarcely one has escaped without fluxion, cold or some disorder.

Needlework in the Sixteenth Century

Needlework panel, embroidered by Mary, Queen of Scots, with a phoenix and the Marian monogram 'M R'.

Sixteenth-century England had a tradition, stretching back over eight hundred years, of producing high quality embroidery: *opus anglicanum* (English work) as it was often called, had long been in demand by the modestly well off to the very rich, by patrons of the arts and by connoisseurs. The items ranged from furnishings, such as hangings for walls and beds, carpets for adorning tables and covers for cushions, to costume embroidery. Fashion for both sexes during the Tudor period called for elaborate embroidery on dress - either complex arabesque ornamentation or linear embroidery in monochrome silks worked in double-running stitch, or sumptuous intermingling patterns of birds, beasts, plants, flowers and fruit. A peculiarity of the age was the demand for embroidered book covers, particularly for Bibles, prayer books and psalteries. Whether the work was meant for domestic or personal use, gold and silver thread were employed lavishly in embroidery, as were pearls: documents also refer to the incorporation of semi-precious stones and jewels.

Contrary to general belief, most Tudor embroidery was professionally produced and done by men. To regulate and maintain manufacturing standards and conditions of work in the face of growing demand, the Broderers' Company procured its first charter from the Crown in 1560. To prevent the

deterioration of any purchased embroideries, most large households kept a professional embroiderer as part of their staff with a room and equipment assigned to his - or her - use: such embroiderers were also expected to make new items, sometimes being assisted by, but more often directing, the women of the household. Any departure from this common practice was a matter for pride, and in 1585 Bess of Hardwick, herself an accomplished needlewoman, while disputing the ownership of a set of hangings with the Earl of Shrewsbury, pointed out that her grooms, women and boys had 'wrought the most part of them' and she 'never had but one embroiderer at one time that wrought on them'.

Skill with a needle was expected of all women. Such skill combined practicality with relaxation, and sometimes solace. It served as a distraction to Catherine of Aragon and her gentlewomen pending her divorce, 'working with their own hands something wrought in needlework, costly and artificially, which she intended to the honour of God to bestow upon some churches'. It served the same end for Mary, Queen of Scots during her captivity. But her devotion to needlework can also be explained by the opportunities it allowed for propaganda, and by the contacts it gave her with well-wishers through presenting her work as gifts.

Taking the Waters

A plan of Bath, made in 1588, and showing the four spa baths then in use: the King's, the Cross, the Common and the Mild Baths. That year, after his exertions in the Armada campaign, the Earl of Leicester died on his way to recuperate at Bath. The Earl of Shrewsbury, on the other hand, patronized the baths at Buxton, which lay near to his estates.

The medicinal properties of waters from certain springs had long been known, and at the beginning of the Tudor era they were, on account of their proven worth, the resorting places of the sick in the hope of a cure. As no scientific explanation could be offered for the variety of cures achieved - although the success rate in treating specific complaints at certain springs was a matter for common knowledge - the remedy was attributed to divine intervention, originally to local deities, later to Christian saints.

Such associations had turned many springs into centres for religious cults and pilgrimages by the end of the Middle Ages. The fraud often perpetrated by con men and the suspect practices of the attendant clergy led to some doubt being cast upon their real efficacy at the Reformation, when the altars, shrines, tabernacles and churches linked with medicinal springs were closed, and the votive offerings removed and destroyed. However, locking and sealing the springs, and the Henrician regime's subsequent ban on drinking their waters or bathing in them, were to no avail. As Sir William Bassett noted to Lord Cromwell in 1538, most people had a 'fond trust' in the waters, and unfortunately in the images and cults linked with them.

Under Queen Mary not only were people once more free to go openly to medicinal springs, but the cults were also revived. However, after the Elizabethan Church Settlement, the association between these springs and Roman Catholicism was a serious stumbling-block in their transformation and evolution into socially approved watering places, or spas, despite the published work of such eminent authorities as William Turner, Dean of Wells and former physician to the Duke of Somerset, which demonstrated the value of the waters at Bath and elsewhere. The successful secularization of the spas is one of the achievements of Elizabethan England, and was largely the work of the nobility.

Bath provided the model which Buxton, Leamington and other spas followed. In addition to its five open-air baths where visitors immersed themselves up to the neck, its pump rooms where they drank the spring water, and its hospitals where long-term patients stayed, Bath had gardens to stroll in and tennis courts for play. Music, dancing and gaming completed the facilities. Such places offered a welcome relaxation from the Court, the capital and business. To many they also offered an escape from the ever-watchful eye of Queen Elizabeth. The Queen's suspicions as to the motives of some of the numerous visitors were not unfounded.

In this rural imprisonment needlework was perhaps Mary, Queen of Scots' only sustaining interest (indeed, it was almost certainly her only real talent). Fortunately, the Scots queen's enthusiasm for embroidery was shared by the Countess of Shrewsbury, and at Tutbury Mary started to go daily with her two ladies-in-waiting to the countess's room. Between the two a great friendship soon developed. Unfortunately, these meetings were not as innocent as they appeared to Shrewsbury. This is clear from the subjects chosen for embroidery, which often had a political meaning - for instance, a cat watching a mouse represents Queen Elizabeth watching Mary.

Earl of Shrewsbury to Sir William Cecil   13 March 1569
Tutbury

This Queen daily resorteth unto my wife's chamber, where with the Lady Levistion and Mrs. Seaton, she sits working with the needle in which she much delights and devising of works, and her talk is altogether of indifferent and trifling matters without any sign of secret dealing or practice...

From insalubrious Tutbury the Earl of Shrewsbury moved the Queen of Scots to his manor house at South Wingfield in Derbyshire during the spring of 1569. On arrival at Wingfield the Queen, always prone to stomach troubles and to arthritis, fell seriously ill. When she recovered, the earl went down with sickness himself. But Shrewsbury's plan to go to the nearby spa of Buxton for a rest cure did not meet with Queen Elizabeth's approval, as she was already only too aware of Mary's capacity for intrigue.

Sir William Cecil to Earl of Shrewsbury   14 August 1569
Farnham

It may please your lordship ... The Queen's majesty, hearing doubtfully of uncertain reports that you should be, or would shortly, depart to the baths at Buxton, demanded of me what I heard thereof from your lordship. Whereunto I could not make any certain answer but in this sort ... that you were earnestly advised of your physicians to go thither for the recovery of your health ... and yet I was assured in so doing you had left a substantial order for attendance upon the Queen of Scots, as should be honourable and sure. Whereupon I found her Majesty somewhat troubled ...

Close surveillance of Mary, Queen of Scots did not prevent the Queen from corresponding with whomsoever she pleased. Cyphered messages sent to the Pope asked for the annulment of her marriage to the Earl of Bothwell; others to the fourth Duke of Norfolk encouraged him in his hope of marrying her. In an effort to step up his watch Shrewsbury transferred Mary to Sheffield Castle in December 1570, and once there he reviewed the orders regulating her household. Notwithstanding Shrewsbury's diligence, Mary was able to maintain contact with her sympathizers. After the discovery of the Ridolfi Plot, whereby Philip II of Spain was to depose Queen Elizabeth and to put Mary on the throne, her household was reduced to sixteen and the number of soldiers guarding her increased to thirty.

Earl of Shrewsbury, orders concerning the household   5 May 1571
of Mary, Queen of Scots

First that all your people which appertaineth to the Queen shall depart from the Queen's chamber or chambers to their own lodgings at 9 o'clock at night, winter and summer, whatsoever he or she be, either to their lodging within the house, or without, or town; and there to remain till the next day at 6 of the clock.

Item that none of the Queen's people shall at no time wear any sword, neither within the house nor when her Grace rideth or goeth abroad, unless the master of the household himself do wear a sword, and no more without my special licence.

Item that there shall none of the Queen's people carry any bow or shafts at no time, neither to the field nor to the butts, unless it be four or five, and no more, being in the Queen's company.

Item that none of the Queen's people shall ride or go at no time abroad, out of the house or town, without my special licence; and if he or they so do, they or he shall come no more in at the gates, neither in the town, whatsoever he or they be, or she.

Item that you or some of the Queen's chamber, when her Grace will walk abroad, shall advert the officer of my ward [i.e. guard], who shall declare the message to me one hour before she goeth forth.

Item that none of the Queen's people, whatsoever he or they be, shall not once offer at no time to come forth of their chamber or lodging when any alarm is given by night or day, whether they be in the Queen's chambers, or in their chambers within the house, or without in the town; and if he or they keep not their chambers or lodging, wheresoever it be, he or they shall stand at their peril for death.

Nor was Shrewbury's own family exempt from this perpetual watchfulness. In 1568 Shrewsbury's second son Gilbert had married Mary Cavendish, and four years later he and his brother-in-law Henry Cavendish were returned as the two knights of the shire for Derbyshire in the Parliament of 1572. The co-membership of these two young men was symptomatic of the marital harmony then extant between Shrewsbury and his wife. While in London for the Parliament Gilbert engaged a new maid for his wife. As a good Talbot son he informed his father: what evidently worried Gilbert was that the new maid had been in the service of the fourth Lord Paget, a well-known sympathizer of the Scots queen.

Lord Gilbert Talbot to Earl of Shrewsbury   25 May 1573
The Court

I have found out a sober maiden to wait on my wife, if it shall so please your Lordship. She was servant unto Mrs. Southwell, now Lord Paget's wife, who is an evil husband, and will not suffer any that waited on his wife before he married her to continue with her. As it behoves me, I have been very inquisitive of the woman, and have heard very well of her behaviour, and truly I do repose in her to be very modest and well given, and such a one as I trust your Lordship shall not mislike; but, if it be so that she shall not be thought meet for my wife, she will willingly repair hither again. Her name is Margaret Butler: she is about twenty-seven years old; Mr. Bateman hath known her long, and thinketh very well of her: she is not very beautiful, but very cleanly in doing of any thing chiefly about a sick body, to dress any thing fit for them. I humbly pray your lordship to send me word whether I shall make shift to send her down presently, for she is very desirous not to spend her time idly. Thus, most humbly desiring your lordship's daily blessing, with my wonted and continual prayer for your lordship's preservation in all honour and health, long to continue, I end.
 Your Lordship's most humble and obedient son,
 Gilbert Talbot

Household Below Stairs

A corner of the vast kitchens at Hampton Court Palace. The kitchens lie at the heart of the 'below stairs': a maze of service rooms and courtyards, which occupy nearly a third of the ground area of the palace.

Each house or castle owned by the nobility had a resident household responsible for running and maintaining the property whether the owner was resident or not. This household was generally called the Household-below-stairs to distinguish it from the entourage which accompanied the owner and occupied the rooms normally shut in his absence, and was thus aptly described as the 'Household-above-stairs'.

Each permanent household was made up of a Kitchen with Larders, a Buttery and Pantry, a Cellar, a Brewery, a Bakery, a Laundry, a Wardrobe, Storehouses and Stables, and each household was intended to be self-sufficient. The various components are largely self-explanatory.

The Kitchen was the area for preparing meat and fish for eating - hardly ever for preparing vegetables and fruit, which played little part in the diet of the great, to the detriment of their digestion, and sometimes of their health. The Buttery was where wine, which was imported largely from France and Spain, was stored in bottles (thus giving it its name, buttery being a variant of bottlery) after it had been brought up from the casks, which were kept in the Cellar; similarly the Pantry was the storeroom for the bread (in Latin *panus*) after its baking.

The Brewery produced the ale and beer which was the staple drink of all classes; drinking well-water or river-water was unwise on account of contamination and pollution, and pure water could only be consumed at certain springs which were known to be disease-free.

The Wardrobe was the store room for cloth, material for new servants' clothes being distributed there annually, and a stock room for repairing the fabrics throughout the house. The Storehouses provided space for the wheat, corn, barley and other crops grown on the neighbouring estates, and sometimes for items bought in, known generically as achates, and which sometimes had a storehouse subdivision of their own called the Achatery or Catery. Each department was headed by an officer, who was often assisted by grooms. In overall charge was nominally a Steward who, because he was also an officer in the Household-above-stairs, was invariably absent.

With the sole exception of the Laundry, Households-below-stairs were predominantly male, women only being employed to any extent if the mistress of the household (that is, the wife of the owner) was in regular or permanent residence. Gardeners and estate officials, some permanently housed there, others occasional visitors, completed this masculine set-up.

On the arrival of the owner with his attendants, it was the duty of the resident household to feed everyone, to keep the entire building clean, and to provide light, heating and hot water throughout.

Shrewsbury's wife did not show the same good sense as Gilbert Talbot when in 1574 the Countess of Lennox passed through Nottinghamshire with her son Charles Stuart. Without consulting her husband, Bess of Hardwick arranged a marriage between her daughter Elizabeth Cavendish and Charles. This marriage alliance with a kinsman of Mary, Queen of Scots and a claimant to the English throne brought down the fury of Queen Elizabeth on the Shrewsburys. Ungallantly but not untruthfully, the Earl threw the blame upon his wife, who for her misdemeanour was briefly imprisoned in the Tower. Bess was never to forgive Shrewsbury for forsaking her in this crisis.

Lord Gilbert Talbot to Countess of Shrewsbury   July 1577

Quoth he, 'Gilbert, what talk had my wife with you?' 'Truly, sir, with as grieved a mind as ever I saw woman in my life, she told me your lordship was vehemently offended with her, in such sort and with so many words and shows in your anger of evil will toward her, as thereby your ladyship said you could not but stand doubtful that all his wonted love and affection is clean turned to the contrary. For your ladyship further said you had given him no cause at all to be offended. You hearing that your embroiderers were kept out of the Lodge from their beds by John Dyckenson's commandment, said to my lord these words in the morning noon, 'Did you give commandment the embroiderers should be kept out of the Lodge?' And my lord answered, 'No'. 'Then,' quoth your ladyship, 'they were kept from their beds there yesternight.' 'And he that did so,' said John Dyckenson, 'had given the express commandment,' which my lord said was a lie and he said it was utterly untrue ... But he cut me off saying it was for no purpose to hear any recital of this matter for if he listed he said he could remember cruel speeches your ladyship used to him, which were such as, quoth he, 'I was forced to tell her she scolded like one that came from the Bank'. 'Then Gilbert,' said he, 'judge you whether I had cause or not.' 'Well,' quoth he, 'I will speak no more of this matter, but she hath such a sort of varlets about her as never resteth carrying of tales, and then uttered cruel words against Owen chiefly, and the embroiderers, over long to trouble your ladyship with. So, being alighted from his horse all this while, said, 'let us get up and be going and I shall have enough to do when I come home.' 'Then', quoth I 'I think my ladyship be at Chatsworth by this time.' 'What,' quoth he, 'is she gone from Sheffield.' I answered, 'by 9 o'clock.' Whereupon he seemed to marvel greatly and said, 'is her malice such she would not tarry one night for my coming?'

As custodian of Mary, Queen of Scots the Earl of Shrewsbury received an allowance of £500 a year. This allowance proved insufficient, and payment was invariably in arrears. Even for a nobleman of Shrewsbury's wealth the inadequacy combined with the irregularity of the allowance was a serious problem, and added to the thankless task of keeping the Queen captive. Shrewsbury raised the matter repeatedly with Lord Burghley over fifteen years, but to no avail.

Earl of Shrewsbury to Lord Burghley   26 July 1580
Sheffield

I do not know what account is made of my charges sustained in the keeping of this woman, but assuredly the very charge of victual of my whole household, with the entertainment I do give to my household servants, is not defrayed with the allowance I have had from her Majesty, besides the which I dare be bold to say the wine, spice and fuel that is spent in my house yearly, being valued, cometh not under the value of £1000 by the year: also the loss of plate, the buying of pewter, and all manner of household stuff, which by them is exceedingly spoiled, and wilfully wasted, standeth me in £1000 by the year; moreover, the annuities I have given my servants, to the end to be the more faithfully served by them and to prevent any corruption that by want they might be provoked into, cometh to above £400 the year; yet do I not reckon the charges to all the soldiers I keep, over that which her Majesty doth allow for them, which being but 6d. a day may be well considered, that men in household, being employed in such painful and careful service, will not be so entertained. I do leave out an infinite number of other hidden charges which I am driven unto by keeping this woman, for [fear of] troubling you so long, but I do trust that her Majesty, of her own consideration, will so well think of these things that she will not abridge anything of that which she hath hitherto allowed. I have in these eleven years of service not pestered her Majesty with my suits ... the world must needs think that either my deserts have been very small, or else her Majesty doth make very small account of me, the which, in her princely nature, I assuredly hope will never do.

Although Shrewsbury was burdened with the task of maintaining Mary, Queen of Scots, his finances were not so straitened (as he would have had Burghley believe) that he was unable to invest elsewhere. His investments related largely to mining or iron production, but on the advice of John Hawkins, Treasurer to the Navy, he also maintained a ship for commerce and for privateering. When early in 1583 Christopher Carlile approached Shrewsbury with a proposal for a voyage to America, Shrewsbury was reluctant to back this voyage with cash, but he wondered if his ship could join in.

Earl of Shrewsbury to Thomas Bawdewyn   20 May 1583
Sheffield

Bawdewyn, where you write to me in your letters of the 14th of this instant, that Mr. Captain Carlile intended shortly to voyage for the discovery of America, and that he requested me to adventure £100 with him, wherein you desire to know my pleasure; for mine own part, you know that I have already many irons in the fire, and sundry occasions, and therefore had rather disburthen myself of some than enter more. But if he like to take my ship with him, and that Mr. Hawkins be contented therewith, I could be the rather drawn to it, because I must set her forth, and furnish her some way ...

I would you should talk with Mr. Hawkins about my ship, and hear his opinion what is best to be done for her. I think the best were to sell her, if I might. I have no liking she should go a scraping, but I would you should see some way with her, because the time of the year passeth space, and I like not she should lie idle. I would you should talk with the tailor, and devise me some jerkin of thin pretty silk that is light and easy, to wear upon my doublet, under my gown or cloak; or else some perfumed leather, with satin sleeves, as the fashion is; wherein I would you should take my son Savile's advice. I would you should remember my chamois jerkin, and hose for winter, but I would have no silver nor gold lace upon it, but some pretty silk lace, and perfumed. I received, as this letter was writing, another letter from you, with Mr. Hawkins' note, and others, of Mr. Carlile's voyage to America; and if Mr. Hawkins like not to have my ship to go with him, I would yet that you should adventure 100 marks [£66 13s. 4d.] with him in this his pretended discovery rather than fail, for his friend's sake, and favourers of the voyage, if he be such a one as you report him to be; and so I cease.

Your lord and master
G. Shrewsbury

The Investment Boom

Shipping in the Pool of London, with London Bridge and the Tower to the left. Nobles were eager to share in wealth gained by overseas trade and the Earl of Shrewsbury was by no means the only peer to have 'many irons in the fire'.

One of the most striking characteristics of the Tudor nobility was their concern not merely to develop the full economic potential of their estates, but also to engage in business on the widest scale. The commercial mentality was particularly noticeable in the reign of Elizabeth I, and at one time it was thought to reflect the attitudes of the 'new nobility' created by the Tudors.

However it can also be found among members of the older families (like the Earl of Shrewsbury), and its origins probably go back to the involvement of English medieval landowners in sheep-raising and the export of wool.

The immediate spur to investment was probably the pressure of the mid-century inflation, both directly on the revenues from landed estates, and indirectly through the government's desire to expand commerce in general. The latter was not only a response to inflation but also a reflection of the prevailing 'Commonwealth' ethos. The first joint-stock company - the Muscovy Company, founded in the last months of Edward VI's reign - was heavily subscribed to by members of Court and Council as well as London merchants. Direct investment by councillors in schemes sponsored by the government increased in Elizabeth's reign, both in the form of metallurgical companies like the Mines Royal (which explored for copper in the Lake District) or the Mineral and Battery Works (which made ordnance),

and in the major oceanic voyages. Many Elizabethan noblemen owned ships - even Shrewsbury, whose lands lay deep in the heart of the country; and these vessels were intended for trade as much as for privateering.

The success of these ventures was mixed. Some of the oceanic voyages produced spectacular returns (Drake's Circumnavigation being the most dramatically successful), but others were equally spectacular disasters. Profitable offices under the Crown or monopolies could be more reliable investments. But these could not claim to be aiding the commonwealth, and the influence of the social and political climate may have been just as important to the investment boom as narrow calculations of profit and loss.

A Hilliard miniature of Sir Francis Drake, the commander of the 1585 expedition which founded the colony of Roanoake.

From 1574 the marriage of the Shrewsburys had steadily deteriorated, and by 1577 it was on the rocks. Occasionally, however, they were able to sink their marital differences, particularly if a matter involving money was likely to go against them. However, a shared cupidity was not sufficient to preserve their marriage. From June 1583 the earl withheld his wife's allowance of £800 a year from her. Angered, Bess suggested that Shrewsbury was having an affair with Mary, Queen of Scots. Although denied by Mary, this imputation led to the ending of her custody under Shrewsbury in August 1584 and her return to Tutbury early in 1585.

Thomas Stringer to Earl of Shrewsbury   15 November 1584
South Wingfield

On Friday last, letters came thither by post from Mr. Secretary that an officer of the Wardrobe, and one of the Cofferer's clerks were dispatched from the Court, and had warrant from my Lord Treasurer for money to supply the wants for Tutbury; and yesterday there came new letters from Mr. Secretary, that the officer of the Wardrobe was sick, and not able to come; so that he was to move your Honour, from her Majesty to continue your provision longer. If that should be so, here is not wine to serve a fortnight; therefore your pleasure must be known for supply, if there be longer stay. I cannot learn of past six quarters of malt in the bailiff of Worksop's hands, and six quarters of multure [inferior] malt here; so that, and all the drink in the house, will serve little more than a month. If her Majesty devised not your remove hither, he or she that devised it were not your friend, to bring you from Sheffield Castle, which is a strong house, and from your provision and people, to this, which is of no strength; and now the ways are foul, and your provision cometh starkly ...

   I did perceive Mr. Secretary wrote to Mr. Chancellor to know how many people were attending of the Scotch Queen, and what her diet was, and how many messes of meat they had daily, and what the charge thereof would be weekly. So that he has returned that the Queen has sixteen dishes at the first and second courses; and the master of the household, and her chief officers have, for them and their servants, ten dishes at the first and second courses ... and for people to guard her, not under one hundred gentlemen, yeomen, and officers, and fifty soldiers; and that she has no furniture of household, neither for herself than her people, but all of your Lordship's. So I judge the Queen's majesty and Council do see to furnish such a house as Tutbury with hangings, the bedding, linens, plate, brass, pewter, and other furniture, which will amount to a huge sum of money ... for though some that were your hollow friends did think your charge not great, now they may see the contrary to their shame.

Harassment by Shrewsbury reached such a pitch that in 1584 Bess had stopped living in any of her husband's houses and had retired to Hardwick, which was part of her patrimony. Bess's hopes of reconciliation came to nothing. The Earl of Leicester and others interceded on her behalf, but to no avail. An inquiry ordered by the Queen ruled in April 1585 that Shrewsbury should take his wife back; honour his financial agreements with her and her Cavendish sons; hand over withheld monies and end all harassment; in return Bess had to settle £500 a year on her husband. The verdict shook Shrewsbury.

Earl of Shrewsbury to Earl of Leicester   30 April 1585
Chelsea

... Since that her Majesty hath set down this hard sentence against me, to my perpetual infamy and dishonour, to be ruled and overran by my wife, so bad and wicked a woman, yet her Majesty shall see that I will obey her commandment, though no curse or plague in the earth could be more grievous to me. These offers of my wife's, inclosed in your letters, I think them very unfit to be offered to me. It is too much to make me my wife's pensioner, and set me down the demesnes of Chatsworth, without the house and other lands leased, which is but a pension in money ...

Shrewsbury's failure to comply with the verdict of April 1585 led to a further commission early in 1586. When the earl obstinately disregarded this confirmation of the earlier verdict Queen Elizabeth commanded him to obey it, and he reluctantly consented. Backed by the Queen and supported by the Court, Bess was reconciled with Shrewsbury. However, the 'peace' was an uneasy one. Bess refused to return certain items removed by her sons, and Shrewsbury refused to welcome her at his Chelsea home.

Earl of Shrewsbury to Countess of Shrewsbury   5 August 1586
Chelsea

Wife ... I answer, that there is no creature more happy and more fortunate than you have been, for where you were defamed and to the world a byword ... I brought you to all the honour you have, and to the most of that wealth you now enjoy ... I told you that you were welcome [at Chelsea] upon the Queen's commandment; but, though you were cleared in her Majesty's sight for all offences, yet I had not cleared you ...

Predictably the reconciliation between Shrewsbury and his countess proved brief. Although Bess believed that those who had been joined together in the sight of God should not be put asunder, her patience was further tested by the increasingly wayward behaviour of her husband. Shrewsbury took a mistress. The Queen protested. Bishop Overton of Lichfield urged him to take Bess back but Shrewsbury refused. In the autumn of 1590 he returned to Sheffield where on 18 November he died.

Bishop Overton of Lichfield to Earl of Shrewsbury   12 October 1590
Eccleshall

Right honourable, my singular good Lord, I am bold according to my promise, to put you in remembrance by letters of some matters already passed between us in talk ...

I cannot see but that it must needs rest and remain a great clog and burthen to your conscience to live asunder from the countess your wife, without her own good liking and consent thereto; for, as I have told you heretofore, it is the plain doctrine of St. Paul that the one should not defraud the other of due benevolence, nor of mutual comfort and company, but with the agreement of both parties, and that also but for a time, and only to give yourselves to fasting and prayer. This is the doctrine of St. Paul, and this doctrine Christ himself confirmed in the Gospel when he forbiddeth all men to put away their wives, unless for adultery, a thing never suspected in my lady your wife ...

But some will say in your Lordship's behalf that the countess is a sharp and bitter shrew, and therefore like enough to shorten your life, if she should keep you company. Indeed, my good Lord, I have heard some say so, but if shrewdness or sharpness may be a just cause of separation between a man and wife, I think few men in England would keep their wives long; for it is a common jest, yet true in some sense, that there is but one shrew in all the world, and every man hath her; and so every man might be rid of his wife, that would be rid of a shrew. My honourable good Lord, I doubt not but your great wisdom and experience hath taught you to bear some time with a woman as with the weaker vessel ... if not for your own sake, yet for the issue of both your bodies, whom she loveth, I dare say as her own life, and would not see by her goodwill to fall into any decay ... although, also, I dare say she wisheth all good unto you for your own sake, as well as theirs, or else she would not be so desirous of your life and company as she is. And, therefore, I beseech your Lordship remove all such conceits far from you as are beaten into your head by evil counsellors, and rather think this unlawful separation, to be a stain to your house, and a danger to your life ...

Prodigy Houses

The courtyard of Kirby Hall, Northamptonshire. Sir Christopher Hatton, later Lord Chancellor, bought the half-timbered house in 1575, even though it was only a few miles from Holdenby where he was building an even larger mansion.

Prodigy houses were houses built by Elizabeth I's subjects, not for themselves, but for the Queen. That is, they were a funcion of the royal 'progress' or summer journey round the country. Until the Dissolution, the monarch had relied mainly on the hospitality of the monasteries for accommodation and entertainment while on progress. Although in origin no more than a fulfilment of one of the Seven Charities, that of feeding the wayfarer, by the end of the Middle Ages, the hospitality shown by the heads of religious houses to the king had come to be one of the more important social functions performed by the monasteries in the regions.

Thus the Dissolution caused a major crisis over suitable stopping points for the King with his Household, but it did not bring the practice of progresses to an end. The retention by the Crown of the sites of certain major abbeys, such as Reading, for prolonged halts proved unsatisfactory and a drain upon the Crown's limited resources. Also Henry's increased reliance after 1540 upon gentle families in the localities was unwelcome both to the families, who could ill afford the financial burden, and to the monarch, whose entourage could not be housed under a single roof.

Under Edward VI and Mary the royal habit of making progresses had been curtailed, but with the accession of Queen Elizabeth in 1558 it was revived. The mere anticipation of a royal visit to some remote parts would set masons and carpenters modifying or extending a house fit for the occasion - and

incidentally making a lasting memorial to it. The Earls of Leicester and Shrewsbury, Lord Burghley and Sir Christopher Hatton had to accept that, on account of their rank or their office, it was necessary to spend more money than even they could afford on houses which they did not need. Hatton rarely visited capacious Holdenby, yet he bought and finished nearby Kirkby. Holdenby, Longleat, Burghley, Theobalds, Wimbledon and Worksop were houses built expressly to honour the Queen, 'for whom we meant to exceed our purses.'

The string of houses designed for the reception of the Court differed from those designed as family homes in that they provided private and public rooms for the Queen's use and extensive lodgings for others. Grandeur was the keynote without and within. Architectural decorum and classical restraint went aesthetically 'out of the window'. Prodigality in design and expense was universal, and home-owners strove to outdo one another in extravagance. These houses were aptly called prodigy houses.

The construction of these gorgeous and exotic palaces sparked off a building craze among the less well-to-do, sometimes country gentlemen of no account outside their localities. Perhaps the most famous of the houses put up in this exuberant phase of construction in late Elizabethan England is outlandish Hardwick Hall, built by the widowed Countess of Shrewsbury for her personal use and that of her granddaughter whom she hoped would be queen.

Shrewsbury's death left Bess the richest woman in England, and free to play an independent role at home and abroad. By 1592 Arabella Stuart was seventeen and unmarried. Since she was a claimant to the throne her marriage was a subject of interest to Queen Elizabeth, who discussed it with Bess of Hardwick. For a year Queen and grandmother considered the suitability of a son of the Duke of Parma as a husband for Arabella, but the death of Parma in December 1592 ended the negotiations. Arabella's wilful character made her supervision a matter for concern, and while the marriage negotiations were in progress Lord Burghley sought assurances as to her welfare.

Countess of Shrewsbury to Lord Burghley   21 September 1592
Hardwick

My good Lord, I was at the first much troubled to think that so wicked and mischievious practices should be devised to entrap my poor Arabella and me ... I will not have any unknown or suspected person to come to my house. Upon the least suspicion that may happen here, any way, I shall give advertisement to your lordship ... Arabella walks not late; at such time as she shall take the air, it shall be near the house, and well attended on. She goeth not to any body's house at all. I see her almost every hour in the day. She lieth in my bedchamber. If I can be more precise than I have been I will be. I am bound in nature to be careful for Arabella; I find her loving and dutiful to me, yet her own good and safety is not dearer to me, nor more by me regarded than to accomplish her Majesty's pleasure ...

Gilbert Talbot had succeeded his father as seventh Earl of Shrewsbury in 1590. At forty-one he was already a martyr to gout, as was the septuagenarian Lord Burghley. Here Shrewsbury exchanges medical lore with his fellow-sufferer.

Gilbert, Earl of Shrewsbury to Lord Burghley   23 January 1594
Handsworth

I heard your lordship was, of late, somewhat visited with the gout ... I would your Lordship would once make trial of my oil of stag's blood, for I am strongly persuaded of the rare and great virtue thereof. In the beginning of this winter I was touched with the gout in the joint of my great toe, and it began somewhat sharply, and yet was I speedily eased ...

As intractable as Shrewsbury's gout was the problem of Arabella Stuart. Throughout the 1590s she had been used as a pawn on the international marriage market by Queen Elizabeth, and she had lived a virtual prisoner with her grandmother, largely at Hardwick. Then in 1602 at the age of twenty-seven Arabella took matters into her own hands and proposed marriage to Edward Seymour, eleven years her junior. As a son of the Earl of Hertford by Catherine Grey, Seymour also had a claim to the throne. The prospect of the union of these two claims alarmed the Council, which early in 1603 sent Sir Henry Brounker to investigate it. Brounker's arrival at Hardwick left the dowager countess with no alternative but to make her excuses to the Queen as best she could. The Shrewsburys, who for a hundred years had stayed clear of side-taking in high politics were entangled at last.

Elizabeth, dowager Countess of Shrewsbury   29 January 1603
to Elizabeth I
Hardwick

I understand by Sir Henry Brounker's letters some part of your Highness' pleasure touching this unadvised young woman here, and do most humbly desire that I may know your Majesty's further pleasure. I cannot yield to your Majesty such humble and dutiful thanks as I am most bound to do for your Majesty's most gracious favour and goodness to me and princely acceptance of my faithful poor service. I will not respect my trouble or charge to do your Majesty any service that shall lie in me during life, but I doubt it is not in my power now to do that service to your Majesty in this matter as I desire, for the bad persuasions of some have so estranged her mind and natural affection from me that she holds me the greatest enemy she hath, and hath given herself over to be ruled and advised by others, so that, the bond of nature being broken, I cannot have any assurance of her good carriage. I cannot but doubt there is another match in working, but who the party should be, I cannot conjecture. Some vain words she hath spoken tending to such a matter, which I thought at the first were to make me more negligent in looking to that which was before discovered. She is borne in hand, as I gather, that she shall have your Majesty's good liking and allowance of anything she doth, and have liberty to have resort to her and herself to go or ride at her own pleasure. For my own part, I should have little care how meanly soever she were bestowed so as it were not offensive to your Highness. So far as my credit doth extend with her, I advise her to attempt nothing without your Majesty's pleasure first known. She saith she will do all duty to your Majesty, but desireth me to forbear to examine her ...

Councillors to Queen Elizabeth

THE CECILS

Rather like the Talbots, the Cecils came of humble origin from the Welsh marches. This fact was an embarrassment to a family with a great sense of its achievement and dignity, and its opponents exploited the matter unmercifully. The fortunes of the Cecils were closely linked with another family with a Welsh background, the Tudors. Richard Cecil, for example, made his career in the Royal Household, where he held a succession of appointments in the Chamber and in the Robes, and it is a measure of his personal standing with Henry VIII that he was one of a small number of household officers remembered under the King's will. By the time of his death early in 1553 Richard Cecil had acquired a series of properties in and around Stamford, and his son William, already a knight, was well launched in his own spectacular political and administrative career.

Coming from a family with a tradition of service to major figures or to the Crown, Cecil was naturally attracted to the Royal Court with its numerous opportunities for advancement in government. He soon became associated with a group of promising young men linked with the household and management of the heir-apparent to the throne; he strengthened this association through his second marriage to a daughter of Sir Anthony Cooke, a Gentleman of the Privy Chamber, revered for his interest in the welfare and education of his children. Mildred Cooke inherited many of her father's qualities: she was rated with Lady Jane Grey as one of the two most learned women in mid-sixteenth-century England, and she was her husband's intellectual equal. Their marriage in December 1545 lasted over forty years, and in an age of arranged and often incompatible marriages, their closeness and abiding affection set them apart from most of their contemporaries.

This remarkable partnership helped Cecil to keep a cool temper, to maintain a detachment and soundness of judgement, and not once

William Cecil, riding his mule. A mule signifies humility; other elements in the picture denote constancy, loyalty, fortitude and nobility. This sort of nobility is closer to Sir Thomas Elyot's than to the Earl of Leicester's.

Somerset. From helping to organize the army of invasion of Scotland in 1547, Cecil went on to become Somerset's personal secretary.

Although imprisoned with Somerset in the Tower after the *coup d'etat* in the autumn of 1549, Cecil soon ingratiated himself with the Earl of Warwick; he received his knighthood on Warwick's elevation to the dukedom of Northumberland in 1551. As Secretary of State and a Privy Councillor Cecil helped to prepare the device settling the succession on Lady Jane Grey and to proclaim her queen, but when public feeling decided the issue in favour of Princess Mary he made his obeisance to her. Mary, perhaps as much on account of his long-standing closeness with Princess Elizabeth as for his part in the succession crisis, did not renew his appointments - although she came to use him as an intermediary between herself and her half-sister.

By the time of Princess Elizabeth's accession in 1558 the new Queen and Cecil were long accustomed to co-operate. Their forty-year partnership in ruling England survived intrigue at court, competition from political rivals, national unrest, international crises, financial uncertainties and a succession of wars.

disrupted his power of application or distracted his eye to the main chance. 'Cautious, sober, minute, something of the Polonius type' with 'a passion for placing everything on record', Cecil came to the attention of the Protector

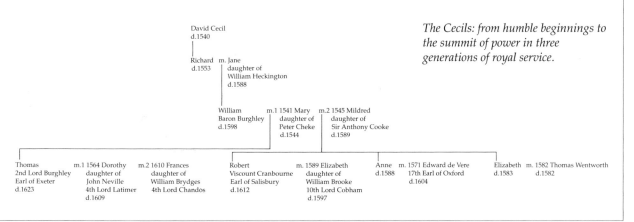

The Cecils: from humble beginnings to the summit of power in three generations of royal service.

William Cecil's rise was meteoric. By the age of thirty he had been Privy Councillor and Secretary of State for twelve months. As Secretary of State and a confidant of the Duke of Northumberland, Cecil might have been expected to support the device for the succession naming Jane Grey as heir to the throne on the death of Edward VI. Cecil, however, shared the general unease over the legality of the measure, and used a genuine illness as a pretext not to perform certain of his duties. Eventually, he did subscribe to the device ('the book') and he helped to proclaim Jane as queen. When popular feeling decided in favour of Princess Mary, Cecil too changed his allegiance. Not long afterwards he drafted 'a brief note of my submission and of my doings' during the succession crisis for Queen Mary's use.

Sir William Cecil   1553

1. First, my submission with all lowliness that any heart can conceive.

2. My misliking of the matter when I heard secretly; whereupon I made conveyance away of my lands, part of my goods, my leases, and my raiment.

3. I also determined to suffer, for saving my conscience ...

4. I did refuse to subscribe to the book, when none of the Council did refuse: in what peril, I refer it to be considered by them who know the duke.

5. I refused to make a proclamation, and turned the labour to Mr. Throckmorton, whose conscience (I saw) was troubled therewith, misliking the matter.

6. I eschewed the writing of the Queen's highness bastard, and therefore the duke wrote the letter himself which was sent abroad in the realm.

7. I eschewed to be at the drawing of the proclamation for the publishing of the usurper's title, being especially appointed thereto ...

Finally, I beseech her Highness that in her grace I may feel some difference from others that have more plainly offended, and yet be partakers of her Highness' bountifulness and grace: and if difference may be made, I do differ from them who I served, and also from them that had liberty after their enforcement to depart, by means whereof they did, both like noble men and true subjects, show their duties to their Sovereign Lady ...

There were problems in Cecil's personal life, too. Thomas Cecil, the offspring of Sir William Cecil's ill-advised student marriage with Mary Cheke, was 'a soft and gentle child' and a disappointment to his father. After being tutored privately he spent a short time at Cambridge and then at one of the Inns of Court. To complete his education Cecil sent Thomas on a tour of the Continent, and to help him while away he set down 'A Memorial' for the nineteen-year-old 'to peruse and put in use'.

Sir William Cecil to Thomas Cecil   1561

... You shall privately every morning before you go out of your chamber upon your knees say the Lord's Prayer, and that with devotion, keeping your mind and intent to the sense of the prayer ...

And after this private prayer every morning, you shall make you ready in your apparel in cleanly sort, doing that for civility and health and not for pride. This done, then shall you at your appointed hour resort to such common prayer as shall be accorded to be said by you and your company ... You shall use the manner of the prayer of the Church of England in Latin. And for your instructions you shall do well to get some small commentary of the Psalter, and after your prayer to peruse the exposition of the words of the New Testament and the Old, daily perusing the hard places...

Also, you shall before you go to sleep every night upon your knees reverently and devoutly ask forgiveness of your offenses, calling them curiously and exactly from the morning through every hour of the day until that time to your remembrance, and not only to remember them but to consider by what occasion you fell unto them, to be sorry for them, to detest them, to make an appointment to avoid the occasions the next day, to beseech Almighty God to guide you in the next day by His Holy Spririt that you fall not unto the like ...

I would that you keep a book like a journal, entering into the same every night all your passages in the day, with the things of moment of that day's travel; and remember this, that although many things worthy your remembrance may appear so fresh to you as you think not need to enter the same into your book, yet trust not your memory therewith but commit it to writing in such sort as at your return you may see as in a calendar your whole doings and travel.

Reports reached Cecil from France that his son was 'dissolute, slothful, negligent and careless' and a series of reproachful letters were sent to Thomas, who was hurt by them.

The Grand Tour

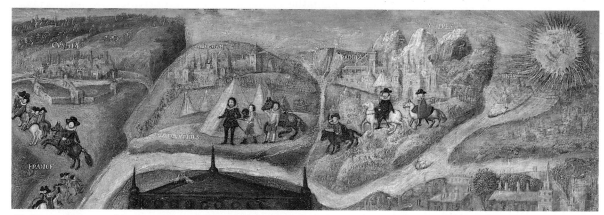

Sir Henry Unton on his Grand Tour of Italy; he began his travels in his nineteenth year, the same age as Thomas Cecil.

At the Reformation the medieval practice of Englishmen from all social classes of going on pilgrimage to Rome, Compostella or Jerusalem came to an end. Similarly the flow of students to universities, medical schools, law centres and theological colleges abroad was disrupted. For the vast majority the only experience of the Continent in the latter half of the sixteenth century was limited to warfare, either through participation in the military expeditions against France and Spain or through service as mercenary soldiers. For some, conscience, religious beliefs and political persuasion forced them into exile at different times: English Protestants found shelter in the Rhineland and Switzerland, and English Catholics in northern Italy, the Netherlands and in Spain. Royal consent became a necessity for foreign travel, but it was not always obtained before departure.

The limited experience of the Continent available through war, diplomacy and trade was sufficient, however, to create a yearning 'to travel countries and to see strange fashions'. A courtier with such a desire was the Devonian Peter Carew who in 1540 received the King's permission to go abroad with several companions. Carew travelled through France into Italy before crossing the Adriatic and continuing through the Balkans to Constantinople; returning to Venice, he went to Budapest and Vienna before journeying home. This two-year excursion brought Carew fame at Court, where King and nobles never tired of hearing what he had seen and done: it also fostered a wish among others to do the same. At first the travellers tended to be men of mature years, such as the second Earl of Bedford who, during the Marian Reaction, found it expedient to seek permission to travel abroad for two years, and got as far as Venice. Within a decade the bulk of travellers were either adolescents or men in their early twenties, accompanied by tutors and financed by their fathers with the ostensible purpose of completing their education.

The key figure in this change, but not its originator, was Sir William Cecil who, in 1560, sent his son Thomas to Paris, Germany and Switzerland. Philip Sidney's tour a decade later set a pattern which became standard, with an emphasis on meeting major political figures, churchmen and intellectuals, learning modern languages and studying the arts in Italy. Unlike Sidney's father, Cecil experienced the hazards that successive parents endured for sending their sons abroad for such tours: filial indiscipline and ingratitude, greater expense than anticipated, unwelcome political, religious and sexual contacts. Later in the 1580s, he was to be acutely embarrassed by his grandson and namesake's flirtation with Roman Catholicism while the boy was in Italy. Yet, notwithstanding such parental distress, the habit of the nobility and gentle families of sending their sons to the Continent to round off their upbringing had been established by 1600, and Grand Tours were to remain a feature of the education of these classes for the next two centuries.

The Law of Treason

Treason was the violation by a subject of his allegiance to the monarch or to the regime. At the accession of Henry VIII the law of treason rested on a fourteenth-century Act which made it treason to plot the King's death, or that of his queen consort or of the heir-apparent, to violate the wife of the King or of the heir-apparent or the King's eldest daughter if unmarried, to levy war in the kingdom, to support the King's enemies in or out of the realm, or to kill the Lord Chancellor or the judges in execution of their offices.

This narrow definition had been enlarged both by judicial interpretation in the courts of law and by more ruthless application regardless of academic arguments by successive kings and their advisers. Thus adverse criticism of a monarch, or simply an expression of astonishment at royal policy ('I marvel the King's grace ...'), without any overt deed as called for by the original statute, could be construed as treason; it helped to create a system of repression, suspicion, allegation and accusation, with no man sure of his friends or enemies, and of spies, some paid agents but more often casual informants. Interpretation, enforcement and precedent combined to create a means to preserve and to extend the Crown's authority in an age without an adequate police force to maintain law and order.

This somewhat loose definition of treason as the ultimate political crime against the monarch and the monarch as the embodiment of the kingdom could well have proved adequate in the sixteenth century, as it had in the late Middle Ages, but for the dynastic problems of the Tudors and the religious break with Rome. These necessitated a revision of the law as it had stood until 1534, and called for regular amendments and modifications over the next seventy years. Also, in 1536, to the established treason of forging the Great Seal was added forgery of other lesser, royal seals as a safeguard of the executive integrity of the Crown, and as a reflection of the burgeoning administrative activity of the period. As a result, legislation setting out what constitutes treason is one of the main threads of parliamentary business under the Tudors.

In its variety of interpretation, treason could be employed as a charge ranging from the greatest in the land such as queens (Anne Boleyn and Catherine

The execution of Mary, Queen of Scots, in the hall of Fotheringhay Castle (1587).

Howard) and the nobility (the third Duke of Buckingham, the Earl of Surrey and the fourth Duke of Norfolk) down to seminary priests, and to more humble peasants distressed by land changes and drunken revellers suspected of destroying royal proclamations. Such a wide net of potential victims inspired further awe for the crown as it was intended to do, but it also fostered the innate tendency of sixteenth-century Englishmen to consult their lawbooks before taking any action.

That was before the event. After an indictment for treason, legal counsel was denied to the accused, which meant almost certain death. In 1572 Norfolk observed: 'I have had very short warning to provide the answer to so great a matter ... The indictment containeth sundry points ... and so draw me into the matter of treason, which are not treasons themselves ... I am brought to fight without a weapon.'

After the premature death of Thomas Parry, Robert Dudley was Cecil's only rival in Elizabeth's esteem. To counterbalance Dudley's claims to the status of a great noble, Cecil had helped to promote the fourth Duke of Norfolk to the Privy Council. But the duke soon over-reached himself. In the autumn of 1568 Norfolk presided over the commission at York to investigate the complaints against Mary, Queen of Scots by her subjects. Rumours about Norfolk's hopes to marry Mary led Queen Elizabeth to transfer the commission to Westminster, but the duke denied the rumours. However, conclusive evidence of Norfolk's duplicity came to light and resulted in his imprisonment on 8 October 1569. Cecil summarized the situation.

Sir William Cecil to Elizabeth I   16 October 1569

The Queen of Scots indeed is and shall always be a dangerous person to your estate. Yet there be degrees whereby the dangers may be more or less. If you would marry, it should be less; and whilst you do not, it will increase. If her person be restrained either here or at home in her own country, it will be less: if it be at liberty, it will be greater. If she be manifested to be unable by law to have any other husband than Bothwell whilst he liveth, the peril is the less: if she be esteemed free to marry, it is the greater ...

   Now for the duke. Whilst he liveth unmarried the hope of matching will continue. And if he shall marry in any other place which of all other things in the end be necessary, all pernicious intents depending upon him shall cease. Again, if he be charged with the crime of treason and shall not be convicted, it shall not only serve, but increase his credit ...

Norfolk's later conduct put him 'within the compass of treason' and, pending his trial, Queen Elizabeth insisted upon the recall of the Spanish ambassador. Before his departure the ambassador organized a conspiracy to assassinate Cecil (recently ennobled as Lord Burghley), but an anonymous letter warned him of the plot.

Anonymous to Lord Burghley   4 January 1572

My Lord, of late I have upon discontent entered into a conspiracy with some others to slay your lordship. And the time appointed, a man with a perfect hand attended you three several times in your garden to have slain your lordship ...

With Cecil secure in the Queen's favour, his daughters became desirable matches for the greatest families. With his much-loved elder daughter Anne married to the seventeenth Earl of Oxford in 1571, Burghley was approached by the sixth Earl of Shrewsbury with a proposal that his fourth son Edward should marry Elizabeth Cecil. Although Burghley was flattered by the prospect of another marriage alliance between his family and the 'old' nobility, he had reservations about a link with the Talbots. Diplomatically, he explained that Elizabeth was too young to be married yet, and he also referred to Queen Elizabeth's suspicions as to his personal dealings with Mary, Queen of Scots - which such a marriage to the son of Mary's gaoler would do little to allay.

Lord Burghley to Earl of Shrewsbury   24 December 1575
Hampton Court

My very good Lord, my most hearty and due commendations done, I cannot sufficiently express in words the inward hearty affection that I conceive by your lordship's friendly offer of the marriage of your younger son ...

There are especially two causes why I do not in plain terms consent by way of conclusion hereto; the one, for that my daughter is but young in years: and upon some reasonable respects, I have determined (notwithstanding I have been very honourably offered matches) not to treat of marrying of her, if I may live so long, until she shall be above fifteen or sixteen: and if I were of more likelihood myself to live longer than I look to do, she should not, with my liking, be married before she were near eighteen, or twenty. The second cause why I differ to yield to conclusion with your lordship is grounded upon such a consideration as, if it were not truly to satisfy your lordship, and to avoid a just offence which your lordship might conceive of my forbearing, I would not be writing or message utter, but only be speech to your lordship's self. My Lord, it is over true, and over much against reason, that upon my being at Buxton last, advantage was sought by some that loved me not, to confirm in her Majesty a former conceit which had been laboured to put into her head, that I was of late time become friendly to the Queen of Scots, and that I had no disposition to encounter her practices ... but to avoid all probable arguments that may be gathered to render me suspected to her Majesty ... if it were understood that there were a communication or a purpose of marriage between your lordship's son and my daughter, I am sure there would be an advantage sought to increase these former suspicions ... My Lord, I pray you bear with my scribbling, which I think your lordship shall hardly read, and yet I would not use my man's hand in such a matter as this is.

The Making of the Tudor Garden

Views of the Privy Garden at Whitehall with left, Prince Edward's nurse, Mother Jack, and right, Henry VIII's jester, Will Somers. Heraldry penetrates even the gardens: the railings round the beds are painted in the livery colours of green and white, while the King's beasts stand on columns. The practice was 'peculiarly English'.

The Earl of Leicester's gardens at Kenilworth rivalled Lord Burghley's at Theobalds, Burghley's son's at Wimbledon, and Lord Lumley's at Nonsuch, which were considered among the wonders of the Tudor age. Often compared with the legendary works of Semiramis in Babylon, these gardens and others were objects of pride visited by a string of Englishmen and continental travellers who rated them as curiosities in their own right, not simply as adjuncts to castles or great houses.

Gardening and the creation of gardens amounted almost to a craze with the Tudor nobility. The initial impulse seems to have been French, and the gardeners who designed and maintained them largely came from France, although herbalists, such as William Turner and John Gerard, were consulted at every stage by the Duke of Somerset and Lord Burghley. The example of Henry VII at Richmond and of Henry VIII at Hampton Court, Whitehall and Nonsuch did not so much as set a fashion as confirm a popular trend. The pleasure ground created at Thornbury during the 1510s for the third Duke of Buckingham combined gardens laid out in squares planted with geometric knots and enclosed by elaborate covered galleries with an orchard and a rose garden laid out with alleys, arbours and aviaries. Changes in taste in the 1530s led to the development of enclosures with square beds divided quarterly, the whole encompassed with walks, hedges with elaborate topiary, sundials, mythological monsters, heraldic beasts and busts. Later mazes, fountains, statuary, obelisks, spheres and urns were introduced, and with these a symbolic meaning was often intended.

The most important change was probably the greater tendency to orientate the principal gardens (open to the general public) with the main rooms or state apartments of the adjoining house and the lesser (privy) gardens with the private quarters used by the owner and his family. Formality was not always an invariable characteristic, as the epithets 'bosky' and 'romancy' applied to the gardens at Stourton (later renamed Stourhead) show. Flowers, shrubs and trees were imported from the Continent and further afield.

The tremendous horticultural achievement of the sixteenth century was swept away with the aesthetic changes of the next two hundred years. No authentic garden from the period survives.

Household Above Stairs

The entourage surrounding a nobleman and his wife resembled a royal court; to some extent the personal households - or 'households-above-stairs' - of the nobility were modelled upon the monarch's court, and like it they were itinerant. Such households provided opportunities for ceremonial and magnificence, which were in contemporary opinion attributes of rank and authority. They offered political and social foci for the regions and localities, and in their opportunities for advancement and patronage they helped to weld together an affinity of kin, servants and clients as supporters and promoters of their lords.

The household-above-stairs was headed by a group

This detail from the 'Sieve' portrait of Elizabeth I c.1580 shows a typical scene in a gallery of the palace.

of three or four men, the steward, comptroller, chamberlain or master, whose function varied from household to household. Its organization reflected the disposition and arrangement of rooms in the public or state apartments of Tudor houses. First was the great hall, which, as in the Middle Ages, provided a common meeting area for the separate establishments of husband, wife and adult offspring, and for visitors with their dependents and for retainers and staff having chambers or lodgings in the building. The sequence of rooms followed for nobleman and wife tended to be great chamber, dining chamber, withdrawing chamber, privy chamber, bedchamber and inner chamber, each room progressively more private, and each with particular servants with carefully defined duties assigned to them, and worked in rotation. In addition to these household officials there were also a secretary and a chaplain, the latter until the Reformation often heading a body of choristers. Some households also included resident musicians, players, fools and celebrities patronized by the owner.

Unlike the household-below-stairs the sexual character was more mixed, with gentlewomen and women-servants in attendance upon the womenfolk and children of the nobility: even so, such households were predominantly male. All employees received an annual livery or maintenance allowance towards clothing: for many, such payments were in kind, and invariably in the owner's colours; so, for instance, the third Duke of Buckingham's household servants were immediately recognizable from their uniform of red and black with badges of knots and swans.

The daily routine of the household-above-stairs centred on the nobleman, his wife and family. It was highly ritualized. The getting up of a nobleman in the morning was a public ceremony as was his going to bed at night. His attendance at chapel involved a procession, and even his saying of prayers in his own bedchamber was not a private matter. However, these ritual performances were secondary to the serving of dinner and supper which was the chief expression of the nobleman's 'state' or rank, and which in their complex preparation and organization involved everybody. Such meals were grand rather than congenial, and were generally conducted in almost total silence.

Burghley may also have begun to have doubts about his existing noble son-in-law, the Earl of Oxford. Oxford, the heir to considerable estates, had been a ward of Burghley's. Despite his great intelligence and many talents he was lazy, untruthful and self-indulgent: added to his undeniable amorality there were suspicions of homosexuality. The naturally parsimonious Burghley found his spendthrift son-in-law beyond comprehension. Oxford learned of his wife's pregnancy while abroad but refused to return home until after the birth of their daughter, when he cast doubt on her legitimacy.

Lord Burghley, memorandum   25 April 1576

No unkindness known on his part at his departure. She made him privy
that she thought she was with child, whereof he said he was glad.
When he was certified thereof at Paris he sent her his picture with kind
letters and messages. He sent her two coach horses. When he heard she
was delivered, he gave me thanks by his letters for advertising thereof.
He never signified any misliking of any thing until the 4 of April at Paris,
from whence he wrote somewhat that by reason of a man of his,
his receiver, he had conceived some unkindness ...

Distressed by the breakdown of Anne's marriage, Burghley wrote to her estranged husband suggesting that she and her daughter should henceforth live with Burghley. This letter irritated Oxford, who had not wanted his marital affairs to become public, even though he had sworn at Court that any child was not his. When Anne appealed to Oxford late in 1581 there was a reconciliation and - eventually - four more children.

Earl of Oxford to Lord Burghley   27 April 1576
Greenwich

... I must let your Lordship understand this much: that is, until I can
better satisfy or advertise myself of some mislikes, I am not determined,
as touching my wife, to accompany her. What they are - because some are
not to be spoken of or written upon as imperfections - I will not deal withal
... And last of all, I mean not to weary my life any more with such troubles
and molestations as I have endured; nor will I, to please your Lordship
only, discontent myself ... This might have been done through private
conference before, and had not needed to have been the fable of the world.

_Burghley had bought the Hertfordshire manor of Theobalds in 1564 in order to provide an estate for his son Robert. Over the next twenty years he constructed one of the most dazzling houses of the Elizabethan age, in 1571-72 spending no less than £2,700 on it. Queen Elizabeth visited Theobalds shortly after raising Burghley to the peerage in 1571, and again in 1572. She returned there in 1583. Extracts from a schedule of accommodation show how the Queen and Court were put up in May 1583.

Schedule of accommodation at Theobalds   August 1583
for Queen Elizabeth and the Court

The Second Stage in the Inner Court.

Over the Gate, a Gallery painted   }
with the arms of the noblemen   }
and gentlemen of England in trees.   }

Southward.

A Chamber, named the Lord Admiral's   }
Chamber, with an inner Chamber   }   The Lord Admiral
opening towards the Garden.   }

The South Side, a third Stage.

A Gallery for the Queen's majesty   }
At the south end in a tower one   }   The Earl of
Chamber, with two pallet-chambers.   }   Leicester

At the east side of the same   }   1. The Gentle-
Gallery, towards the Base Court,   }   women of the
in a garret two Rooms.   }   Privy Chamber.
                                                        2. Their servants.

At the North West End of the Gallery.

Two Chambers, whereof one with a   }   The Gentlewomen
chimney   }   of the Bedchamber.

A Bedchamber in a turret.   The Queen's
                                                       Majesty

Unlike his robust half-brother Thomas, Robert Cecil was frail and had been deformed by a fall as a baby. A lover of books, he was highly intelligent and sophisticated. On completing his education he visited Paris briefly before entering politics. His natural flair for administration soon became apparent and further endeared him to his father, since 1572 Lord Treasurer. Father and son worked virtually hand in glove for fifteen years until Burghley's death in 1598. Even so, Burghley could not resist advising Robert on how to manage his affairs and drafted a set of precepts for him to follow.

Lord Burghley to Robert Cecil   Late 1580s

When it shall please God to bring thee to man's estate, use great providence and circumspection in the choice of thy wife, for from thence may spring all thy future good or ill; and it is an action like a stratagem in war where man can err but once.

If the estate be good, match near home and at leisure; if weak, then far off and quickly. Inquire diligently of her disposition and how parents have been inclined in their youth. Let her not be poor how generous soever ... Neither choose a base and uncomely creature altogether for wealth, for it will cause contempt in others and loathing in thee. Make not choice of a dwarf or a fool, for from the one thou mayest beget a race of pygmies, the other may be thy daily disgrace; for it will irk thee to have her talk, for then thou shalt find to thy great grief that there is nothing more fulsome than a she-fool. Touching the government of thy house, let thy hospitality be moderate and according to the measure of thine own estate, rather plentiful than sparing - but not too costly ... Banish swinish drunkards out of thy house, which is a vice that impairs health, consumes much, and makes no show, for I never knew any praise ascribed to a drunkard but the well-bearing of drink, which is a better commendation for a brewer's horse or a drayman than for either gentleman or servingman ...

Undertake no suit against a poor man without receiving much wrong for therein making him thy competitor. Besides it is a base conquest to triumph where there is small resistance. Neither attempt law against any man before thou be fully resolved that thou hast the right on thy side ...

Towards thy superiors be humble yet generous; with thy equals familiar yet respective; towards inferiors show much humility and some familiarity, as to bow thy body, stretch forth thy hand, and to uncover thy head, and suchlike popular compliments. The first prepares a way to advancement; the second makes thee known for a man well-bred; the third gains a good report ... Yet do I advise thee not to affect nor neglect popularity too much. Seek not to be Essex and shun to be Ralegh.

The Cult of Popularity

Elizabeth I reviewing her troops and winning the 'hearts of her people' at Tilbury in 1588.

Unlike Henry VII, both Henry VIII and Elizabeth I made a point of being seen by their people; it was one way of handling the mystique of royalty to act the role out with public élan, and to accept the desire of their subjects to see them as an act of homage. So ordinary people would be let into palaces to see tournaments, to see Henry on his way to the tennis court or Elizabeth on her way to chapel. And this was not confined to London: their progresses around the country made them highly visible. When May Day 1515 was observed with a banquet in the woods near Greenwich, and the King was served by Robin Hood and his Merry Men, an eye-witness reckoned there were twenty-five thousand spectators - doubtless exaggerating, but suggestively.

Of Elizabeth, in the first careful weeks of her reign, an annalist observed: 'if ever any person had either the gift or the style to win the hearts of people, it was this Queen, and if ever she did express the same it was in that present, in coupling mildness with majesty as she did, and in stately stooping to the meanest sort ... distributing her smiles, looks, and graces so artificially [skilfully] that thereupon the people again redoubled the testimony of their joys.'

The Tudor nobility might make themselves visible, but they normally sought respect for their status, not popularity. Hence the suspicion that the second Earl of Essex's courteous behaviour in public was a deliberate ploy to emulate royal condescension and curry favour with the mob. Everard Guilpin satirized him as 'great Felix' in *Skialethia* (1598): 'Signior Machiavel Taught him this mumming trick, with courtesy to entrench himself with popularity.' Similarly, Shakespeare's Richard II 'Observed [Henry's] courtship to the common people, How he did seem to dive into their hearts With humble and familiar courtesy ... Off goes his bonnet to an oysterwench' (*Richard II*, Act 1, Scene 4). Doubtless Essex's supporters made the connection, if this was the play they commissioned for the eve of his rebellion. 'Popularity' was to be cultivated by Tudor monarchs, not by their subjects.

After the discovery of the Babington Plot in 1586, Burghley's unwavering purpose was to bring Mary, Queen of Scots to her reckoning and to induce Queen Elizabeth to take positive action against her. In September 1586 the Scottish Queen was transferred to Fotheringhay Castle in Northamptonshire, where, after she had been found guilty, she was executed on 8 February 1587. Queen Elizabeth had prevaricated over signing the death warrant as long as possible, and she was deeply annoyed by the speed with which her ministers had put the warrant into effect. She refused to accept two letters of explanation from Burghley, but she accepted the third.

Lord Burghley to Elizabeth I   23 February 1587

Most gracious and mighty Queen, although I am come to no understanding what special means to use to pacify your Majesty's heavy displeasure, so often and grievously expressed both to my friends and many others; whereby I am so overthrown in my weak spirit, as no part of my mind is sound to perform that I ought to do; a torment such as I never felt the like ... Yet such is the miserable condition of my state at this present, differing from others of my company, that though I find my humble submissions to your Majesty, and most lowly requests to be heard, to be still denied, yet comparing in my knowledge your Majesty's natural, princely clemency and compassion with this late accidental quality of your mind, by only one act miscontented, I do turn my face with my fact passed, to behold rather those princely graces which your Majesty hath of God and Nature, than to abide the censure of your mind, now miscontented. Seeking by my defence [not] to have your Majesty in any sort touched, by maintaining any thing against your honour, but to submit my self to your accustomed clemency. And so to be heard, as if your Majesty shall not allow of my answers, yet I may hope to have your concept of my fact in some part alleviated.

I know surely by many experiences your Majesty's sincerity and Christian conscience to be such; as except your Majesty [esteemed me] faulty indeed, your Majesty would not thus extremely use me. And therefore I do not therein think any thing but honorably of your Majesty; as you are persuaded, and as long as your Majesty shall, for lack of my answer, so conceive of me, I can hope of no good end, but only by your mercy. But if your Majesty might be pleased to hear me, though in your conceit as an offender, to answer to such things as move you to think me faulty; indeed I hope in my good God ... either to move your Majesty to temper the severity of your judgement against me, as not being a wilful offender, or to mollify your displeasure with some drops of your princely pity towards me ...

Eventually the Queen was mollified and Burghley was restored to his usual place in Elizabeth's counsels in time to handle the Armada crisis. But by 1595 Burghley's health had started to decline, and increasingly frequent bouts of sickness kept him periodically from Court and Council. Both Queen and minister made light of the septuagenarian's ill health, but Burghley recognized the necessity of his eventual retirement. Behind a show of personal withdrawal from politics he manoeuvred to secure the advancement of his son Robert. A visit by the Queen to Theobalds in May 1591 cost Burghley over £1,000, but it culminated in the knighting of Robert on 20 May, and two months later in Sir Robert's appointment to the Privy Council. Queen Elizabeth had joined in the spirit of her reception at Theobalds by issuing a mock charter which, if it was not actually of her own writing, had her connivance. The hermit addressed in the charter had welcomed the Queen, apologizing for the absence of Burghley, who had retired to a 'cell' to mourn the deaths of his much-loved wife and daughter.

Elizabeth I to 'the Hermit of Theobalds'   10 May 1591
Theobalds

Elizabetha Anglorum id est, a nitore Anglorum Regina formosissima et felicissima. [Elizabeth of the English, that is, in splendour, the most beautiful and most happy Queen of the English.] To the disconsolate and retired sprite, the hermit of Theobalds, and to all other disaffected souls, claiming by, from or under the said hermit, sendeth greeting. Where, in our High Court of Chancery, it is given us to understand that you, Sir Hermit, the abandoned of Nature's fair works, and servant to Heaven's wonders, have (for the space of two years and two months) possessed yourself of fair Theobalds with his sweet rosary, sometime the recreation of our right trusty and wellbeloved Sir William Cecil, knight, leaving to him the old rude repose, wherein twice five years (at his costs) your contemplative life was relieved. In which place Fate inevitable hath brought griefs innumerable (for Love's grief bideth no compare), suffering your solitary eye to bring into his house, desolation and mourning ... whereby Paradise is grown wilderness ... We upon consideration have commanded you hermit to your old cave, too good for the forsaken, too bad for our worthily beloved Councillor. And because we greatly tender your comforts, we have given power to our Chancellor to make out such and so many units (as to him shall be thought good) to abjure desolation and mourning (the consumer of sweetness) to the Frozen Seas and deserts of Arabia Petrosa [Stony Arabia], upon pain of five hundred despites to their terror and contempt of their torment, if they attempt any part of your house again. Enjoining you to the enjoyments of your own house ...

Plays and theatrical performances were the craze of late sixteenth-century Europe. In England, this enthusiasm united rich and poor alike, even if Puritans dismissed it as vicious and ungodly. Both the Queen and the Lord Admiral (second Lord Howard of Effingham) maintained companies, but in the 1590s the most important one was that run by the Lord Chamberlain, which produced plays written by Shakespeare. Unlike the Earl of Leicester, Burghley had no company of his own. However, he was an avid play-goer. Such was his interest that Trinity College wrote for his assistance over a costume when technically it should have raised the matter with a subordinate.

Head and Fellows of Trinity College to Lord Burghley   28 January 1595
Cambridge

Our bounden duty in most humble wise remembered. Whereas we intend for the exercise of young gentlemen and scholars in our college to set forth certain comedies and one tragedy. There being in that tragedy sundry personages of greatest estate, to be represented in ancient princely attire, which is no where to be had but within the Office of the Robes at the Tower, it is our humble request your most honorable Lordship would be please to grant your Lordship's warrant unto the chief officers there, that upon sufficient security we might be furnished from thence with such meet necessaries as are required. Which favour we have found heretofore upon your good Lordship's like honorable warrant: that hath the rather emboldened us at this time. And so craving pardon for this presumption, with remembrance of our daily prayers unto God for the preservation of our Honour's health to his own great glory we humbly take our leave.

Plays and Politics

Theatricals were an important adjunct of Tudor life, a lively source of entertainment and communication at a time when most of the population could not read. Successive monarchs and their grandees employed professional actors to enhance their own magnificence, such as Leicester's lavish entertainment of Elizabeth at Kenilworth in 1575. But they also recognized the subversive potential of 'the quick comedians', especially in matters of religious controversy, and took careful steps to control them. The annual medieval 'mystery' cycles in towns like York, Chester and Coventry (performed by the trade guilds) were 'reformed' and eventually suppressed because of their Catholic associations.

As the century wore on it became increasingly common for companies to tour the country professionally. Their status was uncertain and disputed, however; were they servants of the aristocracy, self-employed entrepreneurs, or merely vagrants and 'masterless men'? From 1572 those who performed in public had to be recognized servants of the peerage. By 1576 the growth of London created scope for regular playing, and the first permanent theatres since Roman times were erected. They were situated in the 'liberties' just north and south of the City, and so outside the control of the city authorities, who resisted these developments on the grounds of moral and public order. The Court defended them, however, claiming they were rehearsing for possible performances before the Queen - such performances being much in demand in the festive season from late November to Shrove Tuesday.

There was much competition for these lucrative commissions, partly because they reflected the status of the troupe's patron; to counter this, in 1583 Elizabeth created her own elite company, the Queen's Men, who dominated the decade but had declined by the great plague of 1593-4. By the late 1590s the privilege of permanent London bases and court performances was restricted to two companies, the Lord Chamberlain's and the Lord Admiral's Men, both patronized by cousins of the Queen.

In educated circles the use of theatricals for political and propaganda purposes was well understood. The gentlemen of Gray's Inn staged *Gorboduc* (1562) by Thomas Norton and Thomas Sackville (later Lord Buckhurst) before the Queen; the mythology is a thin disguise for blunt advice either to marry and beget heirs or to nominate her successors. Elizabeth once remarked to the Spanish ambassador, of a comedy staged at Court, 'This is all against me', indicating that she well appreciated the allegorical advice she was being given, and did not resent it. On another occasion, the Spanish ambassador accused Lord Burghley of instigating public plays ridiculing Philip II, a charge which was not denied.

An extant example of Burghley's shrewd use of theatre is the Theobalds entertainment of 1591, when he had himself 'shadowed' as a Hermit, in retirement from public life after the death of his wife in 1589. The sub-text is clearly a plea to Elizabeth to lighten his load by making his younger son, Robert, Secretary of State. The Hermit reappeared at Theobalds in 1594, making the same plea even more strongly. Robert Cecil apparently had a hand in penning this himself.

Officially, such comments on persons and affairs of state were not allowed on the public stages, but they were tolerated as long as a discreet fictional distance was maintained. After 1581 a court official, the Master of the Revels, was authorized to 'peruse and reform' all plays in the London area to ensure they did not transgress these boundaries.

Masque of Mercury and Diana at Sir Henry Unton's wedding. Francis Bacon advised the choice of colours.

Sir Robert Cecil's advancement during his father's lifetime reached its zenith on his appointment as Principal Secretary in 1596. Notwithstanding Burghley's growing infirmity, father and son then formed a remarkable partnership in government during the closing years of Queen Elizabeth's reign, with greater responsibility gradually shifting to Sir Robert. They communicated almost daily, with Burghley advising on every aspect of business.

Lord Burghley to Sir Robert Cecil   9 June 1598

To my loving son Sir Robert Cecil
    I see you continue your care for me, for which I thank you. I took not your house, for that it was too near the breathing of Westminster. Nor Wimbledon, because of the discommodities in passing the river. But came hither, to my familiar place, although forced to seek a resting place: but want rest.
    As yet I can[not] recover my appetite; only I supped yesternight with 4 or 5 leaves of an artichoke. But this morning I have eaten a small panada [a flavoured porridge made with bread].

In July 1598 Burghley began to fail rapidly. On 10 July he wrote what turned out to be his last letter in his own hand, appropriately to his son Robert. The Queen, whose principal minister he had been for forty years, attended him on his sickbed and fed him with a spoon. He recovered sufficiently to go to a meeting of the Council on 15 July, but this was his last attendance. He died a member of the Church of England, at his house on the Strand in London, on 4 August 1598.

Lord Burghley to Sir Robert Cecil   10 July 1598
[Burghley House, The Strand]

... Only I pray you diligently and effectually let her Majesty understand how her singular kindness doth overcome my power to acquit it who, though she will not be mother, *yet she showed herself by feeding me, with her own princely hand, a dutiful nurse.* And if I may be weaned to feed myself I shall be more ready to serve her on the earth. If not, I hope to be in heaven a servitor for her and God's Church ...
And so I thank you for your partridges.

Burghley was succeeded in his barony by his son Thomas. At the funeral, however, the Queen ordered Thomas to 'mourn as an earl'. Although made President of the Council in the North, the second Lord Burghley endeavoured to avoid this promised elevation in the peerage until, with the general distribution of honours after Elizabeth's death, he consented to receive the earldom of Exeter on 4 May 1605, the same day that his half-brother Robert was raised to the earldom of Salisbury.

Thomas, Lord Burghley to Sir John Hobbard   12 January 1604
Burghley

Your letters found me in such state, as rather I desired three days ease of pain, than to delight to think of any title of honour.

I am resolved to content my self with this state I have a baron. And my present state of living, howsoever those of the world hath enlarged it, I find little enough to maintain the degree I am in. And I am sure they that succeed me will be less able to maintain it than I am, considering there will go out of the baronage three younger brothers' livings.

This is all I can write unto you at this time, being full of pain; & therefore you must be content with this my brief writing. And I give you my very hearty thanks for your good wishes, & think my self beholden to those my friends that had care of me therein. And so I rest,

     Your assured friend,
     Thomas Burghley
I have delivered to your footman ten shillings for his charges.

'Ambitions of Glory'

ROBERT DEVEREUX, EARL OF ESSEX

By origins, the Devereux Earls of Essex, like the Sidneys, were a substantial gentle family made good by the accidents of inheritance, particularly in the female line. Like the Sidneys also, they were drawn into the Dudley orbit. But whereas the Sidneys were cheated of greatness, the Devereux grasped it and were nearly destroyed by it.

In the mid-fifteenth century Sir Walter Devereux, whose main landholdings were in the Welsh marches, married the heiress of the Ferrers of Chartley. Having backed the right side in the Wars of the Roses, he was raised to the peerage as Lord Ferrers of Chartley by Edward IV in 1461. Walter's son John, second Lord Ferrers, scored another matrimonial coup by marrying the eventual heiress of the Bourchiers, Earls of Essex. The Bourchiers, in turn, were the remote heirs of the Bohuns Earls of Hereford, who had died out in the fourteenth century. Over the next two generations the Devereux were able to cash in

both their chips. In 1550 Walter, the third Lord Ferrers, was promoted to the viscountcy of Hereford; finally in 1572 Walter, the fourth baron, was created Earl of Essex as well.

It was a glorious inheritance - if richer in titles than in land. And what land there was, was

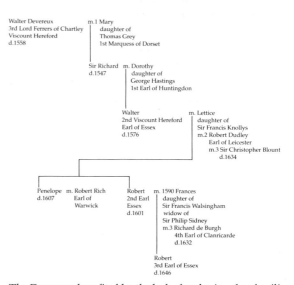

The Devereux benefited by the lack of males in other families.

Robert Devereux, second Earl of Essex. Devereux was clever, well-educated, personally brave and with a real sense of vision. But he never understood the rules of monarchical politics or perhaps he was trying to invent new ones.

bravery in the Netherlands in 1585 and, in a codicil to his will, left him his best swaord. In 1590 Essex secretly married Sidney's widow. It was a deliberate picking up of the mantle. Shortly after, his new father-in-law, the long-serving Secretary of State, Sir Francis Walsingham also died.

Leicester, Sidney and Walsingham had been the three leaders of the anti-Spanish war-party. Essex saw himself as political heir to all three and aspired to combine all their qualities in his own person. Like Leicester he was a great noble and royal favourite; like Sidney he was a soldier and a scholar; finally he determined to emulate Walsingham as a statesman and gatherer of foreign intelligence. Here he relied heavily on the Bacon brothers, Anthony and Francis, who acted almost as 'shadow' secretaries of state to their cousin and rival, Sir Robert Cecil.

Essex's vaulting ambition and Cecil's quieter but shrewder quest for power were bound to clash. At home every appointment turned into a faction struggle between Essex and Cecil (which Cecil almost always won); abroad England's foreign policy became a series of military adventures designed to demonstrate Essex's prowess. All were failures thinly disguised as triumphs; but the disaster of the earl's Irish expedition, too absolute for any pretence, plunged him into the abyss. In 1600 he returned and was executed after the failure of his rebellion.

Essex's folly led inevitably to the rise of Sir Robert Cecil. Elizabeth had hoped that the younger Cecil and Essex would recreate the working relationship between Burghley and Leicester of the great days of the reign. It was not to be.

heavily burdened with debt incurred by the first Earl in Ireland. Walter, the first Earl was aware of the problems. But his son, Robert, the second Earl, who succeeded in 1576, saw only the glory. His father had commended him to Lord Burghley on his deathbed. Instead, events pulled him gradually into the orbit of the Dudley-Sidney connection. His widowed mother married Leicester; Leicester introduced him to Court and he succeeded to Leicester's principal court office of Master of the Horse. The ties with Sidney were more intimate. Sidney had been struck by the young earl's

For centuries Englishmen have had a succession of visions for Ireland, sometimes quite wrongly conceived. For centuries also misfortune has thwarted the realisation of these plans, and in so doing has destroyed the promise of many a brilliant career. One such hopeful visionary was Walter Devereux, first Earl of Essex. Essex had a scheme, as a private adventurer, to establish order in Ulster and to colonize it. To finance this venture he mortgaged his estates to Queen Elizabeth for £10,000. After four years, and after recourse to savage brutality, Essex, frustrated, died of dysentery. He had had another dream, to unite his family with the Cecils, with whom he had stood firm against the aspirations of the fourth Duke of Norfolk. Although rebuffed in 1573 Essex revived the idea on his deathbed. It was equally, and even more disastrously, to fail.

Walter, Earl of Essex to Lord Burghley   21 September 1576
Dublin

My good Lord,
    It were more reasonable that I framed my last speech unto you to this end only, to show myself thankful for your favours past, than to enter into new petitions at such a time as this, when you are sure that your thanks shall die with me; and that my son, by tenderness of years, is far from discretion to judge of such friendships as I must desire to proceed from your lordship in his behalf. Nevertheless, upon the assured confidence that your love to me shall descend to my children, and that your lordship will declare yourself a friend to me, both alive and dead, I have willed Mr. Waterhouse to show unto you, how you may with honour and equity do good to my son Hereford, and how to bind him with perpetual friendship to you and your house. And to the end, I would have his love towards those which are descended from you spring up and increase with his years. I have wished his education to be in your household, though the same had not been allotted to your lordship as Master of the Wards; and that the whole time which he should spend in England in his minority might be divided in attendance upon my Lord Chamberlain [Thomas Radcliffe, third Earl of Sussex] and you, to the end that, as he might frame himself to the example of my Lord of Sussex in all the actions of his life tending either to the wars or to the institution of a nobleman, so that he might also reverence your lordship for his wisdom and gravity, and lay up your counsels and advices in the treasury of his heart.
    I assure myself in God that he will raise up many friends to my posterity, and that this small persuasion shall be sufficient to move your lordship to do good to the son of him who lived and died your true and unfeigned friend. And so to the Lord I commit you, sequestering myself from henceforth from all worldly causes.

And indeed Lord Burghley at first assumed responsibility for the upbringing of the second Earl of Essex. But the marriage of his mother to the Earl of Leicester in 1578 attached him to the Dudley connection, and set the mark on the young earl's development and career. Intellectually precocious, Essex went to Trinity College, Cambridge, where (unusually for a nobleman) he graduated in 1581. Notwithstanding his straitened financial circumstances he was introduced at Court by Leicester, where his 'goodly person' and 'innate courtesy' immediately won him Elizabeth's favour: 'When she is abroad nobody with her but my Lord of Essex, and at night my lord is at cards, or one game or another with her that he cometh not to his lodging till the birds sing in the morning.' His standing with the Queen displaced, but did not oust, her previous favourite, Sir Walter Ralegh. Essex was bitterly jealous of his rival.

Earl of Essex to Edward Dyer   21 July [1587]

Things are fallen out very strangely against me, since my last being with you. Yesternight the Queen came to Northaw ... she came to speak of Ralegh; and it seemed she could not well endure any thing to be spoken against him; and taking hold of one word, *disdain*, she said there was no such cause why I should disdain him. This speech did trouble me so much, that, as near as I could, I did describe unto her what he had been, and what he was; and then I did let her know whether I had cause to disdain his competition of love, or whether I could have comfort to give myself over to the service of a mistress that was in awe of such a man. I spake, what of grief and choler, as much against him as I could, and I think he, standing at the door, might very well hear the worst that I spoke of himself. In the end, I saw she was resolved to defend him and to cross me. From thence she came to speak bitterly against my mother, which, because I could not endure to see me and my house disgraced (the only matter which both her choler and the practise of mine enemies had to work upon), I told her, for my sister she should not any longer disquiet her; I would, though it were almost midnight, send her away that night; and for myself, I had no joy to be in any place, but loth to be near about her, when I knew my affection so much thrown down, and such a wretch as Ralegh highly esteemed of her. To this she made not answer, but turned her away to my Lady of Warwick. So at that late hour I sent my men away with my sister; and after, I came hither myself. This strange alteration is by Ralegh's means; and the Queen, that hath tried all other ways, now will see whether she can by those hard courses drive me to be friends with Ralegh, which rather shall drive me to many other extremities.

The Order of the Garter

The knights of the Garter, c. 1534, in an illumination from the register of the Garter known as the Black Book.

The origins of the Order of the Garter are shrouded in myth. It may commemorate the English victory at Crécy; its insignia of a blue garter may derive from the Countess of Salisbury losing such an item at a ball and Edward III retrieving it and putting it on himself, with the words *'Honi soit qui mal y pense'* [Evil be to him who evil thinks], which is the motto of the Order. At all events it is the oldest order of chivalry in Christendom, a fanciful evocation of King Arthur and his Round Table, and a symbol of nationhood, being dedicated to England's patron saint, St George.

Membership is limited to the sovereign and twenty-five knights, together with favoured foreign princes. Notionally the knights elect new members when there are vacancies, though in reality appointments are the personal gift of the sovereign.

As part of his aim of making the monarchy the fount of all honour, Henry VIII encouraged his courtiers to think of election to the Order as a significant goal, preferable even to grants of money or property as a sign of favour. The Reformation presented some problems for the Garter, which in one sense was a religious guild or fraternity. So did the fact that Mary and Elizabeth were female, and they often chose not to be involved in Garter ceremonials, which somewhat diminished their status.

Essex did not limit his bravado to the Court. He had served under his stepfather, Leicester in the Netherlands, where his personal bravery at Zutphen earned him a knighthood. Sir Philip Sidney bequeathed him his 'best' sword, and this gesture helped to persuade Essex to see himself as Sidney's heir in promoting the Protestant Cause. This personal vision was strengthened when, following the deaths of Leicester and Warwick in 1588 and 1589, many Dudley supporters transferred their allegiance to him. This was given a personal embodiment by his marriage in 1590 to Sidney's widow. Finally, there was his appointment to Leicester's former post as Master of the Horse in 1587 and his creation as Knight of the Garter in 1588. The mastership was the perfect official vehicle for the realization of his personal political vision. An early intimation came in1589 when he joined the expedition to Portugal. Elizabeth, abruptly addressing him as 'Essex', insisted upon his returning to England and to Court.

Elizabeth I to Earl of Essex   15 April 1589
Essex

Your sudden and undutiful departure from our presence and your place of attendance, you may easily conceive how offensive it is, and ought to be, unto us ... Not meaning, therefore, to tolerate this your disordered part, we gave directions to some of our Privy Council to let you know our express pleasure for your immediate repair hither; which you have not performed, as your duty doth bind you ... We do therefore charge and command you forthwith, upon receipt of these our letters, all excuses and delays set apart, to make your present and immediate repair unto us, to understand our further pleasure. Whereof see you fail not, as you will be loath to incur our indignation, and will answer for the contrary at your uttermost peril.

Another opportunity to show himself as Sidney's heir and to prove his worth came in 1596 when he was appointed commander of the land forces in the Cadiz expedition.

Elizabeth I to Earl of Essex   May 1596

I make this humble bill of requests to Him that all makes and does, that with His benign Hand He will shadow you so, as all harm may light beside you, and all that may be best hap to your share; that your return may make you better, and me gladder ...

The expedition of 1596 was a limited success. The port of Cadiz was stormed after the Spanish navy had been forced into Cadiz harbour and destroyed. However, the main quarry, the Spanish treasure fleet coming from America, eluded capture. This did not please Elizabeth and Burghley, but the fact was not allowed to dent either his own or the popular opinion of the earl's 'victory'. To modern eyes Essex's fame as a military commander (even if unwarranted); his appetite for power and above all his popularity, look like advantages. In fact in a monarchy, and particularly under a woman, they were dangerous. In this letter Francis Bacon, Burghley's nephew but Essex's client and adviser, advises the earl to change course: he must recognize his absolute dependence upon the Queen's favour, go for civil, not military office, and pretend to despise 'popularity'. This advice is brilliantly calculated. But Bacon's principal calculation may have been the protection of his own position if Essex, as he clearly foresaw, came unstuck.

Francis Bacon to Earl of Essex   4 October 1596

Win the Queen; if this be not the beginning, of any other course I can see no end … The impression of greatest prejudice is that of a military dependence, wherein, I cannot sufficiently wonder at your lordship's course, that you say, the wars are your occupation … You have property good enough in that greatness. There is none can of many years ascend near you in competition … But I say, keep it in substance, but abolish it is shews. For her Majesty loveth peace. Next, she loveth not charge. Thirdly, that kind of dependence maketh a suspected greatness. Therefore, again, whereas I heard your lordship designing to yourself the Earl Marshal's place, or place of the Master of the Ordnance, I did not, in my own mind, so well like of either, because of their affinity with a martial greatness. But of the places now void I would name to you the place of Lord Privy Seal. For first, it is the third person of the great officers of the Crown. Next, it hath a kind of superintendence over the Secretary. It also hath an affinity with the Court of Wards, in regard of the fees from the liveries. And it is a fine honour, quiet place, and worth £1000 by year … The third impression is of a popular reputation, which … is one of the flowers of your greatness, both present and to come; it should be handled tenderly. The only way is to quench it *verbis* [in words], and not *rebus* [by deeds]; and, therefore, to take all occasions to the Queen to speak against popularity and popular courses vehemently, and to tax it in all others; but, nevertheless, to go on in your honorable commonwealth courses as you do.

Maps and Map-Making

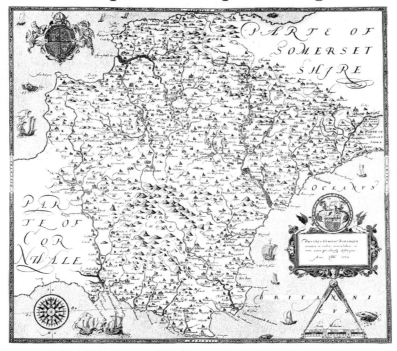

Christopher Saxton's map of Devonshire, 1574. Saxton published engraved maps of all the English counties, which were gathered into the first English Atlas. He was rewarded with the grant of a coat of arms, with the crest of a man with a pair of 'compasses gold'.

In 1561 John Rudd, Dean of Durham, having 'taken some pain in making a platt [plan] of our realm', received the Queen's permission 'to travel more diligently therein for setting forth thereof both fair and more perfect and truer than it hath been hitherto'. Rudd shared a fascination for cartography with Laurence Nowell, tutor to Sir William Cecil's wards. At the same time as this pair and their circle were promoting the idea of mapping England and Wales, the related techniques of draughtsmanship and surveying were undergoing development, partly in response to the ongoing series of wars from the 1530s with the consequent need for up-to-date defences, and partly to meet the increasing requirement by both the Crown and major figures for maps of particular properties. Manuals on surveying had had a ready market from the time of Sir Anthony Fitzherbert's *Book of Surveying* in 1523; the principles of triangulation were generally available from the 1550s, and surveying instruments manufactured by specialists were available in London from the 1570s.

   Crucial to the realisation of the project to survey the kingdom was the support given to Christopher Saxton and John Norden by Sir William Cecil, later Lord Burghley. Burghley appreciated the use of maps throughout his career, even making his own sketch maps of politically sensitive areas. His intervention as Queen Elizabeth's principal minister in regional matters, as well as the Elizabethan regime's close surveillance of the localities, was a spur to surveying the counties. He was also a trendsetter in collecting maps. Saxton's *Atlas* of 1579 was an extraordinary achievement in being both accurate and beautiful: it contained thirty-four county maps and one general map of England and Wales, which were unprecedented in their accuracy. However, Saxton's coverage of regions, not individual counties, and use of scales varying from map to map led to confusion, and induced Norden to start his *Speculum Britanniae*, the first instalment of which appeared in 1593. Norden appended to his maps topographical and historical information, an idea copied by John Speed in his *Theatre of the Empire of Great Britain*. This was eventually published during 1611-12, and then became the standard atlas for the British Isles. Speed also included a novelty which did much to

Maps (continued)

promote demand for the atlas, a set of over seventy town-plans from throughout the kingdom.

The meticulous preparatory work done towards these atlases enhanced the 'upstart art' of estate surveying. Not only was the systematic surveying of the great estates, towns and villages well in hand by the end of the sixteenth century, maps had become familiar features of daily life. They complemented works such as William Lambarde's *Perambulations of Kent* and William Camden's *Britannia*. They occupied pride of place on the walls of houses, and globes were commonplace. They also provided the subject matter for the wall tapestries produced by the Sheldon family at Barcheston in Warwickshire. A revolution in the popular perception of England had taken place.

Late sixteenth-century maps differ from their modern counterparts in lacking countours and rarely showing roads. On the other hand, rivers with their crossings are scrupulously delineated. Relief is suggested by scattered 'mole-hills' that give only a general impression of changes in the landscape. Water-depth along the coastline is more preceisely suggested, particularly near harbours and anchorages, by indicating the rocks and banks of sand or mud which were a hazard to shipping. Other cartographic conventions intimate mainland features: the towns are marked by groups of buildings, villages by smaller clusters, woods by little trees. In fact, the maps show the position of most inhabited places, their relative importance and their distribution among the chief features of the countryside, its rivers, wetlands, forests and hills. The inclusion of deer-parks emphasizes the importance of hunting as a source both of entertainment and of venison to the Tudor nobility and gentry. Also the marking of some 'prodigy' houses, such as Theobalds, was intended to be as much a compliment to the builders of the houses as an indication of general public interest in aristocratic building activity.

Lawrence Nowell's map of Great Britain, c. 1564. This was Sir William Cecil's own pocket copy, with the fold marks still clearly visible. The relationship between them is suggested by the figures on either side: Cecil sitting on an hour-glass, while Nowell is sleeping.

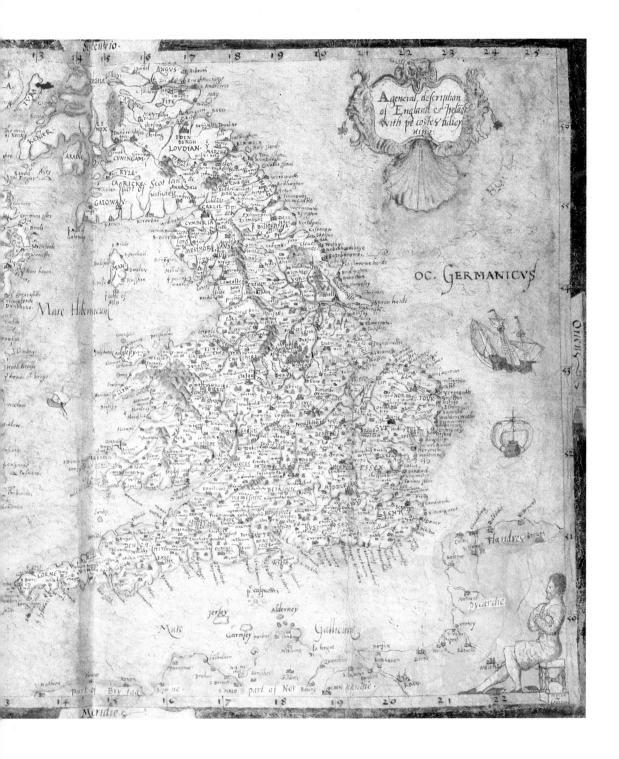

Whether or not he was responding to Bacon's advice, Essex did moderate his behaviour in 1597. His hitherto increasingly strained relations with the Cecils and with Ralegh, his two main rivals and contenders for power, underwent a significant improvement. In June 1597 Essex was given command of the expedition to intercept the Spanish treasure fleet-sailing from America and to seize the Azores. But the 'Islands Voyage' (as it was popularly called) was dogged by unusually bad weather conditions and further highlighted Essex's inexperience and incapacity as commander. Where credit was due, it was again largely Ralegh's. Jealous, Essex had Ralegh court-martialled for insubordination. Still worse, the Spanish navy pursued Essex back to England, and threatened invasion. Here Rowland White writes to Sir Robert Sidney about the Islands Voyage and Essex's frosty reception upon his return.

Rowland White to Sir Robert Sidney   5 November 1597
London

You will expect, now that the Earl of Essex is returned, to hear from me what is done. For himself, he is already disquieted, keeps in, and went not this day to the Parliament; and I heard her Majesty is not well pleased with him for his service at sea, wherein it is alleged, he might have done more than he did ...

The coolness of the reception accorded by Queen, Council and Court to Essex on his return from the 'Islands Voyage' was not what he had expected. Distressed at Lord Admiral Howard of Effingham's creation as Earl of Nottingham, Essex withdrew to his house at Wanstead. There he took the conventional adulation of the Queen as Gloriana to its highest pitch. The ploy worked. Made Earl Marshal (with precedence over the Lord Admiral) late in December 1597 he returned triumphantly to Court.

Earl of Essex to Elizabeth I   late November or December 1597
[?Wanstead]

Madam ... least your Majesty should wonder at my coming away so soon, I crave leave to put your Majesty in mind what a stranger I was made today, which doth so ill fit with my past fortune and my mind at this present, as I had rather retire my sick body and troubled mind into some place of rest, than, living in your presence ... be one of those that look upon you afar off.

But the earl marshalship was precisely the military office which Bacon had counselled him most to avoid. In addition he had been appointed Master of the Ordnance as well (also on Bacon's forbidden list). That meant that, by an unprecedented piece of pluralism, all three chief military offices were in the same hands. Doubts about Essex's ambition - at home as well as abroad - were magnified. At the same time, Essex's view of Elizabeth soured. A difference in Council over policy towards Ireland during 1598 led, it is said, to the earl blurting out that the Queen's 'conditions were as crooked as her carcase.' Convinced as to the rightness of his ideas for Ireland Essex barred the appointment of Lord Mountjoy as Lord Lieutenant, and instead in March 1599 he was made Lord Lieutenant himself. Within six months both Essex's Irish policy and his political reputation were in ruins. He returned to Court in defiance of an express order to remain in Ireland, in an attempt to justify himself. He was committed to the care of Lord Keeper Egerton in October 1599 and became a subject for popular sympathy. Further incriminatory revelations about his handling of Irish rebels led to the Queen declining to act on the Council's recommendation to release him. Prayers were then said in London at Christmas for his restoration to favour. A further manifestation of support for Essex was the publication of a print depicting Essex on horseback with his titles of honour and military feats. The image was near to the representation of the monarch as knight-defender of the people which appears on the reverse of the Great Seal. The implication was that Essex would fulfil this role better than Elizabeth. And the challenge was driven home by the description of Essex as 'God's Elect'. Rowland White reports on the furore and the banning of the engraving (and indeed of all representations of noblemen apart from the Queen herself).

Rowland White to Sir Robert Sidney   February 1600
London, Baynard's Castle

The Earl of Essex is well again, and walks up and down the house [York House] and garden at my Lord Keeper [Sir Thomas Egerton]'s; small hope of grace or liberty appears. Her Majesty, as it seems, constant in her just conceived displeasure against him, will have the world see that he hath deserved this punishment laid upon him. Some say, 'He shall be called to public question'; some are of another opinion.

    Some foolish idle headed ballad-maker of late caused many of his pictures to be printed on horseback, with all his titles of honour, all his services, and two verses underneath that gave him exceeding praise for wisdom, honour, worth; that Heaven and Earth approve it, God's elect, with such words as hath occasioned the calling of them all in again.

The Essex Rebellion

Henry Wriothesley, third Earl of Southampton, one of Essex's confederates in his rebellion. The picture commemorates Southampton's subsequent imprisonment, with a view of the Tower top right, the dates of his imprisonment and the uncontrite motto, which means 'Undefeated in chains'.

Even before the Irish expedition, Essex's star was on the wane. Essex was constantly vexed that he and his nominees were passed over for posts and honours that he felt were their due. He blamed the Cecils, Ralegh and Cobham for coming between him and Elizabeth. In Ireland he contemplated using the forces under him against his enemies at Court, if not against Elizabeth herself.

Failure in Ireland led to disgrace, restraint, banishment from Court, the loss of his principal revenues and the constant threat of prosecution. By the beginning of 1601, however, Essex was desperate and drew up plans to take the Court by force, with the support of relations and close allies. They flocked to Essex House, closely watched by Cecil's spies. On 7 February a group of them commissioned Shakespeare's company, the Lord Chamberlain's Men to put on a performance of a play about Richard II, very likely Shakespeare's own, at the Globe. Grumblers commonly likened Richard, surrounded by base-born flatterers, to Elizabeth; Richard, of course, was deposed. The conspirators' aim was not to incite a mob, but to steel their own

resolve. That evening the Council ordered Essex to appear before them, but he declined, saying he feared a plot against him.

The following day, Sunday, the Council made a pre-emptive move; they sent Lord Keeper Egerton, the Earl of Worcester, Sir William Knollys and the Chief Justice, all former friends of Essex, to see him in the Queen's name. Essex panicked, held them hostage and took to the streets with about two hundred followers, crying: 'For the Queen! For the Queen! A plot is laid for my life!' As one who had always courted commons, he hoped for popular support, but none was forthcoming. He found all routes blocked and retired in disarray to Essex House, only to find that his hostages had been released.

The Queen's forces, under Nottingham, now laid siege to the house and sent Sir Robert Sidney to negotiate with his old patron. Essex vacillated between fighting to the last and lapsing into the remorseful melancholia that was to characterize his final days. Under Nottingham's threat to blow up the house he finally surrendered. He was tried and executed on 25 February, privately, in the Tower.

Such 'popularity' only made the Queen and Council more determined to bring Essex to trial. The earl was brought before a specially constituted court in June 1600. This advised clemency and Essex was released from captivity. But he was not 'freed from her Majesty's indignation.' When a summons to Court eventually came in February 1601, it was accompanied by an anonymous warning that his plan to return there with a show of force had been disclosed. Essex panicked, and this sparked a rebellion from Essex House. When the popular rising did not take place, he surrendered. Brought to trial in Westminster Hall on 19 February, he was found guilty and beheaded. In his testimony at the trial Sir Robert Cecil contrasted Essex's failure with his own success.

Sir Robert Cecil at the Earl of Essex's trial   19 February 1601

My Lord of Essex, the difference between you and me is great. For wit, I give you pre-eminence: you have it abundantly. For nobility also I give you place: I am not noble, yet a gentleman. I am no swordsman: there also you have the odds. But I have innocence, conscience, truth and honesty to defend me against the scandal and sting of slanderous tongues, and in this court I stand as an upright man, and your lordship as a delinquent ...

Queen Elizabeth survived Essex by just over two years, dying on 24 March 1603. Within two months of the Queen's death Cecil, although confirmed in his post as Principal Secretary, was wistfully regretting her departure. The age of Elizabeth I now had the aspect of halcyon days.

Lord Cecil to Sir John Harrington   29 May 1603
[?Greenwich?]

... give heed to one that hath sorrowed in the bright lustre of a court ... It is a great task to prove one's honesty, and yet not spoil one's fortune. You have tasted a little hereof in our blessed Queen's time, who was more than a man and, in troth, sometimes less than a woman. I wish I waited now in her Presence Chamber ... I am pushed from the shore of comfort and know not where the winds and waves of a court will bear me ... Farewell, good knight; but never come near London till I call you. Too much crowding doth not well for a cripple, and the King doth find scant room, to sit himself, he hath so many *friends* as they choose to be called ...

Index

Further Reading

For those wishing to pursue further the themes central to this volume the following books are recommended.

S. Adams, 'Eliza Enthroned? The Court and its Politics', in C. Haigh (ed), *The Reign of Elizabeth I*, 1985
S. Adams, 'The Dudley Clientèle, 1553-1563', in G.W. Bernard (ed), *The English Nobility in the Sixteenth Century*, 1991
G.W. Bernard, *The Power of the Early Tudor Nobility: A Study of the Fourth and Fifth Earls of Shrewsbury*, 1985
G.W. Bernard, *War, Taxation and Rebellion in Early Tudor England: Henry VIII, Wolsey, and the Amicable Grant of 1525*, 1986
S.T. Bindoff, *Tudor England*, 1950
J. Buxton, *Sir Philip Sidney and the English Renaissance*, 1964
A. Cecil, *Robert Cecil, First Earl of Salisbury*, 1915
H.W. Chapman, *Lady Jane Grey*, 1962
P. Collinson, *The English Captivity of Mary Queen of Scots*, Sheffield History Pamphlets, 1987
W.B. Devereux, *Lives and Letters of the Devereux, Earls of Essex*, 1853
M.H. Dodds and R. Dodds, *The Pilgrimage of Grace, 1536-1537, and the Exeter Conspiracy, 1538*, 2 vols, 1915
G.R. Elton, *Reform and Reformation*, 1977
G.R. Elton, *Policy and Police: The Enforcement of the Reformation in the Age of Thomas Cromwell*, 1972
A. Fraser, *Mary, Queen of Scots*, 1969
Fulke Greveille, 'A Dediction to Sir Philip Sidney' in J. Gouws (ed), *The Prose Works of Fulke Greville, Lord Brooke*, 1986
S.J. Gunn, *Charles Brandon, Duke of Suffolk c. 1484-1545*, 1988
S.J. Gunn and P.G. Lindley (eds), *Cardinal Wolsey: Church, State and Art*, 1991
J. Guy, *Tudor England*, 1988
P.J. Gwyn, *The King's Cardinal*, 1990
A. Haynes, *The White Bear: Robert Dudley, The Elizabethan Earl of Leicester*, 1987
D.E. Hoak, *The King's Council in the Reign of Edward VI*, 1976
R. Howell, *Sir Philip Sidney: The Shepherd Knight*, 1968
E.W. Ives, *Anne Boleyn*, 1986
M.E. James, *Society, Politics and Culture: Studies in Early Modern England*, 1986
M. Levine, *The Early Elizabethan Succession Question, 1558-1568*, 1966
W.T. MacCaffrey, *The Shaping of the Elizabethan Regime*, 1968
W.T. MacCaffrey, *Queen Elizabeth and the Making of Policy, 1572-1588*, 1981
H. Miller, *Henry VIII and the English Nobility*, 1986
J.E. Neale, *Queen Elizabeth*, 1934
A.F. Pollard, *England under Protector Somerset*, 1900

The ceiling of the Great Chamber at the Charterhouse displays the Duke of Norfolk's heraldry.

A.F. Pollard, *Thomas Wolsey*, 1929
C. Read, *Mr Secretary Cecil and Queen Elizabeth*, 1955
C. Read, *Lord Burghley and Queen Elizabeth*, 1960
E. Read, *Catherine, Duchess of Suffolk*, 1962
W.C. Richardson, *Mary Tudor, The White Queen*, 1970
J.M. Robinson, *The Dukes of Norfolk: a quincentennial history*, 1982
A.L. Rowse, 'Bess of Hardwick: Builder and Dynast' in *Eminent Elizabethans*, 1983
J.J. Scarisbrick, *Henry VIII*, 1968
J.J. Scarisbrick, *The Reformation and the English People*, 1984
W.A. Sessions, *Henry Howard, Earl of Surrey*, 1986
D.R. Starkey, *The Reign of Henry VIII: Personalities and Politics*, 1985
D.R. Starkey, *The English Court from the Wars of the Roses to the Civil War*, 1987
L. Strachey, *Elizabeth and Essex*, 1928
F.W. Steer, *Henry Howard, the Poet Earl of Surrey*, 1977
M. Tucker, *The Life of Thomas Howard, Earl of Surrey and Second Duke of Norfolk, 1443-1524*, 1964
R. Virgoe, 'The Recovery of the Howards in East Anglia, 1485 to 1529', in E.W. Ives et al (eds), *Wealth and Power in Tudor England*, 1978
M.W. Wallace, *The Life of Sir Philip Sidney*, 1915
N.J. Williams, *Thomas Howard, Fourth Duke of Norfolk*, 1964
D. Wilson, *Sweet Robin: A Biography of Robert Dudley, Earl of Leicester 1533-1588*, 1981
J. Wormald, *Mary, Queen of Scots: A Study in Failure*, 1988

PICTURE CREDITS
Note: t = top, b = bottom, c = centre, r = right, l = left.

1 Henry VIII Shilling. British Museum, London, Department of Coins and Medals. 3 Henry VIII Gold Sovereign. British Museum, London, Department of Coins and Medals. 7 Table Desk belonging to Henry VIII, English, c 1525. Victoria & Albert Museum, London, no. W29-1932. 10t Letter Patent to Gilbert Talbot, Deputy of Calais, appointing receivers of payments due under treaty with Etaples, 1510. British Library, London, Add. Ch. 74075. 10b Letter signed by Duke of Norfolk, 1546. British Library, London, Cotton. MS. Titus, B.I, f.101. 11 Henry VIII, painting after Holbein. Hever Castle, Kent/Woodmansterne. Ltd. 17l Arms of Robert Sidney, Viscount Lisle, later Earl of Leicester, early 17th century. College of arms, London, MS. E. 16, f. 33v. 17r Arms of Thomas Cecil, Earl of Exeter, early 17th century. College of Arms, London, MS. E. 16, f. 24v. 18l Henry VII and Elizabeth of York, bronze-gilt tomb effigy by Torrigiano in Westminster Abbey. Woodmansterne Ltd. 18r Mary Queen of Scots, oil on panel after Nicholas Hilliard, c 1610. National Portrait Gallery, London, no. 429. 20l Henry VIII with Henry VII, ink and watercolour by Hans Holbein, 1536-7. National Portrait Gallery, London, no. 4027. 20r Henry Howard, Earl of Surrey, oil on canvas by William Scrots, c1550. National Portrait Gallery, London, no. 5291. 24l A procession of Elizabeth I, painting attributed to Robert Peake the Elder, c 1601. Private Collection. 24r Rcbert Devereux, 2nd Earl of Essex, line engraving by Thomas Cookson. British Museum, London, Department of Prints & Drawings, no. 07-283. 31 The Great Harry, engraving from an original draawing in a 16th century list of the Kings ships. Magdalene College, Oxford/The Mansell Collection, London. 32-3 The Embarkation from Dover of Henry VIII for France, 1521 or 1532, by an unknown artist. By Gracious Permission of HM the Queen. 35 Coronation of Henry VIII and Catherine of Aragon, 1509, from a pamphlet by Stephen Hawes. Cambridge University Library, Rare Book Sel. 5.55 36 Robes of the Peers, drawings by an unknown artist, 16th century. British Library, London, Add. MS. 6113, f. 61v. 38 Mary Tudor with her second husband, Charles Brandon, Duke of Suffolk, painting by unknown artsit. By Permission of the Marquess of Tavistock, and the Trustees of the Bedford Estate. 41 Trumpeters summon Challengers to the Joust, from the Great Tournament Roll of Westminster. College of Arms, London. 42-3 Henry VIII jousting before Catherine of Aragon at the Tournament of 1511, to Celebrate the Birth of Henry, Prince of Wales, from The Great Tournament Roll of Westminster, College of Arms, London. 46 Catherine of Aragon, painting by Miguel Sittow, c 1502. Kunsthistorisches Museum, Vienna. 47 Henry III and his Court at a Ball Celebrating the Marriage of Anne, Duc de Joyeuse to Margaret de Lorraine-Vandémont, oil on canvas attributed to Hermann van der Mast, c 1581-4. Musée National du Chateâu de Versailles, no. MV 5636/© Photo R.M.N. 50 Cardinal Thomas Wolsey, panel by an unknown artist. National Portrait Gallery, London, no. 32. 51 Wolsey delivers the Great Seal to the Dukes of Norfolk and Suffolk, from 'Cavendish's Life'. The Bodleian Library, Oxford, MS. Douce 363, f.71. 54 Henry VIII in his Privy Chambers, drawing by an unknown artist. British Museum, London, Department of Prints & Drawings/ Fotomas Index, London. 57l Francis I, painting by Jean Clouet. The Louvre, Paris/© Photo R.M.N. 57r Charles V, painting by Titian. Prado, Madrid/Scala 61 Pages from an Album of Designs of Armours built at the Royal Armouries, Greenwich, c 1589, by the Master Workman, Jacob Halder. Victoria and Albert Museum, London, no D. 586-614-1894/the Bridgeman Art Library, London. 62-3 Meeting of Henry VIII and the Emperor Maximilian I at Theronanne, 1513, painting by an unknown artist. By Gracious Permission of HM the Queen. 67 Opening of The Act in Restraint of Appeals to Rome of 1553, published by the King's Printer. British Library, London, Printed Books, 506.d.31.(4). 71 Thomas Howard, 3rd Duke of Norfolk, painting by Hans Holbein, 1539. By Gracious Permission of HM the Queen. 74 Initial of Earl Marshal and Heralds, Isabella Stewart Gardiner Museum, Boston, MS. 3. T/8, f.26. 75 Anne Boleyn, painting by an unknown artist. Hever Castle, Kent/ Woodmansterne Ltd. 79 Henry VIII reading in his Bedroom, illuminated by Jean Maillard, from the King's Psalter, c 1540. British Library, London, Royal MS. 2A XVI. f.3. 82 St James' Church, Louth, Photograph by John Meek. 83 Thomas Cranmer, oil on canvas by Gerlach Flicke, 1546. National Portrait Gallery, London, no. 535. 86 Detail from Portrait of Henry Howard, Earl of Surrey, oil on canvas by William Scrots, c 1550. National Portrait Gallery, London, no.5291. 87 Tomb of 3rd Duke of Norfolk and his second wife Elizabeth Stafford, Framlingham, Suffolk. Courtauld Institute of Art, London. 90 Jane Seymour, painting by Hans Holbein. Kunsthistorisches Museum, Vienna/The Bridgeman Art Library, London. 91 South Porch, Church of St Peter and St Paul, Lavenham, Suffolk. Photograph by John Meek. 95 Thomas Cromwell, 1st Earl of Essex, oil on panel after Holbein. National Portrait Gallery, London, no.1727. 98 Page from the 'Booke of Falconre'. Fotomas Index, London. 99 Anne of Cleves, miniature by Hans Holbein, 1539. Victoria and Albert Museum, London, no. P153-1910. 102 Detail from Edward VI and The Pope, oil on canvas by an unknown artist, c 1548-9. National Portrait Gallery, London, no. 4165. 106 Catherine Howard, miniature by Hans Holbein, c 1540-2. By Gracious Permission of HM the Queen. 110 Banners of the Dukes of Ferrare, Norfolk, Buckingham and Suffolk, from the 'Book of Standards'. College of Arms, London, MS.I.2. 111 Kenninghall Place, Norfolk. Photograph by John Meek. 118 Detail from Edward VI and The Pope, oil on canvas by an unkown artist, c 1548-9. National Portrail Gallery, London, no. 4165. 122l Elizabeth I, miniature by Nicholas Hilliard, c 1580. Private Collection/The Bridgeman Art Library, London. 122c The Gresley Jewel, miniature by Nicholas Hilliard, c 1590. Private Collection/The Bridgeman Art Library, London. 122r Charles Howard, Lord Howard of Effingham, miniature attributed to Rowland Lockey, 1605. National Maritime Museum, Greenwich, London/The Bridgeman Art Library, London. 123 Detail from Edward VI, panel by an unknown artist. National Portraity Gallery, London, no. 5511. 126 Catherine Parr, oil on panel attributed to William Scrots, c 1545. National Portrait Gallery, London, no. 4618. 131 The Strand Front of Somerset House, c 1550. Sir John Soane Museum, London. 135 West end of Westminster Hall, the Court of King's Bench, left, and Court of Chancery, right, drawing attributed to Hollar. British Museum, Department of Prints & Drawings. 138 Lady Jane Dudley (née Grey), panel attributed to Master John, c 1545. National Portrait Gallery, London, no.4451. 139 Detail from The Family and Descendants of Sir Thomas More, painting by Rowland Lockey, c 1593-4. Victoria and Albert Museum, London, no.P15-1973. 146 Robert Dudley, Earl of Leicester, panel by unknown artist. National Portrait Gallery, London, no. 447. 147 Elizabeth I: the Armada portrait, oil on panel, English School, 16th century. Private Collection/The Bridgeman Art Library,, London. 150 Mary I of England and Philip II of Spain, oil on canvas English school, 17th century. National Maritime Museum, Greenwich, London, no. BHC 2952. 151 Elizabeth's entry into London, 1559, drawing by an unknown artist, c 1560-70. College of Arms, London, MS. M.6. 158 Seating Plan for the opening of Parliament at Blackfriars, 1523, drawing by Garter King of Arms. By Gracious Permission of HM the Queen. 162 The St. Bartholomew' Massacre, 1572, oil on panel by François Dubois. Musée Cantonal des Beaux-Arts, Lausanne, no. 729. 163 Detail of Title Page from John Foxe's: Actes and Monuments, 1593. The Mansell Collection, London. 171l Resolution of a Council of War signed by the Commanders of the English Fleet, 1588. British Library. London, Add. MS. 33740, f. 6. 171r The Fleets off Berry Head and engagement near Portland Bill, from the Armada Charts, coloured engraving, 1590, by Augusine Ryther, after Robert Adams. National Maritime Museum, Greenwich, London/The Bridgeman Art Library, London. 175 Veiw of London, drawing by van der Wyngaerde, 1550, taken from facsimile edition of 1881-82. Original drawing in the Ashmolean Museum, Oxford. Photograph by Norman Brand. 178 Tomb of Catherine Duchess of Suffolk. St. James' Church, Spilsby. Photograph by John Meek. 182l Title Page from John Gerarde's Herball, 1597. The Bodleian Library, Oxford. 182r Sir William Butts, painting by Hans Holbein. Isabella Stewart Gardner Museum, Boston. 183 Oak Chest, English c 1637. Victoria & Albert Museum, London/The BridgemanArt Library, London. 184l Thomas Howard, 4th Duke of Norfolk, oil on panel by Hans Eworth, 1563. Private Collection. 184r Margaret Audley, Duchess of Norfolk, oil on panel by Hans Eworth, 1562. Private Collection. 185 The 4th Duke of Norfolk's New Testament, with his Last Message written while in the Tower. By Permission of his Grace The Duke of Norfolk. 187t Funeral Procession of Philip Sidney. Fotomas Index, London. 187b Funeral Procession of Elizabeth I. British Library, London, Add. MS. 35324, f. 37v. 190 Design for a Clock by Hans Holbein, presented by Sir Anthony Denny to Henry VIII on New Year's Day, 1544. British Museum, London, Department of Prints and Drawings. 191 Durham Cathedral. Woodmansterne Ltd. 194 Plan of the Manor grounds of Moulsham, 1591, by J. Walker. British Museum, London, Department of Prints & Drawings. 198 Doctor Latimer Preaching before Edward VI in the privy-garden at Westminster, from Foxe's: Actes and Monuments, 1593. The Mansell Collection, London. 207 Monument to Blanche Parry, St. Faith's Church, Bacton, Hereford and Worcester. Photograph by John Meek. 211 The Castle and Town of Carrickfergus in Ireland, c 1560. British Library, London, Cotton MS. Augustus I. ii.42. 214-215 An Allegorical Scene: Virtue Confronts Vice, Painting by Isaac Oliver, c 1590-95. State Museum of Art, Copenhagen. 219l Robert Dudley, Earl of Leicester, drawing by Federigo Zuccaro, 1575. British Museum, London, Department of Prints & Drawings. 219r Sir Thomas Elyot, drawing by Hans Holbein. By Gracious Permission of HM The Queen. 222 Sir Philip Sidney, oil on canvas by an unknown artist. National Portrait Gallery, London, no. 2096. 223 Christ Church, Oxford, design by John Bereblock to illustrate a Latin dialogue by Thomas Neale, 1566. The Bodleian Library, Oxford, MS Bodl. 13, f. 5v/The Mansell Collection, London. 226 Map of Virginia, drawn by John White, c 1585. British Museum, London. 231 Standard of George Talbot, Earl of Shrewsbury, from the Book of Standards. College of Arms, London, MS.I.2. 234 'Phenix' from the Oxburgh Hangings. Victoria & Albert Museum, London, no. T29-1955. 235 Map of Bath, by W. Smith, 1588. British Library, London, Sloane MS. 2596, f. 39v. 239 The Kitchen at Hampton Court Palace, London. Courtesy English Heritage. 243t Visscher's veiw of London, 1616, from facsimile published by the London Topographical Society. British Library, London. 243b Sir Francis Drake, miniature by Nicholas Hilliard, 1581. National Portrait Gallery, London, no. 4851/The Bridgeman Art Library, London. 247 Inner Court from the Loggia, Kirby Hall, Northamptonshire. Courtesy English Heritage. 251 William Cecil, 1st Baron Burghley Riding his Grey Mule, oil on canvas, English School, 16th century. The Bodleian Library, Oxford. 254 Detail from Sir Henry Unton, panel by an unknown artist, c 1596. National Portrait Gallery, London, no. 710. 255 Contemporary Sketch of Execution of Mary, Queen of Scots, 1587. British Library, London, Add. MS, 48027. 258 Detalls from The Family of Henry VIII, painting by an unknown artist. By Gracious Permission of HM The Queen. 259 Detail from Elizabeth I: the 'Sieve' portrait, oil on canvas by Quentin Massays the younger, 1583. Pinacoteca Nazionale, Sienna/Scala. 263 Elizabeth I at Tilbury, oil on panel, English School, 17th century. St. Faith's Church, Gaywood/The Bridgeman Art Library, London. 267 Detail from Sir Henry Unton, panel by an unknown artist, c 1596. National Portrait Gallery, London, no. 710. 271 Robert Devereux, 2nd Earl of Essex, painting after Marcus Gheeraerts the Younger. National Portraita Gallery, London, no. 180. 274 Henry VIII Enthroned, Flanked by Knights of the Garter, illumination from the Liber Niger, c 1534. By Permission of the Dean and Canons of Windsor. 277 Map of the County of Devonshire, by Christopher Saxton, 1574. British Library, London, Department of Maps. 278-279 Map of Great Britain, by Lawrence Nowell, c 1564. British Library, London, Add. MS. 62540. 282 Henry Wriothesley, 3rd Earl of Southampton, painting by John de Critz the Elder. 1601-3. Duke of Buccleuch and Queensbury/Robert Harding Associates, London. 284 Poster Advertising William Kemp, 1600. Fotomas Index, London. 291 Charterhouse , London. Photograph by John Meek.

Endpapers: Letter from Queen Elizabeth I to Thomas Randolph her agent in Scotland, 1566. British Library, London, Lansdowne. MS. 8, f. 95. Letter from Henry VIII to Cardinal Wolsey, c 1520-21. British Library, London, Add. MS. 19398, f. 44.

Front Cover: Top Left Henry VIII, painting after Holbein. Hever Castle, Kent/Woodmansterne Ltd. (detail) Top Centre Anne Boleyn, painting by an unknown artist. Hever, Castle, Kent/Woodmansterne Ltd. (detail) Top Right Thomas Howard, 3rd Earl of Norfolk, painting by Hans Holbein. By Gracious Permision of HM The Queen. (detail) Bottom Left Henry Wriothesley, 3rd Earl of Southampton, painting by John de Critz The Elder,1601-3. Duke of Buccleuch and Queensbury/Robert Harding Associates, London. (detail) Bottom Centre The Embarkation from Dover of HenryVIII for France, 1521 or 1532, by an unknown artist. By Gacious Permission of HM The Queen. (detail) Bottom Right Elizabeth I: the 'Sieve' portrait, oil on canvas by Quentin Massays the Younger, 1583. Pinacoteca Nazionale, Sienna/Scala. (detail)

Back Cover: Henry VIII and Will Somers, illumination by Jean Maillard from the King's Psalter, c 1540. British LIbrary, London, Royal MS. 2A. XVI, f. 63v.

The right honourable Thomas Cicell, Earle of Excester Baron Burghley Knight of the moste Noble order of the Garter &c.

HONI SOIT QVI MAL Y PENSE

COR VNVM VIA VNA

Robert Sidney Viscount Lisley Baron of Penßhurst Lord Chamberlayne to the Queenes Maiestie and Knight of the most honourable order of the Garter.

HONI SOIT QVI MAL Y PENSE

QVO FATA VOCANT

The founder of the Tudor dynasty, Henry VII, and his Queen, Elizabeth of York, sculpted by Torrigiano on their tomb in the Henry VII Chapel, Westminster Abbey.

The Tudor dynasty, which (like so many noble families) only lasted three generations.

HENRY VII
1485-1509

Margaret d.1541 — m.1 1503 JAMES IV of Scotland d.1513 — m.2 1514 Archibald Douglas 6th Earl of Angus d.1557

HENRY VIII 1509-47
m.1 1509 Catherine of Aragon divorced d.1536
m.2 1533 Anne daughter of Thomas Boleyn Earl of Wiltshire d.1536
m.3 1536 Jane daughter of Sir John Seymour d.1537
m.4 1540 Anne of Cleves divorced d.1557
m.5 1540 Catherine daughter of Lord Edmund Howard d.1542
m.6 1543 Catherine daughter of Sir Thomas Parr widow of 1 Sir Edward Burgh 2 John Neville 3rd Lord Latimer m.4 1547 Thomas Seymour Baron Seymour of Sudeley d.1548

MARY I 1553-58
ELIZABETH I 1558-1603 d.1536
EDWARD VI 1547-53

Mary m.1 1514 LOUIS XII of France d.1515 m.2 1515 Charles Brandon Duke of Suffolk d.1545

Scottish Royal Family STUART

Charles Stuart m. Elizabeth Cavendish, Earl of Lennox stepdaughter of 6th Earl of Shrewsbury

Catherine Grey m. Edward Seymour Earl of Hertford

Talbot Earl of Shrewsbury

Brandon Duke of Suffolk

Howard Duke of Norfolk

13th Earl of Arundel

Seymour of Wolf Hall

JAMES IV m. Margaret Tudor

Mary Tudor m. Charles Brandon Duke of Suffolk

HENRY VIII m.2 Anne Boleyn
HENRY VIII m.3 Jane Seymour
HENRY VIII m.5 Catherine Howard
HENRY VIII m.6 Catherine Parr m.4 Baron Seymour of Sudeley

Thomas Howard m. Margaret 4th Duke of Norfolk widow of Henry Dudley

Henry FitzRoy Duke of Richmond m. Mary Howard

Jane Grey m. Guilford Dudley

Anne Seymour m. John Dudley

Robert Devereux 2nd Earl of Essex

Lettice Devereux m. Robert Dudley Countess of Essex

Sir Henry Sidney m. Mary Dudley

Frances m. widow of Sir Philip Sidney

Devereux Earl of Essex

Sidney of Penshurst

Robert Dudley Earl of Leicester

John Dudley Duke of Northumberland

English Royal Family TUDOR

The connections of the dynasties of Brandon, Grey, Howard, Seymour, Dudley, Talbot and Sidney with eachother and the royal dynasties of Tudor and Stuart.

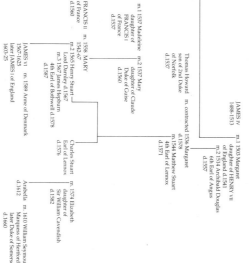

Mary, Queen of Scots, with crucifix and rosary, as the pious Catholic captive of Elizabeth 1. Queen of Scotland and (by marriage) of France, and heir to England, Mary's ill-luck and folly cost her all three crowns, and eventually her head. But her wily son James VI of Scotland succeeded unopposed on Elizabeth's death in 1603 as James I, the first English King of the Stuart dynasty.

JAMES IV 1488-1513 m.1 1503 Margaret daughter of HENRY VII of England d.1541 m.2 1514 Archibald Douglas 6th Earl of Angus d.1557

Thomas Howard son of 2nd Duke of Norfolk d.1571 m. contracted 1536 Margaret daughter of Claude Duke of Guise d.1560

JAMES V 1513-42 m.1 1537 Madeleine daughter of France FRANCIS I of France d.1537 m.2 1537 Mary daughter of Claude Duke of Guise d.1560

FRANCIS II of France d.1560

MARY 1542-87 m.1 1558 Francis son of FRANCIS I of France d.1560 m.2 1565 Henry Stuart Lord Darnley d.1567 4th Earl of Lennox d.1571 m.3 1567 James Hepburn 4th Earl of Bothwell d.1578

Charles Stuart Earl of Lennox d.1576 m. 1574 Elizabeth daughter of Sir William Cavendish d.1582

JAMES VI 1567-1625 later JAMES I of England 1603-25 m. 1589 Anne of Denmark d.1619

Arabella d.1612 m.1610 William Seymour later Duke of Somerset d.1660 Marquess of Hertford

The Stuart dynasty, showing the double claim of James VI to the English throne.